Critical Cyberculture Studies

EDITED BY

David Silver and Adrienne Massanari

WITH A FOREWORD BY

Steve Jones

New York University Press

NEW YORK AND LONDON

NEW YORK UNIVERSITY PRESS
New York and London
www.nyupress.org

Library of Congress Cataloging-in-Publication Data
Critical cyberculture studies / edited by David Silver and Adrienne
Massanari ; with a foreword by Steve Jones.
p. cm.
Includes bibliographical references and index.
ISBN-13: 978-0-8147-4023-1 (cloth : alk. paper)
ISBN-10: 0-8147-4023-5 (cloth : alk. paper)
ISBN-13: 978-0-8147-4024-8 (pbk. : alk. paper)
ISBN-10: 0-8147-4024-3 (pbk. : alk. paper)
1. Computers and civilization. 2. Internet—Social aspects.
3. Cyberspace—Social aspects. I. Silver, David, Ph. D.
II. Massanari, Adrienne.
QA76.9.C66C744 2006
303.48'33—dc22 2006008884

New York University Press books are printed on acid-free paper,
and their binding materials are chosen for strength and durability.

Manufactured in the United States of America

c 10 9 8 7 6 5 4 3 2 1
p 10 9 8 7 6 5 4 3

Contents

Acknowledgments

David Silver wishes to acknowledge all contributors to *Critical Cyberculture Studies* for their hard work and good ideas. He also wishes to thank Becky Lentz and the Ford Foundation who made it all possible.

Foreword

Dreams of Fields: Possible Trajectories of Internet Studies

Steve Jones

Fielding Internet Studies

A good place to begin a discussion of the field of internet studies is with the notion of whether there is a "field" that one can "view" from any perspective. I do think one can best describe internet studies as a field. A discipline, though, it is not. Disciplines are traditionally marked by departments in colleges and universities. They are usually denoted by a canon (whether for better or worse) and by a curriculum. While we have internet institutes, centers, units, what-have-you, there is not a canon, nor curricula, nor departments.

I am not particularly bothered by this fact, nor do I think scholars working in the field of internet studies should be concerned about it. My own "home" discipline is communication, and for decades there have been debates about whether communication is a discipline or a field or something else altogether (perhaps it is an "interdiscipline," as some have designated internet studies). There was an infamous, though it seems now often forgotten, issue of the *Journal of Communication* titled "Ferment in the Field" that was published in 1983. It had a couple or so dozen "names" in the field write about whether communication was a field, a discipline, etc. I remember reading it in graduate school, and reading D. Charles Whitney's (1985, p. 142) remarkable response to it in another journal, in which he wrote, concerning the mixture of many disciplines within communication, that "the questions communication researchers are asking are too crucial for us to be left alone." I hope the same can be said of internet studies, that the questions we are asking are so interesting and important as to cause others to join us in asking them, and I even more so hope that we welcome them.

What stood out for me then about communication, as it does now about internet studies, is how little the debate has mattered since. I look at the youth of the participants in the Critical Cyberculture Studies symposium (not that I am old, really . . . but no matter how the midlife-crisis siren calls on me to digress I will resist), and I wonder how those working in internet studies will fare over time, how they, we, will make a difference. Will we struggle against the things we do not like about academic life? Will we seek to create environments and opportunities that we wish for the field of internet studies? What will we do to make things better? Because I see things in communication little changed from the way they were in the early 1980s, when I entered that field, so I wonder what we will see of internet studies if, fate willing, we may reconvene in twenty years at another Critical Cyberculture Studies symposium to examine the paths it took.

I know that the comparison between internet studies and communication is at least a little of the "apples and oranges" variety. Of course, there were departments of communication even before 1983, so the debate about the ferment in the field was different than it may be in internet studies, and indeed if there is any ferment in internet studies it is not coming from discussions of whether there is a discipline or a field but, I think, from whether there is anything at all. This is not unlike the situation many other fill-in-the-blank studies (women's studies, African-American studies, Jewish studies, Catholic studies, to name but a few at my own university) found themselves in decades ago. To borrow from Jan Fernback's (1999) comment concerning online community, what I find people asking me about internet studies in various ways is whether "there is a there there." I am asked things like "Where should I go to get a degree in internet studies?" and "What are the classic texts in the field?" These are basic questions concerning a field, ones that require an answer, but are not the kind that I find the scholars themselves are all that much asking, nor are they ones to which there is an easy or ready answer. In that 1983 issue of the *Journal of Communication*, the invitation given to contributors was to write "on the state of communications research today: the relationship of the research with respect to social issues and social structure; and the tactics and strategies for reaching their goals." When it comes to internet research, I wish we would ask ourselves to undertake these tasks ourselves. But we will need to answer some more-basic questions than those so that we can consolidate what we have gained to this point, and I think we have gained quite a lot.

If I were for a moment to dream of a field, my dream for internet studies would be the same as the one I had, and still have, for communication. That dream begins with interesting questions, bright students, smart colleagues, and the means and will to work together and share knowledge, insight, and curiosity. For me, that dream has by and large been lived, and I have been very fortunate in that regard. But the reason I know that I have lived it and that it has not been simply a dream is that in a dream having the means and the will would have been simple, easy matters.

The Internet in the Academy

That it has not been easy to find the means and the will to work with others is by no means the fault of internet studies or communication. If anything is to blame, it is the fact of working in a scholarly system (in my case in the United States, but it is a model taken up in many other places in the world) that emphasizes original work and too often merely substitutes individual work for it and that emphasizes competitiveness while promoting collaboration. It is a system that values commerce (in the form of research grants, student numbers, and other quantifiable measures that translate into money) while touting prestige, all the while never making clear what in fact "counts" among the myriad ways one may be evaluated, whether by peers, administrators, or the public.

It may end up being one of the greatest ironies in contemporary higher education that at a time when internet-based creative and collaborative technologies are all the rage—with new ones seemingly invented every other month, reported on in the media, and added to the lexicon (*blog, wiki, p2p, podcast*—the list goes on and will no doubt grow further)—that the academy's own use of those technologies lags behind that of the public and that of students. In a recent survey of college faculty internet use that I conducted, the vast majority of faculty (over 90 percent) use e-mail, but fewer use instant messaging (24 percent) and fewer still use new internet tools like blogs and wikis. Part of the reason for this is no doubt that it takes time for technology to prove its value. Why change one's teaching and work habits unless one can be certain of a benefit (pedagogical, professional, personal, or all of the above)? One respondent wrote that "faculty use of the internet is only limited by their knowledge/ability and by their imaginations," but within the academy what structures are in place to encourage faculty to learn about new technologies and unleash their imaginations in this domain? What might internet researchers contribute to the deployment and use of the internet in higher education?

Internet in Practice, in Theory

One of the things that may keep us from making a contribution is the ages-old division in the academy between theory and practice. Consider that the disciplines most often represented at meetings of the Association of Internet Researchers are those in the social sciences and that the struggle for legitimacy of those disciplines in the academy has regularly involved a defense of engagement against theory. Should it be a surprise that internet studies may face a similar struggle?

Perhaps it should, because if internet studies is to be truly multidisciplinary then it must embrace a multitude of disciplines, ones from the arts, engineering, law, and medicine, among others. Why must internet studies have any discipline(s) as primary? Furthermore, why must internet studies replicate any of the struggles and debates that have been part of what has resulted in the academy's present disciplinarity?

Simply from the standpoint of practice versus theory (a debate all too common in my home discipline of communication) it makes little sense to continue the debate when that energy could be better spent learning both practice and theory. It is worthwhile to consider what could be valuable for internet researchers to know about the internet from a practical standpoint. By practice I mean, in very broad terms, the programming, engineering, and standards development related to the internet. Is it important to know something about how the internet works? Why? Did those who studied other media like television or newspapers know how those media worked? In most cases they did not, but I believe such knowledge would not hurt scholarship and would in fact enhance it. And such knowledge certainly need not be opposed to theory; rather, it ought to complement it. Indeed, to be good theorists and critical scholars of the internet we should know something about the conditions in which it develops, if only so that we can begin to answer any question that begins with "Why?"

But there is a more important reason to engage in learning about prac-

tices associated with internet use, history, and development: because doing so can help us expand the scope of our knowledge and our questioning.

As an example, consider the primacy of text in internet studies. We
have done terrific work thus far in internet studies to understand the nature of text-based online interaction. But we have done little more than
that. Think about it: what *are* the interactions on the internet? They are
far more than text. They may also be sound (voice, music, and various
beeps, blurts, and pings), image (old and new, archival and live, still and
motion), or some combination of those, with or without text. Sure, the
internet is evanescent (just ask Brewster Kahle). It is hard to study, particularly when one focuses on anything other than text, but *we have to study
and understand other than text on the internet.* As a brief but important
aside, even when we do study and analyze text, let us ask why it is that we
largely choose text from the same kinds of sources (newsgroups, MUDs,
etc.) and treat virtually all text the same? The internet's earliest history
is one of textual interaction, but it has developed into a highly visual
medium. What caused the development, the evolution from text to image?
How can we create new methods and tools for understanding text and
image?

Understanding, or at least paying attention to, internet practices can
also help us understand the phenomenology and ontology of the internet.
To put that in another, somewhat simplistic way: we are too quick to use
the vocabularies to which we ourselves have become accustomed through
our own internet use. But what if we problematize some of the basic terms
we casually use, like *e-mail* or *Web*? For example, what is email in terms of
its experience, its perception? Is it text only or graphical? Is it fast, slow,
easy to read, hard to understand? What does it mean to its users? How did
we get where we are in e-mail's development, and how does that development tie in to e-mail use? In a follow-up to the "Ferment in the Field"
Journal of Communication issue, Joli Jensen (1993, p. 67), in an article titled
"The Consequences of Vocabularies," noted the importance of being self-
reflexive about how we go about naming the objects and subjects of our
study: "In doing such mappings, explorations, and definitions, we create
what we pretend to merely describe."

As somewhat of an aside, perhaps the most important reason to be self-
reflexive is the possibility that disciplinarity may creep in through the back
door. We all bring to our own scholarly endeavors various intellectual
backgrounds, approaches, and interests, most often formed while graduate

students, whether we studied in strongly disciplinary or highly interdisciplinary programs. Those of us working from an academic institutional base (as are the majority of scholars in the United States) also bring with us, whether deliberately or not, interests focused and shaped, whether subtly or not, by the institutions and units within which we work. There is nothing sinister or dire about this. However, it becomes problematic when such focus and shaping tends toward the exclusionary. For example, at the conferences of the Association of Internet Researchers the preponderance of work presented is oriented toward the social impacts of the internet. There may be many explanations for that orientation, not the least important being that the internet's social impacts may simply be interesting to many people. But it may also be that the disciplinary backgrounds and situations of those attending the conferences are such that social impacts come to the fore. Judging by my own observations, the majority of presenters have degrees in, or are in departments that belong to, the social sciences.[1] The social networks of attendees may in turn reinforce the substance and/or impression of conference content and may also dissuade those outside the network from attending, leading to self-exclusion or exclusion by default. In that case, in addition to being self-reflexive, one must ask, "What are we missing?" not in the sense of gaps in our own work (important as those are) but in the sense of ascertaining what we are overlooking entirely and why. We are all poorer, in a sense, for associating if our associations are not clearly and forthrightly inclusive in word and in deed.

There are other areas that are largely escaping our study. One is the realm outside human-to-human interaction on the internet. Not only are there bots online with which we interact, but there are also other computers and machines with which we interact—and machine-to-machine communication, on our behalf, is an interesting area to examine, too. There is what we might call an invisible internet, that which is infrastructure: protocols, standards, and algorithms. Although the internet's infrastructure has always been important (after all, the internet's existence is, despite the frontier rhetoric associated with its origins, based on standards and agreements), as network connections become ubiquitous and pervasive the infrastructure will play an increasingly important role in managing our online interactions. If you think interface design matters to the ways we use computers and the internet, I am betting infrastructure design will matter far more. I am reminded of a dinner in St. Paul in 1987 at which James Carey said, regarding new communication technologies, that "we should listen to the engineers." I parsed his comment then, and now, in light of his very brief comments in the *Journal of Communication*'s "Ferment" issue and, in particular, in light of a comment he made therein that "cultural studies is an attempt to think through a theory or vocabulary of communications that is simultaneously a theory or vocabulary of culture" (1983, p. 313). What do we know about the theory or vocabulary of those who code and create, and what do we know about its consequences for internet users?

Conclusion: Detours through Theory, Practice

I do think it is important for us to attend to matters of theory and vocabulary because they remind us of the multiple layers at which power and ideology operate when it comes to the internet. As Joli Jensen (1993, p. 68) put it, "Our understanding of what we are up to in communication study has been based in a belief in a neutral 'world out there' waiting for us to figure it out." This is not an attitude we can afford to mirror in internet studies if our work is to matter to the academy, and the world, at large. Too much of what comes across my desk in journals, books, unpublished manuscripts, and conference papers is purely descriptive, work done largely without regard to matters of practice, power, and ideology and, further, largely without theory. The internet is far from a "neutral 'world out there'" that we can figure out without engaging it and ourselves in complex and complicated ways. That it typically comes to us at a screen's remove should not remove from our consideration the realities (socially, politically, economically, or otherwise constructed) within which those who use it live and within which the hardware and software, markets and marketing operate.

I should note that I do not intend to close with a shrill "call to theory," nor a "call to practice," because these alone are not enough. Jensen rightly warns against the "consequences of expertise" particularly in the realm of theory: "The danger is greatest, it seems to me, in the theoretical mode, because loyalties are to theories, not empirical evidence or lived experience" (p. 73). We must remember that theory is politically and ideologically motivated. We detour through it, to borrow a phrase from Larry Grossberg. Likewise, practice is never a mere "act," for every practice calls into question other practices upon which one does not act. While theory can give us insight into meaning, practice can give us insight into materiality, effect, and power.[2]

Indeed, what brought me around, so to speak, in regard to the ferment in the field of communication, were the interactions I had with Grossberg beginning in the late 1970s. That was my introduction to the ferment in cultural studies, and I think that ferment has as much or more to offer internet studies as it did communication. Grossberg's (1993, p. 89) admonition, in his essay in the *Journal of Communication*'s ferment follow-up, that we "(reject) the application of a theory known in advance as much as (we reject) the possibility of an empiricism without theory" is crucial. It is also crucial that we be "driven . . . by (our) own sense of history and politics" (p. 89). In short, the practices he identified of cultural studies can inform our own work:

> [Be committed] to the fact that reality is continually being made through human action.

> [Be] continuously drawn to the "popular," not as a sociological category purporting to differentiate among cultural practices but as the terrain on which people live and political struggle must be carried out in the contemporary world.

> [Be committed] to a radical contextualism, a contextualism that precludes defining culture, or the relations between culture and power, outside of the particular context into which cultural studies imagines itself to intervene. . . . cultural practices cannot be treated as simply texts, as microcosmic representations . . . of some social other." (pp. 89–90)

I will leave it to you to think about the relationships between culture and the internet in Grossberg's formulations, and about the moments at which one might substitute the word "internet" for the word "culture" in them. The opportunities and contexts in which internet studies can intervene meaningfully are numerous, too numerous for us to be deterred by traditional disciplinary boundaries, perhaps even too important for us to be deterred by traditional institutions. The burden is on us, then, to determine how best to move forward while learning from our own and others' many disciplinary pasts and institutional histories.

NOTES

1. As AIR's founder and as someone with a Ph.D. in communication I can take some responsibility for this, perhaps, for it is likely that my own social network contributed to its early disciplinarity regardless of my efforts, personal as well as AIR-related, at multidisciplinarity.

2. It should be noted that it is only for brevity's sake that I am positing these (theory and practice) in the form of a dualism.

REFERENCES

Beam, R. A., and Kim, E. P. S. (2003). Technology-induced stressors, job satisfaction and workplace exhaustion among journalism and mass communication faculty. *Journalism & Mass Communication Educator, 57*(4), 335–351.

Carey, J. W. (1983). The origins of the radical discourse on cultural studies in the United States. *Journal of Communication, 33*(3), 311–313.

Dennis, E. E., Meyer, P., Sundar, S. S., Pryor, L., Rogers, E. M., Chen, H. L., and Pavlik, J. (2003). Learning reconsidered: Education in the digital age. *Journalism & Mass Communication Educator, 57*(4), 292–317.

Fernback, J. (1999). There is a there there: Notes toward a definition of cybercommunity. In *Doing Internet Research: Critical Issues and Methods for Examining the Net.* Ed. Steve Jones, 203–219. Thousand Oaks, CA: Sage.

Grossberg, L. (1993). Can cultural studies find true happiness in communication? *Journal of Communication, 43*(3), 89–97.

Jensen, J. (1993). The consequences of vocabularies. *Journal of Communication, 43*(3), 67–74.

Journalism and Mass Communication Educator. (2003). *58*(4), Winter.

Ogan, C., and Chung, D. (2003). Stressed out! A national study of women and men journalism and mass communication faculty, their uses of technology, and levels of professional and personal stress. *Journalism & Mass Communication Educator, 57*(4), 352–368.

Voakes, P. S., Beam, R. A., and Ogan, C. (2003). The impact of technological change on journalism education: A survey of faculty and administrators. *Journalism & Mass Communication Educator, 57*(4), 318–334.

Whitney, C. W. (1985). Ferment and the field. *Communication Research, 12*(1), January, 133–143.

Introduction

Where Is Internet Studies?

David Silver

Internet studies. New media studies. Digital media studies. Digital arts and culture studies. Cyberculture studies. Critical cyberculture studies. Networked culture studies. Informatics. Information science. Information society studies. Contemporary media studies.

Naming, not to mention mapping, an academic field is a tricky proposition.

In their 1982 book, *Learning the Library*, Anne K. Beaubien, Sharon A. Hogan, and Mary W. George suggest that the growth of academic disciplines often follows four stages. First, disciplines begin with a *pioneering stage*, an intellectual movement formed by a collection of "mavericks" interested in sharing ideas, collecting data, and testing hypotheses. Their work is often developed within the classroom and most often distributed through informal means like personal correspondences, newsletters, and journalistic features. Next comes the *elaboration stage*, a period of growth marked by an increased number of participating scholars and an established but not yet codified set of terminologies and methodologies. This is also the stage during which an organization, usually national, is established and an academic journal, chapters in books, and college courses begin to appear.

Following this is the *proliferation stage*, during which the community of scholars grows dramatically and becomes international in scope. As the output of findings grows, so do the number of conferences and journals, as well as the number of languages through and between which ideas and data are shared. At this stage, undergraduate majors are established, textbooks and monographs are published, and a somewhat agreed upon set of methodologies takes shape. This is also where "twigging," or the formation of subfields, begins. Finally, we witness the *establishment stage,* which is characterized by traditional markers of academic legitimacy, including the introduction of academic departments, graduate dissertations, federal and private funding, and endowed chairs. Publishers begin to devote series to the discipline, universities establish centers, and the community of scholars negotiates—and renegotiates—a canon. Further, the field witnesses intellectual stratification, often between theoretical and applied research, and a proliferation of subfields.

Using the four stages as a signpost, Internet studies appears to be rapidly approaching disciplinary status. Indeed, many of the traditional markers of an academic discipline are, for better or worse, in place, thriving and growing: a community of scholars; conferences and symposia; journals, journal articles, anthologies, monographs, and textbooks; university courses, common curriculum, and majors; theses and dissertations; theories and methodologies; and academic centers.

There are many communities of scholars interested in the social, political, and cultural elements of new media. Some of these communities are more international than others. To date, the largest and most academically mainstream is the Association of Internet Researchers, or AIR (http://www.aoir.org/). Established in 1998, AIR has hosted six international conferences—at the University of Kansas, in 2000; at the University of Minnesota, Minneapolis, in 2001; in Maastricht, the Netherlands, in 2002; in Toronto, Canada, in 2003; at the University of Sussex, United Kingdom, in 2004; and in Chicago, Illinois, in 2005—and attendance, an excellent and healthy mixture of mostly graduate students and faculty, runs in the high hundreds. With an increasingly international executive committee and a listserv with more than a thousand subscribers, AIR continues to bring together scholars from across the disciplines and around the world.

AIR is by no means the only umbrella under which to huddle. The Institute of Network Cultures (http://www.networkcultures.org/) has hosted numerous conferences and symposia, and the institute's founder, Geert Lovink, is one of the key players in the Next Five Minutes conferences (http://www.next5minutes.org/), which seek to bring together activists, artists, and academics to trace and transform tactical media. In Germany, the German Society for Online Research (http://www.dgof.de/) continues to network German and German-speaking scholars of new media, while the diverse and deep thinkers of Ciberpunk (http://www.ciberpunk.net/)

continue to generate groundbreaking work in Spanish cyberculture. Moreover, the Digital Games Research Association (http://www.digra.org/) continues to host international conferences that welcome academics, practitioners, and players of digital games.

For a field of study focused on and rooted firmly in new media, we have generated a fair share of print-based findings. As I argue elsewhere (Silver 2000), the twin pillars of cyberculture studies are virtual communities and online identities, and much of the work is derived from Howard Rheingold's *The Virtual Community: Homesteading on the Electronic Frontier* (1993) and Sherry Turkle's *Life on the Screen: Identity in the Age of the Internet* (1995). These two topics were (and continue to be) explored, explicated, and problematized by a range of subsequent works, primarily in anthologies, including Mike Featherstone and Roger Burrows's *Cyberspace/Cyberbodies/Cyberpunk: Cultures of Technological Embodiment* (1995), Sara Kiesler's *Culture of the Internet* (1997), David Potter's *Internet Culture* (1996), Fay Sudweeks, Margaret L. McLaughlin, and Sheizaf Rafaeli's *Network and Netplay: Virtual Groups on the Internet* (1998), and Steve Jones's enormously influential trilogy of anthologies *CyberSociety: Computer-Mediated Communication and Community* (1995), *Virtual Culture: Identity and Communication in Cybersociety* (1997), and *Cybersociety 2.0: Revisiting Computer-Mediated Community and Technology* (1998). As the new millennium dragged itself in, metastudies of the field appeared (and continue to appear), including Thomas Swiss's *Unspun: Key Concepts for Understanding the World Wide Web* (2000); David Bell and Barbara Kennedy's *The Cybercultures Reader* (2000); David Gauntlett's *Web.Studies: Rewiring Media Studies for the Digital Age* (2000); David Bell's *An Introduction to Cyberculture* (2001); David Trend's *Reading Digital Culture* (2001); Geert Lovink's *Dark Fiber: Tracking Critical Internet Culture* (2003); and Noah Wardrip-Fruin and Nick Montfort's *New Media Reader* (2003).

Along the way, academic journals—print-based and online—flourished, affording multiple outlets for new findings, reworkings of theories and methods, and collectively built canons. For the time being, some of the most influential journals include *Convergence: The Journal of Research into New Media Technologies*; *CTheory* (http://www.ctheory.net/); *ebr* (http://www.altx.com/ebr/threads/pages/info.htm); *First Monday* (http://www.firstmonday.org/); *Game Studies* (http://www.gamestudies.org/); *Information, Communication & Society*; *The Information Society*; *Journal of Computer-*

Mediated Communication (http://jcmc.indiana.edu/); *M/C: Media & Culture* (http://www.media-culture.org.au/); *New Media & Society*; *Surveillance & Society*; and *Teknokultura* (http://teknokultura.rrp.upr.edu/).

These books and articles have found numerous audiences, especially among students who flock to undergraduate and graduate courses in new media and digital culture. What is striking, however, is that while many of the courses are offered through Internet studies and other new/digital media programs, the majority are found within traditional disciplines such as American studies, anthropology, communication, cultural studies, ethnic studies, gender/women's studies, informatics, journalism, linguistics, management studies, psychology, and sociology, to name just a few.[1] This cross-pollination suggests a fertile field, an *interdiscipline*, from which traditional disciplinary approaches can help inform our understanding of new sites of study, and from which such sites can tweak traditional methods and theories. Indeed, the ultimate artifact of a field's pedagogical maturity, the textbook, is abundant, ranging from Erik Bucy's *Living in the Information Age: A New Media Reader* (2002) to Crispin Thurlow, Laura Lengel, and Alice Tomic's *Computer Mediated Communication: Social Interaction and the Internet* (2004).

While new media and digital culture make their way into traditional disciplines, clusters of interdisciplinary collaborations have generated many diverse centers of cyberculture studies. Across Europe, academic centers have been built: Austria's International Center for New Media (http://www.icnm.net/); Denmark's Center for Computer Games Research (http://game.itu.dk/); Great Britain's Oxford Internet Institute (http://www.oii.ox.ac.uk/); the Netherlands' Institute of Network Cultures (http://www.networkcultures.org/) and Govcom.org (http://govcom.org); and Spain's Biblioteca de las Indias Electrónicas (http://www.lasindias.org/). In Australia, fibreculture (http://www.fibreculture.org/) serves as an umbrella organization for many Australian universities and scholars interested in digital media. In Singapore, the Singapore Internet Research Centre (http://www.ntu.edu.sg/sci/sirc/) conducts research related to the Internet across Asia. And finally, in the United States, a number of academic centers have appeared, including Pacific University's Berglund Center for Internet Studies (http://bcis.pacificu.edu/); Virginia Tech's Center for Digital Discourse and Culture (http://www.cddc.vt.edu/); University of Maryland, Baltimore County's Center for Women and Information Technology (http://www.umbc.edu/cwit/); University of Minnesota's Internet Studies Center (http://www.isc.umn.edu/) and the Institute for New Media Studies (http://www.inms.umn.edu/); and the University of Washington's Resource Center for Cyberculture Studies (http://www.com.washington.edu/rccs/).

So where do we stand? We have a community of scholars, some arranged internationally, others nationally. We have academic organizations that host large and largely international conferences on the field, as well as a diverse array of symposia for multiple subfields. We have books (and book series), anthologies, and journals. We have both undergraduate and graduate courses, which have helped proliferate the field with theses and dissertations on the topic. And we have academic centers and institutes. But do we have a common set of theories and methodologies?

Yes and no.

Drawing heavily from cultural studies and cultural theory, scholars of new media have weaved into their work the theories of Jean Baudrillard, Judith Butler, Gilles Deleuze and Felix Guattari, Michel Foucault, Donna Haraway, and Paul Virilio, to name a few. Yet rarely—James Katz and Mark Aakhus's (2002) theory of apparatgeist comes to mind—have we generated new theories of our own. We have applied traditional methods and approaches such as content analysis, cultural history, discourse analysis, and ethnography in novel and admirable ways, and in the case of ethnography, we have significantly altered it to include digital domains (Baym 2000; Danet 2001; Hine 2000; and Miller and Slater 2001). In some cases, including Steven M. Schneider and Kirsten Foot's (2005) "Web sphere analysis" and Joe Walther's (1996) "hyperpersonal communication framework," we have derived altogether new approaches.

It can be argued that a commonly shared set of theories and methodologies is a sign of an academic field's development and sophistication. It can also be argued that such commonly held approaches signal ossification, stagnation, and a lack of imagination. I favor the side of a temporarily canonless field of study (Silver 2004). If and when the canon appears, replete with acceptable theories, methods, and methodologies, I surely hope its foundations are pliable enough for whatever meets us in the future.

We have a young field of study, one that, depending on with whom one speaks, stretches back only five, ten, or fifteen years. In other words, what we have is a field of study *under construction*—with boundaries not yet set, with borders not yet fully erected, and with a canon not yet established. As such, we have a field of study ripe for growth and twigging, becoming and re-becoming, imagined and reimagined. Now, before the mold is set, is the time for experimentation.

Critical cyberculture studies is, in its most basic form, a critical approach to new media and the contexts that shape and inform them. Its focus is not merely the Internet and the Web but, rather, all forms of networked media and culture that surround us today, not to mention those that will surround us tomorrow. Like cultural studies, critical cyberculture studies strives to locate its object of study within various overlapping contexts, including capitalism, consumerism and commodification, cultural difference, and the militarization of everyday life. Although the origins of critical cyberculture studies rests firmly in academia, it is most fully realized when it moves beyond campus and is built, challenged, and rebuilt with as many publics as possible. Above all, critical cyberculture studies scholars have high goals: we seek to use our collective understanding of new media and their environments to alleviate suffering and oppression and to accelerate freedom and justice. We take our field—and our world—quite seriously.

For the sake of this volume and to encourage further dialogue on the matter, I wish to highlight three crucial elements of critical cyberculture studies: historical contexts, social contexts, and cultural difference.

Historical Contexts

The twentieth century welcomed, among many other things, a dizzying array of new and once-new media. Radio, film, television, computers, and the Internet are merely the major players. Naturally, all of these technologies are historically specific, and their origins, development, adoption, and distribution merit critical attention. By critical attention I mean something beyond (or, perhaps, in addition to) the monthly hagiographies found in *Wired* magazine. For, as Daniel Czitrom notes in *Media and the American Mind,*

> Considered as an institution, each medium that evolved from the work of individual inventors and entrepreneurs was later subsumed into larger corporate or military contexts. The key roles played by small concerns and amateurs in the early history of new communications technologies are too often forgotten. Yet the importance of corporate and military settings for

technological progress and of the accompanying support by large capital investments and highly organized research teams clearly intensifies the closer one gets to the present. (1982, 185)

As we embark on the newest chapter of new media, it is important to engage in what we may call "critical histories of the recent past." This means situating our studies of, say, blogs, Moveon.org, and Grand Theft Auto within larger historical landscapes, including early developments of the Internet and early developments in modern computing, and investigating the ways in which these technologies emerged from within a complex web of corporate and military interests. But it also means looking backward to histories of other once-new media such as radio, television, and, as Jonathan Sterne smartly suggests in this volume, sound recording.

Social Contexts

Back in the day, early adopters of the Net took pleasure in knowing that most people had no knowledge of what would soon be called cyberspace, let alone of more "tangible" elements like e-mail, ftp, and unix commands. Today, of course, cyberculture is everywhere, especially in the West—in sitcoms and sci-fi, in political campaigns and political mobilizations, in *Wired* and *Women's World,* in URLs printed on public billboards and scrawled on bathroom walls. For better or worse, this larger technoscape is our site of study.

Nearly fifteen years ago, Constance Penley and Andrew Ross began their anthology *Technoculture* with wise words:

> Technologies are not repressively foisted upon passive populations, any more than the power to realize their repressive potential is in the hands of a conspiring few. They are developed at any one time and place in accord with a complex set of existing rules or rational procedures, institutional histories, technical possibilities, and, last, but not least, popular desires. (1991, xiv)

We must do the same with new media and continue to examine how they are built within and shaped by consumer capitalism, how they are developed, brought to the market, and continually monitored by military interests, and how they are discursively constructed by an array of other media forms, most of which encourage us to consume stuff we never needed. Simultaneously, we must continue to explore individual and collective agency, a social context in itself, a set of decisions that sometimes leads us in directions that were not preprogrammed.

Cultural Difference

In 1993, Rheingold wrote that "because we cannot see one another in cyberspace, gender, age, national origin, and physical appearance are not apparent unless a person wants to make such characteristics public" (26). He was wrong then, and it is doubtful, after multiple governmental reports, academic studies, and plain common sense, that he still subscribes to such a belief. Critical cyberculture studies approaches cultural difference—human elements of race and ethnicity, gender, sexuality, age, and disability—not as an afterthought or a note inserted under "future studies" but, rather, front and center, informing our research questions, frameworks, and findings.

The bad news is that we have a long way to go. The good news is that work in the area is finally beginning to appear. To date, issues of gender online have received the most critical attention with works like Lynn Cherny and Elizabeth Reba Weise's *Wired Women: Gender and New Realities in Cyberspace* (1996), Wendy Harcourt's *Women@Internet: Creating New Cultures in Cyberspace* (1999), Susan Hawthorne and Renate Klein's *CyberFeminism: Connectivity, Critique and Creativity* (1999), Eileen Green and Alison Adam's *Virtual Gender: Technology, Consumption and Identity* (2001), Mary Flanagan and Austin Booth's *Reload: Rethinking Women + Cyberculture* (2002), and Lori Kendall's *Hanging Out in the Virtual Pub: Masculinities and Relationships Online* (2002). Works that explore the intersections among new media, race, and ethnicity are far fewer yet include significant contributions like Beth E. Kolko, Lisa Nakamura, and Gilbert B. Rodman's *Race in Cyberspace* (2000), Alondra Nelson, Thuy Linh N. Tu, and Alicia Headlam Hines's *Technicolor: Race, Technology, and Everyday Life* (2001), Lisa Nakamura's *Cybertypes: Race, Ethnicity, and Identity on the Internet* (2002), and Emily Noelle Ignacio's *Building Diaspora: Filipino Cultural Community Formation on the Internet* (2005). Studies of sexuality online remain understudied, yet contributions like John Edward Campbell's *Getting It On Online: Cyberspace, Gay Male Sexuality, and Embodied Identity* (2004) are steps in the right direction. Likewise, critical studies of age and ageism remain largely under the radar, with exceptions like Karen E. Riggs's *Granny @ Work: Aging and New Technology on the Job in America* (2003). And finally, while scholars in technical communication and informatics are beginning to work on issues of disability, little has been done to integrate the burgeoning field of disability studies with the more culturally inflected field of critical cyberculture studies.

Although the majority of this volume's contributors are from the United States, scholars from Canada, China, Denmark, Great Britain, the Netherlands, and Puerto Rico give the anthology a modest and much needed international perspective. Moreover, contributors represent a spectrum of disciplinary affiliations, including art history, city and regional planning, communication, film studies, game studies, journalism, library and information sciences, media studies, psychology, radio-television-film, sociology, speech communication, technical communication, and visual culture. Although a handful of authors are senior scholars, the majority are junior —graduate students, newly minted PhDs, and untenured professors.

Critical Cyberculture Studies is divided into four section: Fielding the Field; Critical Approaches and Methods; Cultural Difference in/and Cyberculture; and Critical Histories of the Recent Past.

Part I: Fielding the Field

In "The Historiography of Cyberculture," Jonathan Sterne questions the seemingly ahistorical construction of "new" media and offers an alternative historiography of contemporary media culture via sound. The next three chapters interrogate the field of study by situating it within larger and overlapping developments. In "Cultural Difference, Theory, and Cyberculture Studies: A Case of Mutual Repulsion," Lisa Nakamura argues for a more proactive inclusion of theories of cultural difference. In "How We Became Postdigital: From CyberStudies to Game Studies," Espen Aarseth advocates approaching digital culture via game studies and suggests a number of productive avenues that such a direction generates. In "Internet Studies in Times of Terror," David Silver and Alice Marwick encourage readers to take a step back in order to reflect upon the forces of militarization that have always accompanied, informed, and helped shape new technologies—as well as the academic study of such technologies.

Part I concludes with chapters by Wendy Robinson and McKenzie

Wark. In "Catching the Waves: Considering Cyberculture, Technoculture and Electronic Consumption," Robinson provides an excellent survey of what may be called a "second wave" of cyberculture studies, one that brings together new and "old" media technologies and that reminds us that commercial and consumer imperatives help shape such technologies. In "Cyberculture Studies: An Antidisciplinary Approach (version 3.0)," Wark questions not only the disciplinarity of new media studies but also the utility of disciplinary-based forms of knowledge. As we think through the development of our field of study, we would be wise to consider his words: "The disciplines arise not as a necessary means of managing the abundance of knowledge but, to the contrary, as an artificial means of maintaining the scarcity of access within a regime of knowledge/media predicated on a politics of hierarchy and arbitrary division and an economics of exclusion" (pp. 69–70 in this volume).

Part II: Critical Approaches and Methods

In "Finding the Quality in Qualitative Research," Nancy K. Baym outlines a number of problems found in qualitative research in general and qualitative research in digital media in particular, followed by a set of principles that can mitigate such problems. In "Web Sphere Analysis and Cybercultural Studies," Kirsten Foot puts forth the concept of the "Web sphere" as a productive unit of analysis and discusses methods of Web sphere analysis that can help us explore the complex web of online interactions. In "Connecting the Selves: Computer-Mediated Identification Processes," Heidi J. Figueroa Sarriera brings the field of study into dialogue with contemporary developments in psychology, especially as they relate to notions of subjectivity.

The next two chapters, by Christian Sandvig and Beth E. Kolko, situate the field within Internet infrastructures and cultural policy. In "The Structural Problems of the Internet for Cultural Policy," Sandvig argues for an "infrastructural cultural policy," one that takes technical, social, and legal elements into consideration and encourages creative and proactive involvement on the part of public-interests advocates. This chapter meshes nicely with Kolko's "Cultural Considerations in Internet Policy and Design: A Case Study from Central Asia," which brings together Internet policy and design, focusing especially on efforts currently under way in Central Asia.

Part II ends with four different approaches to cyberculture studies. In "Bridging Cyberlife and Real Life: A Study of Online Communities in Hong Kong," Anthony Fung leads us through a much needed exploration of the overlaps between off- and online interactions by examining community-building practices of young Hong Kong gamers. Blanca Gordo, in "Overcoming Institutional Marginalization," raises similar issues by investigating the conditions and social processes of community-based organizations working to integrate digital media and low-income communities. Part II concludes with Greg Elmer's "The Vertical (Layered) Net: Interrogating the Conditions of Network Connectivity," a useful analysis of the ways in which new media are vertically integrated, and Stine Gotved's "The Construction of Cybersocial Reality," a provocative approach that combines culture, structure, and the Internet to better understand social interactions online.

Part III: Cultural Difference in/and Cyberculture

Part III explores the intersections of contemporary notions of cultural difference and digital media and culture. In "E-scaping Boundaries: Bridging Cyberspace and Diaspora Studies through Nethnography," Emily Noelle Ignacio bridges diaspora studies with cyberculture studies, paying special attention to notions of identity and nation. In "An Interdisciplinary Approach to the Study of Cybercultures," Madhavi Mallapragada continues this convergence, adding postcolonial studies and media/cultural studies to the mix. Shifting from theory to practice, Bharat Mehra, in "An Action Research (AR) Manifesto for Cyberculture Power to 'Marginalized' Cultures of Difference," argues how action research can and *should* invigorate the field of study, especially when applied toward social justice and community enfranchisement.

In "Cyberstudies and the Politics of Visibility," David J. Phillips investigates issues of identity, not only online but also with regard to the researcher, and develops these questions with an analysis of surveillance technologies. Frank Schaap, in "Disaggregation, Technology, and Masculinity: Elements of Internet Research," continues this examination of identity, with a focus on masculinity. Closing Part III is Kate O'Riordan's "Gender, Technology, and Visual Cyberculture: Virtually Women," an exploration of gender and visual culture via an analysis of the simulated newsreader Ananova.

Part IV: Critical Histories of the Recent Past

Part IV offers four critical histories of what could be called "new media's recent past," with special attention paid to the processes of commercialization and commodification. In "How Digital Technology Found Utopian Ideology: Lessons from the First Hackers' Conference," Fred Turner injects the field with a much needed dose of history, tracing the libertarian ethos often attached to cyberculture to the first Hackers' Conference in 1984. In "Government.com: ICTs and Reforming Governance in Asia," Shanthi Kalathil investigates recent e-government initiatives in Asia, in light of developing commercial applications. The book's coeditor, Adrienne Massanari, in "Dot-Coms and Cyberculture Studies: Amazon.com as a Case Study," performs a rhetorical analysis of one of the most successful, and boastful, dot.coms, Amazon.com. Traveling from Seattle to New York, Gina Neff, in "Associating Independents: Business Relationships and the Culture of Independence in the Dot-Com Era," examines the media and cultural negotiations behind Silicon Alley, New York's hypercommercialized version of the so-called new economy.

Critical Cyberculture Studies purports neither to represent a comprehensive view of what the field is nor to suggest a master blueprint of what it should be. Instead, it serves as an invitation to scholars to consider a few new directions, directions that we believe to be too important to ignore and too interesting to leave unexplored. If, as discussed earlier, the field is still "under construction," then *Critical Cyberculture Studies* offers some strategic elements and ingredients that may help to build a more inclusive, more critical, more dynamic, and more interesting field of study.

NOTES

1. For a large yet not nearly comprehensive list of relevant syllabi, see "Courses in Cyberculture" at the Resource Center for Cyberculture Studies, http://www.com .washington.edu/rccs/courselist.asp.

REFERENCES

Baym, Nancy K. 2000. *Tune in, log on: Soaps, fandom, and online community.* Thousand Oaks, CA: Sage.

Beaubien, Anne K., Sharon A. Hogan, and Mary W. George. 1982. *Learning the library: Concepts and methods for effective bibliographic instruction.* New York: R. R. Bowker.

Bell, David. 2001. *An introduction to cyberculture.* London and New York: Routledge.

Bell, David, and Barbara Kennedy, eds. 2000. *The cybercultures reader.* London and New York: Routledge.

Bucy, Erik P., ed. 2002. *Living in the information age: A new media reader.* Belmont, CA: Wadsworth Thomson Learning.

Campbell, John Edward. 2004. *Getting it on online: Cyberspace, gay male sexuality, and embodied identity.* Binghamton, NY: Harrington Park Press.

Cherny, Lynn, and Elizabeth Reba Weise, eds. 1996. *Wired women: Gender and new realities in cyberspace.* Seattle: Seal Press.

Czitrom, Daniel J. 1982. *Media and the American mind: From Morse to McLuhan.* Chapel Hill: University of North Carolina Press.

Danet, Brenda. 2001. *Cyberpl@y: Communicating online.* Oxford, UK: Berg.

Featherstone, Mike, and Roger Burrows, eds. 1995. *Cyberspace/cyberbodies/cyberpunk: Cultures of technological embodiment.* London: Sage.

Flanagan, Mary, and Austin Booth, eds. 2002. *Reload: Rethinking women + cyberculture.* Cambridge, MA: MIT Press.

Gauntlett, David, ed. 2000. *Web.studies: Rewiring media studies for the digital age.* London: Arnold.

Green, Eileen, and Alison Adam, eds. 2001. *Virtual gender: Technology, consumption and identity.* London: Routledge.

Harcourt, Wendy, ed. 1999. *Women@Internet: Creating new cultures in cyberspace.* London: Zed Books.

Hawthorne, Susan, and Renate Klein, eds. 1999. *CyberFeminism: Connectivity, critique and creativity.* North Melbourne, Australia: Spinifex Press.

Hine, Christine. 2000. *Virtual ethnography.* London: Sage.

Ignacio, Emily Noelle. 2005. *Building diaspora: Filipino cultural community formation on the Internet.* New Brunswick, NJ: Rutgers University Press.

Jones, Steve, ed. 1995. *CyberSociety: Computer-mediated communication and community.* Thousand Oaks, CA: Sage.

———, ed. 1997. *Virtual culture: Identity and communication in cybersociety.* Thousand Oaks, CA: Sage.

———, ed. 1998. *Cybersociety 2.0: Revisiting computer-mediated community and technology.* Thousand Oaks, CA: Sage.

Katz, James E., and Mark Aakhus, eds. 2002. *Perpetual contact: Mobile communication, private talk, public performance.* Cambridge: Cambridge University Press.

Kendall, Lori. 2002. *Hanging out in the virtual pub: Masculinities and relationships online.* Berkeley: University of California Press.

Kiesler, Sara, ed. 1997. *Culture of the Internet.* Mahwah, NJ: Lawrence Erlbaum.

Kolko, Beth E., Lisa Nakamura, and Gilbert B. Rodman, eds. 2000. *Race in cyber-space*. New York: Routledge.

Lovink, Geert. 2003. *Dark fiber: Tracking critical Internet culture*. Cambridge, MA: MIT Press.

Miller, Daniel, and Don Slater. 2001. *The Internet: An ethnographic approach*. Oxford, UK: Berg.

Nakamura, Lisa. 2002. *Cybertypes: Race, ethnicity, and identity on the Internet*. New York: Routledge.

Nelson, Alondra, Thuy Linh N. Tu, and Alicia Headlam Hines, eds. 2001. *Technicolor: Race, technology, and everyday life*. New York: NYU Press.

Penley, Constance, and Andrew Ross, eds. 1991. *Technoculture*. Minneapolis: University of Minnesota Press.

Potter, David, ed. 1996. *Internet culture*. New York: Routledge.

Rheingold, Howard. 1993. *The virtual community: Homesteading on the electronic frontier*. Reading, MA: Addison-Wesley.

Riggs, Karen E. 2003. *Granny @ work: Aging and new technology on the job in America*. New York: Routledge.

Schneider, Steven M., and Kirsten Foot. 2005. Web sphere analysis: An approach to studying online action. In *Virtual methods: Issues in social research on the Internet*, edited by Christine Hine. 157–170. Oxford, UK: Berg.

Silver, David. 2000. Looking backwards, looking forward: Cyberculture studies 1990–2000. In *Web.studies: Rewiring media studies for the digital age*, edited by David Gauntlett. 19–30. London: Arnold.

———. 2004. Internet/cyberculture/digital culture/new media/fill-in-the-blank studies. *New Media & Society*, 6(1), 55–64.

Sudweeks, Fay, Margaret L. McLaughlin, and Sheizaf Rafaeli, eds. 1998. *Network and netplay: Virtual groups on the Internet*. Menlo Park, CA: AAAI Press.

Swiss, Thomas, ed. 2000. *Unspun: Key concepts for understanding the World Wide Web*. New York: NYU Press.

Thurlow, Crispin, Laura Lengel, and Alice Tomic, eds. 2004. *Computer mediated communication: Social interaction and the Internet*. Thousand Oaks, CA: Sage.

Trend, David, ed. 2001. *Reading digital culture*. Malden, MA: Blackwell.

Turkle, Sherry. 1995. *Life on the screen: Identity in the age of the Internet*. New York: Simon and Schuster.

Walther, Joe. 1996. Computer-mediated communication: Impersonal, interpersonal, and the hyperpersonal interaction. *Communication Research*, 23, 3–43.

Wardrip-Fruin, Noah, and Nick Montfort, eds. 2003. *The new media reader*. Cambridge, MA: MIT Press.

Part I

Fielding the Field

Chapter 1

The Historiography of Cyberculture

Jonathan Sterne

We are at a turning point in the analysis of so-called new communication technologies.[1] Even though we are used to thinking of them as new, these technologies are not nearly as new as they were ten, twenty, or thirty years ago. Claims for the revolutionary promise of digital technologies are dissipating as well: advertisers have moved to "digital lifestyle" campaigns that represent digital technologies as commodities to be integrated into everyday life rather than as epochal forces that will transform it. Meanwhile, scholarly treatments of so-called new media are getting more nuanced. While some conservatives and otherwise recalcitrant sorts still argue for the revolutionary power of "new" technologies, the technophilic position is at least somewhat less acceptable in serious scholarship than it was five years ago. With perseverance and good fortune, they'll become even less respected as time passes. Similarly, critical scholars are less likely to present simple critiques of technological determinism and e-topian discourse (to borrow a term from Crawford [2003]) and are more likely to expand the scope of their studies either to offer robust descriptions of digital media or to connect the remaining e-topian discourses with broader social and political currents.

So in many ways, cyberculture studies—whatever you take the field to be—has made significant strides in the past five years. It has more conferences, more journals, and more good scholarship. Ah, signs of progress![2] In other ways, however, we are still at the very beginnings of a specifically academic and critical historiography of cyberculture; we ought to step back and reflect for a moment. Some habits of historical and methodological thinking have begun to crystallize in cyberculture studies. Many of our analytical categories were developed in the 1980s and 1990s, and many of them persist into the supposedly new moment we now inhabit. In a sense, we are mirrors of our object: as we take each step, we carry forward a history that we have not yet fully grasped, and that history in part shapes our action on the present stage. In fact, most of our scholarly histories of cyberculture in one way or another recapitulate narratives available from corporations heavily invested in the digital media economy, or stories told online by self-described "pioneers" themselves (our language still hasn't quite given up on the frontier mythos) or cheerleader journalists.

In this essay, I will challenge you, dear reader, to think more broadly and bravely about what counts in the domain of cyberculture studies. I will do so by exploring some aspects of contemporary media culture via sound. But my point is much bigger than "gee, people should talk about sound." Rather, my point is that we need to be careful in our object construction. Or, to borrow a social scientific phrase, we need to be more sensible in our "research design."

Sound might seem like an odd theme to crop up in an essay with a title as grand as "*The* Historiography of Cyberculture." We already assume that an essay bearing such a grandiose title would discuss cyberpunk authors and sci-fi flicks, hackers and phone phreaks, defense systems, university networks and home computers, MUDs and MOOs, browsers and user groups, VR helmets and wearable media, Web sites and information economies, and sites of new industry. All of these objects are legitimate objects of cyberculture study—and elsewhere I've considered many of them. But if we assume that these are the proper objects of cyberculture study *before* we read the essay, then we are also assuming that the most important parts of our historiographic work are finished—that we already know what cyberculture is and where it comes from. I aim to trouble that certainty in this short piece.

Let us start with a banal example: a story on special effects in *The Matrix Reloaded* in the May 2003 issue of *Wired* magazine. As the author explains, the production studio created its fight scenes from elaborate composites of sampled images. Rather than creating an artificial reality and filming it, the editors built motion sequences out of countless still images of actors and locations—taken from every imaginable angle. In a word, they "sampled" images and created a totally fabricated scene from them:

> The standard way of simulating the world in [computer graphics] is to build it from the inside out, by assembling forms out of polygons and applying computer-simulated textures and lighting. The ESC [a visual

effects firm] team took a radically different path, loading as much of the real world as possible into the computer first, building from the outside in. This approach, known as image-based rendering, is transforming the effects industry.

A similar evolution has already occurred in music. The first electronic keyboards sought to re-create a piano's acoustic properties by amassing sets of rules about the physics of keys, hammers, and strings. The end result sounded like a synthesizer. Now DJs and musicians sample and morph the recorded sounds of actual instruments.

Instead of synthesizing the world, [ESC effects-guru John] Gaeta cloned it. To make the Burly Brawl, he would have to build the Matrix. (Silberman 2003)

The *Wired* writer immediately picks up on the analogy between sampling sounds and sampling images, and points out that the *Matrix*'s "Burly Brawl" fight scene was indeed "sampled." For all the academic critiques of *Wired*, I wonder how many of us scholars would have picked up on that obvious parallel as quickly as a *Wired* journalist. While visual design is very much at the center of cyberculture studies, the auditory dimension is almost always left out. One need only look at the available bibliographies. Beyond Steve Jones's work (Jones 1993 [discussed below]; Jones 2000; Jones 2002) and a few other notable mentions like Mark Dery's references to music in *Escape Velocity* (1996), Sean Cubitt's chapter on sound in *Digital Aesthetics* (1998), or a passing mention of sound synthesis in Lev Manovich's *Language of New Media* (2001), one has to leave the field entirely to find interesting writing on digital audio that is not simply commentary on MP3s and file sharing (for example, Meintjes 2003; Rothenbuhler and Peters 1997; Taylor 2001; Theberge 1997).[3] In other words, the history to which Silberman refers is often left out of academic histories of cyberculture. Indeed, a great many writers in cyberculture studies have taken the field to be a subspecies of visual culture (for example, Druckrey 1996; Manovich, forthcoming; Mitchell 1995; Robins 1996). It is one thing to claim that there is a visual dimension to cyberculture and that cyberculture might well connect up with other aspects of visual culture. It is another to subsume cyberculture under the rubric of visual culture, and this is my concern here.

There are many possible explanations for why sound is so neglected by cyberculture scholars. We could blame it on the organization of the disciplines: while "visual culture" is an object of study and a set of problems recognized across many humanities and social sciences (and one can find various kinds of "visual studies" positions advertised in many fields), "sound studies" is only an emergent term. Even though there exists a massive interdisciplinary archive of scholarship about sound, many of these writers are only beginning to notice one another, much less be noticed by people in other fields. Although there is some merit to the "organization of the disciplines" story, it is ultimately unsatisfying because cyberculture scholars have been quite creative in other areas of object construction. Yes, "visual culture studies" is an available scholarly orientation. And as Lisa Nakamura points out elsewhere in this volume, scholars of the Internet are only now waking up to the fact that it is filled with pictures as well as texts. But why has digital audio fared even worse than images in cyberculture studies?

A more robust answer lies in our historiography. Consider the available histories of digital media. Although the compact disc was the first digital medium widely adopted by consumers, it is rarely discussed in histories of cyberculture. For all our self-congratulation about moving into a new period of cyberculture studies, here is where the millennial specter still haunts us. Is it possible that CDs fare so poorly in our histories because so few people thought of them as "revolutionary" in any significant way? Because compact discs were a new storage medium that neither responded to nor required significant changes in practices and habits of music listening, they do not fit the model of new technology as "revolutionary."[4] While computers, networks, and various aspects of virtual reality have populated the available histories and prehistories of cyberculture, CDs warrant a footnote at best. The same can be said for digital sound synthesis, sampling, and digital audio recording in general (with the exception of the scholars cited above).

Sound is, pardon the pun, a blind spot of cyberculture historiography. Consider this "visual culture" narrative of the history of "virtuality," an important theme in cyberculture studies:

> Virtuality is a buzzword for the 1990s, a seemingly new way of experiencing the outside on the inside. . . . Some critics have wanted to call [it] a radical break with the past, heralding a transformation of everyday life unequalled since the Industrial Revolution. Others have insisted that there is relatively little new here, recalling a panoply of once-forgotten visual devices from the panorama to the stereoscope and zootrope that immersed the viewer in a seemingly real environment. For all the bluster, a middle way seems fairly

clear. Virtuality has certainly been experienced before, perhaps as long as people have been sufficiently distracted by an artist's skill to take a picture briefly for reality. On the other hand, computer-generated environments offer the chance to interact with and change this illusory reality, an opportunity that no previous medium has been able to provide. At root, the question is the relationship between the human body and space, mediated by the sense of sight (Mirzoeff 1998, p. 181).

Nicholas Mirzoeff ought to be applauded for his attention to the tensions between historical continuity and change in the description of the present. And, to be fair, he is writing about cyberculture in the context of a reader on visual culture. But as I have argued elsewhere, even if we presuppose the "hegemony of the visual" (I do not), hegemony does not mean the totality of vision, and therein lies the rub. Mirzoeff's media history is entirely partial because he collapses media history into visual history. If virtuality has been experienced as long as people have been willing to take pictures for reality, then what about human-produced sounds? Next to (and before) panoramas, zootropes, and stereoscopes lies a history of automata, musical instruments, and architectural acoustics designed to produce synthetic auditory experiences. Whether these are "virtual" in the same way that we talk about virtuality today is open to question. But they are better and more preponderant examples of the phenomena Mirzoeff points to through reference to nineteenth-century visual technologies. We should be wary of collapsing the history of virtuality or any other dimension of cyberculture too quickly into the visual.

My criticism of the visual culture orientation is not just a matter of inclusion. Consider Mirzoeff's claims that "computer-generated environments offer the chance to interact with and change this illusory reality, an opportunity that no previous medium has been able to provide" or that "at root, the question is the relationship between the human body and space, mediated by the sense of sight" (p. 181). Both of these claims are simply untrue and leave out perhaps the most important and mundane experience of virtual space in twentieth-century media: audio recording. As Steve Jones (1993) has written, audio engineers have been producing one or another form of "virtual space" for most of the twentieth century through the use of careful microphone placement, synthetic echo and reverberation, and artificial manipulation of listeners' stereo fields. Indeed, many of the problems now faced by Virtual Reality (VR) designers were first faced in the areas of sound design for audio recordings.

(Jones also deserves kudos for pointing out the visual bias of new media theory ten years ago; if only we'd listened!) Ken Hillis (1999) has smartly connected the visual obsession in VR theory with more tactile issues surrounding bodily motility—the experience of moving through the space and the connection between a VR helmet (or glasses or other head-mounted display) and a glove that measures movement. Hillis's point is that virtuality is not simply a visual experience but a multisensory one. Indeed, if virtuality is not defined as a purely visual experience, then it has a century-long history to be unearthed: the same problems of spatiality and motility were addressed over a century ago in early experiments with stereo audition and in attempts to use audio to give listeners a sense of spatial position (Bell 1880; Sterne 2003a, pp. 156–157).

The same kind of history exists regarding representations of information. "Audialization" is a term coined by Honor Harger (2003) to refer to the process whereby information is made more comprehensible by rendering it as sound. It is the auditory equivalent of the more familiar "visualization" of information, but in fact, it is older and more fully established. In fields such as radio astronomy, sound is often converted into images for easier scientific apprehension and comprehension. Yet sometimes sound provides more information than sight. For instance, the rotation of a pulsar becomes much more comprehensible when it is actually heard by a listener. As with spatialization, attempts to comprehend and analyze phenomena by converting them into sound (or merely attending to their sonic characteristics) have a history much longer than that of cyberculture. For instance, from the second decade of the nineteenth century, physicians used stethoscopes to audialize the otherwise imperceptible interiors of their patients' bodies (Sterne 2003a, pp. 99–136).

What do these histories of auditory media mean for cyberculture scholarship? At the most basic level, auditory media have, over the past century, developed in areas that are now considered central themes in cyberculture studies. Long before Virtual Reality hit the scene, there were media experiences designed specifically as artificial media experiences, and many of the so-called new problems of cyberculture have already been dealt with in the auditory realm. This is true for artificial senses of space; it is true for a sense of artificial or "pure" media experience; and it is true for even basic issues like interface design: for example, in Trevor Pinch and Frank Trocco's history of the Moog synthesizer, there is a very interesting chapter on debates over whether to control synthesizers through pianolike keyboards or through sets of knobs, sliders, and switches (Pinch and Trocco 2002, pp. 53–69).

As my auditory examples suggest, our available histories of cyberculture are highly selective. They would seem even more selective if we explored the olfactory, tactile, and gustatory dimensions of sensory media history. Though the "postmodern turn" has held much less sway over historical writing than its ethnographic counterpart, it is widely accepted that when we write a history, the inclusions and exclusions are the result of conscious, methodical choices by the historian, and not simple, empirical facts "out there" that the historian has apprehended. History is the act of writing about the past. The past itself is always a step away from its description (on the disjuncture between historical description and its object, see Derrida 1976; Lacapra 1985; and White 1978; on the postmodern turn in historical writing, see Jenkins 1997 and Novick 1988).

One of the most important choices a historian makes is that of periodization. Periodization is, most simply, how we mark periods in our histories. The simplest periodization of cyberculture studies would be a binary operation: there was analog, and now there is digital. Nicholas Negroponte's much-maligned *Being Digital* (1995) implies this kind of all-or-nothing approach. The opposite is not much more fruitful: cyberculture is simply the latest version of trends we can identify since the invention of writing. Books like Tom Standage's *Victorian Internet* (1998) are useful because they show that claims about the power of new media recur across historical periods, but taken too far, the argument turns into a claim that there is nothing new under the sun. Other writers have attempted to bridge the gap through the rather dubious notion of "prehistory," which implies periods very clearly: everything before cyberculture leads up to it. Yes, there are times when we must, as C. Wright Mills (1959, p. 154) said, "study history in order to get rid of it," but as of yet we have a relatively limited historical palette for cyberculture.

Of course, many histories do take more nuanced approaches. Mirzoeff attempts to distinguish between old and new visual technologies in the account cited earlier. We can also find many standard periodizations of cyberculture history by technology: computers → personal computers → Internet; by art: avant-garde art → cyberpunk → cyberculture; and even by economics: fordism → postfordism. My point is not to catalog the approaches but rather to point out what is at stake in choosing them: once we define our periods, we set our limits. We make choices about inclusion and exclusion. I am arguing that we should attend to those choices with much greater care. We should treat the historical periods in our writing less like self-evident categories in our data and more like problems to be considered and debated. We should place object construction at the very center of our intellectual project.

I borrow the phrase "object construction" from Pierre Bourdieu and his collaborators (Bourdieu, Chamboredon, and Passeron 1991; Bourdieu and Wacquant 1993). Bourdieu believed that the two most important moments in social research were the "epistemic break" and the "construction of the object." As a sociologist, Bourdieu saw many other people in his field who accepted their research problems as they were defined by policy bodies or journalistic reports. Those scholars accepted prepackaged or, in Bourdieu's words, "pregiven" research problems that carried with them the assumptions of the institutions in which they were defined. If scholars do not make an "epistemic break" with the existing ways of defining a problem, they risk importing unwanted and unexamined institutional or personal biases into their work (I am *not* arguing for unbiased work, only that we attend to our biases and choose them with care). Once we have broken with existing assumptions, we then must begin defining our object of study: we have to classify it, figure out its "inside" and "outside," and choose a method with which to approach it. This is an especially important issue in the study of technology, where there are strong institutional imperatives for certain kinds of technological study (I develop this further in Sterne 2003b).

If we cannot assume what does and does not count as cyberculture in our histories, then for each study we do, we need to reclassify it. Each time we approach a new question or object in cyberculture studies, we need to figure out what is "inside" the category of cyberculture and what is "outside" it. Once we make these distinctions, we need to choose research methods appropriate to our objects. In other words, these are not questions on which the field should settle but, rather, questions with which we should constantly wrestle. This is *especially* important in cyberculture studies. Consider the very unfortunate and bad habit of many cyberculture scholars who use the term "technology" synonymously with "digital technology," as if other kinds of technologies had never existed. The first step in a sensitivity to history as a problem is to attend to the differences between our subject and a long, complex, and significant history of technology that spans the entirety of human civilization. This elision points to another important dimension of periodization and historical object construction: cyberculture scholars need to develop a better sense of how cyberculture fits into larger phenomena. If we give up the everything-or-nothing-is-new approach, if we expand the range of technologies and practices admitted to the domain of cyberculture studies, we will also have to develop coherent explanations of how the history of cyberculture fits into larger histories like communication history, cultural history, political history, and the history of technology. Indeed, what goes for the past also goes for the present: we will need accounts of the relationship between cyberculture as a specific domain and the larger domains of culture, politics, media, and technology.

As the field enters a new phase, we need a richer sense of the history of cyberculture and the larger histories of which cyberculture is a part. This will help us break out of some of the methodological ruts in scholarship on contemporary phenomena as well. As works like Haraway's "Cyborg Manifesto" (1991), Turkle's *Life on the Screen* (1995), Stone's *War of Desire and Technology at the Close of the Mechanical Age* (1995), and a small group of others become staples of cyberculture syllabi, fleets of studies that reproduce their methods and conclusions have emerged. But we should not blame our canonical authors for their mediocre imitators: their works are staples of cyberculture syllabi precisely because they innovated in their time. They came up with new objects and new approaches, and they challenged us to think differently. Now that they have won us over (on at least a few points) we would do well to take a lesson from their scholarly ethic rather than from their conclusions. Ultimately, our job is to invent and not to repeat.

In this chapter, I have explored some gaps in cyberculture scholarship by criticizing its visualist bias and gesturing toward sound history. But it should be clear that my purpose is not to wag a finger and say, "you all should be studying sound." Far from it. My foray into sound and historical method offers a warning. My critique here is quite easy, almost too easy in way, and it leads me to wonder what other aporias we carry with us as cyberculture scholars. After about a decade of criticizing millennial claims for digital media, we are only just now finding robust alternatives for historical and contemporary description of cyberculture. We are very much at the beginning of object construction, and we are in a moment when it might be good to spend a little more time looking over our shoulders and gazing at our navels (though we need not do it all in print). Ultimately, we have no choice as critical, responsible intellectuals but to refuse the temptations of pregiven problems, ossified methods, and familiar conclusions. Our jobs require the hard work of object construction. The alternative is oblivion.

NOTES

1. Many thanks to Carrie Rentschler and Fred Turner, who made comments on earlier versions of this essay. Thanks also to David Silver, Adrienne Massanari, and the other contributors to the book for their comments on the piece and an inspiring occasion on which to present an earlier version.

2. But even as our field and object begin to stabilize, we should be wary of false closure: for instance, in twenty years will there be an "Internet" for Internet scholars to study?

3. Mike Ayers's forthcoming edited collection, *Cybersounds,* could be an important bridge between scholarship on cyberculture and scholarship on digital music and audio.

4. Oddly, CDs were "revolutionary" in at least one way: they were able to artificially prop up the music industry's lagging sales for over a decade. The film industry followed the CD model with its move to the DVD standard, with outstanding results: the DVD is the most quickly adopted format in the history of consumer electronics.

REFERENCES

Bell, A. G. (1880). Experiments in Binaural Audition. *American Journal of Otology.*
Bourdieu, P., Chamboredon, J.-C., and Passeron, J.-C. (1991). *The Craft of Sociology: Epistemological Preliminaries.* New York: Walter de Gruyter.
Bourdieu, P., and Wacquant, L. J. D. (1993). *An Invitation to Reflexive Sociology.* Chicago: University of Chicago Press.
Crawford, A. (2003). The City in the Future Perfect: Information Technology, Utopianism, and Urban Life. Ph.D. dissertation, Department of Communication, University of Pittsburgh.
Cubitt, S. (1998). *Digital Aesthetics.* Thousand Oaks, CA: Sage.
Derrida, J. (1976). *Of Grammatology.* Baltimore: Johns Hopkins University Press.
Dery, M. (1996). *Escape Velocity: Cyberculture at the End of the Century.* New York: Grove Press.
Druckrey, T. (ed.). (1996). *Electronic Culture: Technology and Visual Representation.* New York: Aperture.

Haraway, D. (1991). "Cyborg Manifesto." In *Simians, Cyborgs and Women*. New York: Routledge.

Harger, H. (2003). Broadcasting Media. Paper presented at Musical Constellations in the Digital Age, Zagreb, Croatia, 8 April.

Hillis, K. (1999). *Digital Sensations: Space, Identity and Embodiment in Virtual Reality*. Minneapolis: University of Minnesota Press.

Jenkins, K. (ed.). (1997). *The Postmodern History Reader*. New York: Routledge.

Jones, S. (1993). A Sense of Space: Virtual Reality, Authenticity and the Aural. *Critical Studies in Mass Communication*, 10: 238–252.

Jones, S. (2000). Music and the Internet. *Popular Music*, 19: 217–230.

Jones, S. (2002). Music That Moves: Popular Music, Distribution and Network Technologies. *Cultural Studies*, 16: 213–232.

Lacapra, D. (1985). *History and Criticism*. New York: Columbia University Press.

Manovich, L. (2001). *The Language of New Media*. Cambridge, MA: MIT Press.

Manovich, L. (forthcoming) *Info-Aesthetics*. Cambridge, MA: MIT Press.

Meintjes, L. (2003). *Sound of Africa! Making Music Zulu in a South African Studio*. Durham, NC: Duke University Press.

Mills, C. W. (1959). *The Sociological Imagination*. New York: Oxford University Press.

Mirzoeff, N. (1998). Introduction to Part III, pp. 181–188 in *The Visual Culture Reader* (ed. N. Mirzoeff). New York: Routledge.

Mitchell, W. J. (1995). *City of Bits: Space, Place and the Infobahn*. Cambridge, MA: MIT Press.

Negroponte, N. (1995). *Being Digital*. New York: Knopf.

Novick, P. (1988). *That Noble Dream: The "Objectivity" Question and the American Historical Profession*. New York: Cambridge University Press.

Pinch, T., and Trocco, F. (2002). *Analog Days: The Invention and Impact of the Moog Synthesizer*. Cambridge, MA: Harvard University Press.

Robins, K. (1996). *Into the Image: Culture and Politics in the Field of Vision*. New York: Routledge.

Rothenbuhler, E., and Peters, J. D. (1997). Defining Phonography: An Experiment in Theory. *Musical Quarterly*, 81: 242–264.

Silberman, S. (2003). MATRIX[2]: Bullet Time Was Just the Beginning. *Wired*, 11 (May). Available online at http://www.wired.com/wired/archive/11.05/matrix2.html.

Standage, T. (1998). *The Victorian Internet: The Remarkable Story of the Telegraph and the Nineteenth-Century's Online Pioneers*. New York: Walker.

Sterne, J. (2003a). *The Audible Past: Cultural Origins of Sound Reproduction*. Durham, NC: Duke University Press.

Sterne, J. (2003b). Bourdieu, Technique and Technology. *Cultural Studies*, 17: 367–389.

Stone, A. R. (1995). *The War of Desire and Technology at the Close of the Mechanical Age*. Cambridge, MA: MIT Press.

Taylor, T. (2001). *Strange Sounds: Music, Technology and Culture*. New York: Routledge.

Theberge, P. (1997). *Any Sound You Can Imagine: Making Music/Consuming Technology*. Hanover, NH: Wesleyan University Press.

Turkle, S. (1995). *Life on the Screen: Identity in the Age of the Internet*. New York: Simon and Shuster.

White, H. (1978). *Tropics of Discourse: Essays in Cultural Criticism*. Baltimore: Johns Hopkins University Press.

Chapter 2

Cultural Difference, Theory, and Cyberculture Studies
A Case of Mutual Repulsion

Lisa Nakamura

In a famous and oft-quoted formulation, postcolonial feminist critic Gayatri Spivak asks in an essay of the same name, "Can the Subaltern Speak?" This query brings to mind an answering one: can the subaltern read . . . any of the essays and books that Spivak, Homi Bhabha, and Judith Butler have written? Bhabha and Butler won second and first place in the 1998 annual prize for bad prose handed out by *Philosophy and Literature,* and even their strongest supporters would be hard put to describe their expository style as anything but dense.[1] The irony here, of course, is that their theories deal exclusively with the state of the marginalized, abject, nonnormative subject under capitalism, colonialism, and other manifestations of power and hegemony in Western culture.

So clearly, there is no shortage of theoretical firepower if one is looking for critical theories of cultural difference. However, there is a telling disconnect in the way that "theory" has disseminated itself in cyberculture studies. There is certainly no lack of postmodernists, cyberfeminists, posthumanists, poststructuralists, and even Frankfurt School approaches to cyberculture studies. However, the "post" in "postmodern" is emphatically *not* the "post" in "postcolonial" in the case of studies of new technologies. As a result, like numerous other anthologies, David Trend's excellent *Reading Digital Culture* (2001) features essays by Zizek, Guattari, Virilio, and Ronell, all well-known critical theorists of culture and technology. However, there are no "theory" articles on cultural difference in the book: those that do deal with the topic appear in a separate section of the collection and are by either digital artists, ethnographers, or other nontheory types.

This enshrinement of "high theory" in the first section of this quite typical anthology serves to establish cyberculture studies' academic chops, lending it a type of institutional legitimacy that is dearly purchased. For as anyone who has tried to teach students Zizek, Guattari, or even Haraway's work in an Internet and cultural studies class has most likely discovered, requiring students to use one of these essays to analyze actual new media objects is like trying to teach someone to tie their shoes with their teeth. It can be done with a great deal of effort, but the results are not pretty, and the feeling one gets is that the whole business could have been a lot easier using a different method.

This leaves teachers (and scholars) in a pickle, especially if they are trying to teach theory, cultural difference, and cyberculture studies together. For somehow these three objects seem mutually repellant, like socks from the dryer with the wrong kind of static charge. Anthologies such as Steve Jones's *Cybersociety 2.0* (1998) may work well for a traditional mass communication class, but its social-science-influenced approach makes it less useful in a cultural or media studies class. Jones's anthology does, however, actually make reference to and in some cases does close readings of specific examples from the Internet, a feature conspicuously absent from Zizek, Guattari, and company, who appear never to have used the Web, much less stooped to including screenshots in their work to illustrate their points.

This poses serious problems to the discipline of cyberculture studies, for it cannot take its place in cultural studies' most respected journals such as *Social Text, Representations, American Quarterly, Critical Inquiry,* and *Cultural Studies* until it can engage with the existing body of critical theory that informs other studies of media such as film, literature, and to a growing extent television. On the other hand, it cannot be relevant and teachable to students studying the Internet at the university unless it helps them to do their work, which is to analyze actual interfaces and new media objects in their papers. It cannot be useful to other scholars if it is neither teachable nor citable. (I have never been able to work any of the scholars that I mention above into anything I have written except Haraway, and I have tried hard). And last and in a sense most important, cyberculture studies cannot be socially responsible if it continues to ignore the contemporary constellation of racism, globalization, and technoculture in which the Internet is implicated.

This chapter will speculate as to the possible reason that we are in this state of affairs as a discipline and suggest some fixes for it.

In 1995, Michael Heim wrote of cyberspace, "today, naïve questions like What is it? And How do I connect to it? have evolved into trickier questions like Am I for or against cyberspace? What position do I take regarding its social benefits? Now that we have crossed the electronic frontier, how does our society measure cyberspace? This is where most of us could learn from the dialectic."[2]

Heim describes the "digital dialectic" as opposing hateful cynicism about the Internet to cyber-utopianism. Ironically, Heim's "trickier questions" sound totally irrelevant today, while his more naïve ones have become intensely interesting, as the past few years have seen the dominance of broadband for the home and all types of media convergence on the Internet. The striking thing about this dialectic is that race is not mentioned as having anything to do with it.

In 2003, I served as a subchair for paper-proposal reviewing for the Association of Internet Researchers conference, and in that capacity I read other reviewers' comments, since part of my job was to break ties in case of disagreement. I was struck by a comment from one reviewer: she wrote of one proposal she rejected that it was "too nineties." What precisely does the "nineties" signify in terms of cyberculture study?

First of all, it is nineties to say that the jury on cyberspace is still out— it is in, and it is neither the threat that people feared nor the utopia that people hoped. David Silver's (2000) influential periodization of cyberculture studies into three distinct stages (popular cyberculture, cyberculture, and critical cyberculture studies) confirms this idea. Michael Heim's claims aside, that dialectic is over.

I am going to convey my opinions on the state of current cyberculture scholarship in the form of a much maligned but paradigmatic feature of nineties cyberculture: that is, as a "wired, tired, and expired" list. This form, imported directly from the magazine we love to hate, *Wired,* celebrates the ephemerality of cyberculture, and my revision of it means to track the short expiration dates of its academic study from a humanities perspective. This exercise is meant to raise the question of how we might create a rigorous critical methodology to apply to an object that defines itself in terms of rapid change.

> *Wired*: empire, the Web, Wi-Fi and broadband, political economy, history/industry approaches, blogs, file sharing, visual culture, social death, cultural studies, gaming, *The Matrix*, the digital divide (but tiring fast), the body

> *Tired*: identity, disembodiment, the subject, online community and
> anything starting with the term "online," "cyber," "virtual," or "e,"
> avatars, interfaces, discourse, gender, critical theory, *Blade Runner,*
> the body
>
> *Expired*: CD-ROMs, virtual reality, MUDs and MOOs, terms like IRL
> and VR, *Wired,* hypertext, multimedia, newsgroups, semiotics, the
> body

There are a few things that pop right out of this list: while visual culture,
Wi-Fi, and broadband are all wired (and all mutually constitutive: the new
graphics-rich Internet of the millennium owes its deployment of images
to faster data-connection speeds), textuality, like hypertext, is expired. In
the early days of the field, however, rhetoricians and artists and writers
emphasized hypertextuality and textuality generally as the Internet's greatest offering to users. Considering the way that the Internet has become a
media storage, viewing, and distribution vector, it is high time that scholars of visuality and visual culture update the existing work on the Internet
as a text medium.

You may notice that "the body" is in every category. The body is the
Lazarus of cyberculture studies—everybody is sick of seeing it around, but
it just won't die. As you can see, the digital divide came into vogue right
around the same time that it got highjacked to empty it of its referentiality
to race and repurposed to signify general inequities in access (this is now
usually read as class). *Where is race in this picture?* Race was never on any
of those lists, because it was never "wired" and thus had no chance to
become tired or expired: critical race theory was never a dominant form of
cyberculture critique.[3] The only way to explain this glaring omission is
through a theory of mutual repulsion.

The matter of race in cyberspace has gone from not being talked about
at all to being talked about very little. In 1996, Cameron Bailey wrote that
"very few of the thinkers currently probing into cyberspace have said a
word about race," and this is still true.[4] What is interesting is that this
limited discourse is to be found in some rather unexpected places. Early
critics of cyberspace like Richard Markley mention racism as a potential
problem in the medium, but since this objection was buried within a
plethora of less salient ones it tended to get lost. Generally, critiques of
cyberspace in terms of race conformed to two types: example based or
theoretical. The first type, exemplified by the collection I edited with Beth

Kolko and Gil Rodman, entitled *Race in Cyberspace* (2000), was an every-thing-but-the-kitchen-sink approach: if it had anything to do with race and cyberspace, it went in there. We did tend to favor those articles that did close analysis of specific examples, though.

The second type of critique was much higher-profile critical theory writing by established scholars like Sandy Stone or Haraway that had a more consistent critical approach and gave tantalizing glimpses of a racial critique but didn't actually do it (however, Haraway is much closer than people give her credit for). As I read back I find that writers like Jennifer Gonzalez (2000) were doing detailed analysis of actual cyberspace objects that integrate analysis of images of race online with theoretical approaches such as postcolonialism, feminism, and global culture. However, the ob-jects in Gonzalez's analysis were art Web sites that were esoteric and not within the realm of most users' or students' experience. This made her article difficult to teach and to relate to popular uses of the Internet such as gaming and the commercial Web.

At the present time there are some intensely fuzzy distinctions between cyberspace studies, cyber/technoculture studies, new media studies, and Internet studies (I would make an argument for the latter as a distinct field). Barry Wellman and Carolyn Haythornthwaite's book *The Internet in Everyday Life* (2002) proposes a useful fourth stage, at least by implica-tion. A thriving popular culture has developed on the Internet, and it has become a part of many people's everyday lives. And I believe that until academic studies of cyberculture examine the popular Internet as a part of everyday the field will be irrelevant.

How Cyberculture Studies Got Respectable

Reading Digital Culture's table of contents demonstrates the legitimation of cyberculture studies as part of the domain of critical theory. What was lost in this transition were two things: specificity and relevance. You can teach those essays exactly the same now as when they were first published, which in cyberculture studies means that it was either outstandingly good (i.e., Haraway) or outstandingly vague and not really about any particular new media object (i.e., Zizek).

As programs in ethnic studies and women's studies have learned, throw-ing in your institutional lot with high theory is a gamble and a bargain:

you trade respectability for relevance and accessibility. Postcolonial theory, one of the more successful academic disciplines that gives racial representation a central position in its critique, is interested in cyberspace but (like cyberculture critical theorists) only in ways that tend to show up as glancing, tantalizing asides to larger projects. Ngugi wa Thiongo (1998, p. 118), a venerable postcolonial theorist, writes, "In cyberspace resides the possible merger of the four aesthetic systems of the written, the oral, the theatrical, and the cinematic. Cyberspace orature may turn out to be the great oral aesthetic system of the future." African American cultural theorist Paul Gilroy (2000) attributes a tremendous, if vaguely delineated, potential to cyberspace, but he does so only in passing and without clear elaboration as to how cultural difference can be expressed in this medium.

Problems with teaching cyberculture are invisible to scholars who are either at the top or the bottom of the academic food chain. Two years ago I was at the bottom because I was responsible for teaching four classes per semester as an English professor at a state university with no resources for frills like cyberculture courses and with a heavy emphasis on general education. (Of course, the other end of that chain is represented by richly compensated research scholars who are paid not to teach at all but, rather, to write their deep thoughts without the distractions of student contact. I had plenty of student contact, to the tune of a couple hundred of bodies a year, but we talked mainly about paragraph development and thesis statements, not the Internet).

Once hired by UW Madison's Communication Arts department, which has an interest in cyberculture studies and a reasonable teaching/research balance, I found it profoundly unuseful to teach articles that are based on critiques or descriptions of virtual reality (Maggie Morse's *Virtualities,* much of Stone's and N. Katherine Hayles's work, and Zizek all take this tack). Most students will never use virtual reality equipment and have a difficult time seeing virtual reality as having much to do with their experiences using the Internet. And why should they? I don't either.

Why is it important to teach the popular Internet at this stage of the game? It is necessary if we are to avoid the mistake that other disciplines made of enshrining exercises in form and obscurity that students can't relate to and that you can't make popular arguments about. Cyberculture studies is grounded in cultural studies, which evolved to perform rigorous academic analysis of music videos, commercials, television, fashion, food, and other popular cultural forms that established academic disciplines wouldn't address but that people actually used and related to in their daily lives. The Internet is a daily technology, but virtual reality isn't.

Gaming is a daily technology too, and we need to do more research on it. People deep in the throes of gaming addiction are maybe not the people you'd expect to find writing meticulously researched, theoretically incisive academic articles, but on the other hand, the kind of personal engagement and detailed knowledge of the interface and interactivity that comes from *personal use* cannot be feigned. I was a MUD addict for a couple years, and there was no way I could have done my work without that experience. You rarely get the feeling that critics of postmodernism and technology like Baudrillard have been truly immersed in the Internet; it is not a lived practice for them. People who write about the mechanics of immersion and virtuality but have clearly not felt them are not compelling advocates for their force.

On the other hand, it's a big deal for me when iVillage changes its site design, in almost exactly the same way that it is a big deal when my neighborhood gets new traffic islands or when the roads I commute on are torn up for construction. It means that I physically have to do different things to read my playgroup bulletin board for my daughter Laura.

So how do we solve the problem of mutual repulsion? How do we make cyberculture studies a field of inquiry that as *a matter of course* employs critical race theory and theories of cultural difference and that employs close visual analysis of popular Internet objects in order to accomplish this? This is my dream of what the field needs to be, because I've seen what the field has become without it: initially wired on its own frontier metaphors, full of tired dialectics about the mind/body split without taking into account that some bodies are raced differently from others and thus part of a different dialectic, and expiring into esoteric and ungrounded arguments about the virtual subject and disembodiment. Internet studies needs to meld close interface analysis with issues of identity and to match considerations of form, the user, and the interface with an attention to the ideologies that underlie them.

NOTES

1. See Steve Fuller, "Whose Bad Writing?" *Philosophy and Literature* 23, no. 1 (1999): 25; and "*Philosophy and Literature* Is Pleased to Announce the Winners of

the Fourth Bad Writing Contest, 1998," available at http://www.yorku.ca/nollaig/
links/bwc.htm.

2. This quotation is from the anthologized version of Michael Heim's "The
Cyberspace Dialectic," in *The Digital Dialectic*, ed. Peter Lunenfeld (Cambridge,
MA: MIT Press, 1999), 25.

3. I was hurrying to finish *Cybertypes* before someone else wrote a single-
authored book on the subject of race and cyberculture. I shouldn't have bothered.

4. This quotation is from the anthologized version of Cameron Bailey's "Virtual Skin: Articulating Race in Cyberspace," in *Reading Digital Culture,* ed. David
Trend (London: Blackwell, 2001).

REFERENCES

Bailey, Cameron. 2001. "Virtual Skin: Articulating Race in Cyberspace." In *Reading
Digital Culture,* edited by David Trend, 332–46. London: Blackwell.
Fuller, Steve. 1999. "Whose Bad Writing?" *Philosophy and Literature* 23, no. 1: 174–80.
Gilroy, Paul. 2000. *Against Race: Imagining Political Culture beyond the Color Line.*
Cambridge, MA: Belknap Press of Harvard University Press.
Gonzalez, Jennifer. 2000. "The Appended Subject: Race and Identity as Digital
Assemblage." In *Race in Cyberspace,* edited by Lisa Nakamura, Beth Kolko, and
Gil Rodman, 27–50. New York: Routledge.
Heim, Michael. 1999. "The Cyberspace Dialectic." In *The Digital Dialectic,* edited
by Peter Lunenfeld, 25–45. Cambridge, MA: MIT Press.
Jones, Steve. 1998. *Cybersociety 2.0: Revisiting Computer-Mediated Communication
and Community.* Thousand Oaks, CA: Sage.
"*Philosophy and Literature* Is Pleased to Announce the Winners of the Fourth Bad
Writing Contest, 1998." 1998. Available at http://www.yorku.ca/nollaig/links/
bwc.htm.
Silver, David. 2000. "Looking Backwards, Looking Forwards: Cybercultures Stud-
ies 1990–2000." In *Web.Studies: Rewiring Media Studies for the Digital Age,*
edited by David Gauntlett, 19–30. London: Arnold.
Thiongo, Ngugi wa. 1998. *Penpoints, Gunpoints, and Dreams: Towards a Critical
Theory of the Arts and the State in Africa.* Oxford, UK: Clarendon Press.
Trend, David. 2001. *Reading Digital Culture.* London: Blackwell.
Wellman, Barry, and Caroline A. Haythornthwaite. 2002. *The Internet in Everyday
Life.* Malden, MA: Blackwell.

Chapter 3

How We Became Postdigital
From CyberStudies to Game Studies

Espen Aarseth

In the year of this writing, 2003, the number of transistors printed on silicon chips will have exceeded the number of characters printed on paper worldwide. By now, all of our public and personal media have become more or less digital. The feeling of excitement and wonder about all things cyber- that characterized the 1990s has been replaced by familiarity and business-as-usual. Finally, Web newspapers have started to make rather than lose money, while paper-based newspapers are finding it hard to recruit new readers from the younger generations (Berthelsen 2003). To the cultural researcher, the once marginal and exotic cyberculture (remember *Mundo 2000*?) has been subsumed by mainstream culture, and cyberdiscourse is finally ready to be integrated into the traditional research discourses. *We can all go home now.*

But even if cyberculture is all over (and all over the place), some areas have emerged that cannot be subsumed by traditional sectors of academia. One such field is the cultural genre of digital gaming. Not quite art, not quite children's culture, not quite, or should I say, not *only*, mass media, games are going through a renaissance that promises to produce the richest and most varied cultural interface we have yet seen.

The Rise and Fall of Digital Studies

The predicament of digital studies can be characterized by the paradox of successfulness, akin to Groucho Marx's membership paradox. The more mainstream and popular the field's object becomes, the less the need for special treatment or attention. Here is an example of a more advanced case: From the late 1980s, the budding field of historical computing (historians using computer-assisted methods such as statistics and databases) had international conferences and a worldwide organization, as well as regional and national ones. The field quickly grew, but suddenly it stopped growing, and in 1999 the yearly conference had to be canceled because of lack of expected participation. What had happened? Did this mean that the historians' use of computing was merely a fad, a bubble that burst along with the inflated "new economy"? Not at all.

The field of historical computing was formed so that its practitioners could have a place to meet, exchange ideas, and receive merit for their scholarly output. In the beginning, they had been few and far between, so it made sense to organize themselves in a special interest group. But eventually, the mainstream history conferences and journals opened up and welcomed the computer-assisted historians to their main events and publications. Computer-assisted historiography was no longer viewed with indifference or suspicion. And so the special interest group, focused on method and technology rather than content, was no longer necessary.

One wonders if the field of cyberstudies or digital studies (if such fields even exist within identifiable boundaries today) may not experience the same rise and fall, perhaps within the same fifteen years. At present, the international Internet research organization (Association of Internet Researchers—AIR), perhaps the largest and most visible cyberculture research community, is a highly successful, growing movement with participants from a large number of disciplines, including communication and media studies, law, psychology, ethnography, political science, and linguistics, to name just a few. By the look of it, things are going very well. But even so, there seems to be an element of doubt about the scope of the field: The conference CFP mentions "digital art," a topic that is quite orthogonal to the Internet, and also it mentions something called the "The Post-Internet Age." Perhaps AIR will become the APIR, in an attempt to stay current? Already, socially successful technologies like SMS are expanding the AIR horizon beyond the Internet as such. Being online does not equal being on the Internet, and it never did. For example, as late as around 1988, computer magazines published articles about e-mail without mention of the Internet. And still today, in that most online of all online societies, Japan, online means mobile phones, not the Internet, which relatively few people have in their homes there.

But what happens when the difference between doing "Internet/online research" and doing "research" becomes hard to see? When, say, Web-based newspapers are simply called newspapers, and e-literature has become literature? Or when TV is completely digitized and transmitted via digital networks? We may not be looking more than ten to fifteen years ahead here, probably less. Will the Internet or even the "post-Internet" suffice as a scope, when already it is cracking up?

Most likely this is a generational thing. Young, untenured scholars need to get recognition for their work and band together across disciplines. But what happens when they get tenure? When the cybergeneration becomes department chairs? As in the case of the computing historians, it seems likely that cyberstudies at that point will run out of steam, or should I say glue. Just as cyberculture is already all over the place, so will cyberstudies be assimilated into the old disciplines. Cyberethnography will become ethnography, cyberlaw will become law, and cybermedia will become media.

It is of course of limited value and hard to predict what exactly will happen. A better question is perhaps, Will any part of cyberstudies survive intact, after the reassimilation into the mother disciplines?

Games Research—101 Disciplines or One?

One candidate for such longevity is the study of video and computer games (increasingly referred to as digital games—but for no good reason). The study of games has a long but thin tradition;[1] only in the last two or three years have games been the object of a broad and increasing attention from a number of disciplines (just like the Internet). There are already five independent and interdisciplinary research traditions that cover some aspect of games:

- Game Theory, a branch of mathematics and economics that is not really about games at all but about making sequential decisions in competitive situations with limited knowledge
- Play Research, a tradition focused on understanding children's play with contributions from ethnography, psychology, and pedagogics
- Gaming and Simulation, an experimental field that explores and creates games for use in learning situations; i.e., games as explorative tools, not entertainment
- Board Game Studies, the historical study of board games and their evolution

- The Philosophy of Sport, the study of physical games—sometimes a theoretical companion to university athletics programs.

These independent traditions have very different goals and means and little or no interaction with or even awareness of one another. In addition, their interdisciplinary natures make them vulnerable to logistics and university politics. None of them sees computer games as an important area in itself.

And now, enter computer game studies, like the other game disciplines with little or no regard for previous and neighboring efforts and with yet another set of research agendas. This particular emerging game research field is perhaps even wider and more disparate than the other four combined, yet it seems already set to become more developed and (hopefully) also more departmentalized than they are. However, what is computer game research, and can it become one field? Since computer games are simulations that in principle can contain any element of (popular) culture or reality that a game designer can think of, there is very little, perhaps nothing, that could not, somehow, find its way into these games, from beach volleyball to medieval heraldry. Also, nearly all existing fields of research are relevant, or can be made relevant, through their perspectives, methods, or objects of study. The list is practically endless.

A few years ago, the Humanities dean at a Texas university brought a few local game developers to a meeting with the provost to discuss a possible new undergraduate program for game developers. So, what courses did they think would be most useful? Medieval history and ancient mythology!

I once tried to imagine what academic field in my own university (the University of Bergen) could not be applied to game research, and I could only come up with one, namely, dentistry. Of course, when I mentioned this at the games conference in Tampere in 2002, there was a dentist in the audience who protested! So any academic field or discipline can probably be brought to bear.

The problem, then, becomes one of coherence. Are we talking of one and the same field? Already there are journals and conferences covering various subparts of the game field; some focus on the technical, some on development, and some on cultural and aesthetic issues. So can we have game studies as a monolithic, separate field? Probably not. But there seems to be an excellent opportunity for an interdiscipline or for several related viable subfields that cover various main aspects, such as those mentioned earlier.

The Case for Game Studies

While many subfields of cyberstudies, such as the study of digital art or of e-literature, can and should easily be studied in its "mother disciplines" (the Art History or English or Literature department), game studies does not have such a mother field to fall back into. It could, like film studies, be seen as part of media studies, but there are strong reasons why this might not be a good idea. The most compelling of these is that games, unlike film, are not a medium but a broad category of systems that exist across media, and they are capable of using different media. Take chess: it can be played online or against a machine or on a board or by post-card or in the heads of two blindfolded expert players. Between Tetris to EverQuest (EQ), there is a vast gap in all relevant dimensions: technologically, socially, aesthetically, cognitively, economically, and so on. Tetris and EQ are far from being in the same medium, and to group them together in the same "medium studies" is probably not going to reveal anything interesting. Games are not media; they do use media but many different ones.

The problem also arises when we try to define games or "computer games." It is such a broad field that it might just be too broad to constitute a meaningful, practicable academic area. One strategy would be to turn away from games in general and look at a more coherent subfield, such as what I have elsewhere termed "games in virtual environments" (Aarseth 2003a), that is, games that take place in some kind of virtual world, unlike card or dice games, computerized or not. Here we do get the problem that noncomputerized games like Monopoly and Dungeons & Dragons also fall under our definition, but that is only a problem if we insist that the "digital" is an overriding category, which is both an arbitrary and technology-fetishizing thing to do. As we now know, the online/offline distinction is not a very good one.

The study of games in virtual environments, then, becomes a tentative approach to a phenomenon that could not be subsumed by an umbrella discipline, because games have none. It might still be too optimistic to assume that this will happen, but at the moment it is more likely than not, especially given all the programs and even, in the United States, dedicated vocational schools, like Full Sail School of Game Design and Development in Florida or DigiPen Institute of Technology in Washington State, that have emerged in the past few years. Granted, most of these have a very practical and technical focus, but like any other mainstream entertainment industry there will also be room for theoretical and "content"-oriented issues.

Games as Cyberculture

Also, let me make the case that the study of digital games is, or could very well be, a new core field that arises from the ashes of cyberculture studies. Here is why:

- Games (computer games and online computer games) combine culture, aesthetics, and technology in a new way.
- Games display all the signs of cyborgness (that nineties word!) and identity experiments.
- Games like EverQuest are vast community experiments, a kind of avant-garde society infrastructure that reconfigures our social roles and networks.
- Games encourage user activity and creativity and subvert the corporate entities that produce them.
- Games are a new mode of communication (in fact, several modes) with networking, space, and simulation as core elements.
- Games are used by the grassroots to make political and satirical statements (e.g., racist games, Bush/Michael Jackson/Bin Laden games, even presidential campaign games).
- Games are a semi-post-literate, global culture.

To sum up, there is probably not one characteristic commonly ascribed to cyberculture that could not be found in the gaming sector. This indicates that the world of computer games is a perfect test bed for cyberculture studies. Perhaps, in time, it will be the field in which cyberstudies has the strongest resonance and the longest dominance.

Toward a Game Studies Department

If, as I have suggested here, "games in virtual environments" is a viable empirical focus for our new scholarly field, we are still left with the conundrum of how to come up with a good disciplinary or methodological approach. Are we going to analyze the players, the aesthetic aspects, or the technology? Should we look at the cultural industry of games or the social aspects? Inevitably, our choice of focus will be predetermined by our backgrounds and by our methodological preferences, which is not exactly a rational, disinterested way to establish a discipline.

There are three main perspectives (or virtual-world game components) that readily lend themselves to a "postdigital" game studies field: the gameplay, the rules or structure of the game, and the game world. These three components tend to attract different methodological and disciplinary approaches:

- Game-play: sociology, ethnology, psychology, pedagogy ("player studies")
- Game-structure: game design, economics, computer science/AI ("design studies")
- Game-world: art, aesthetics, history, cultural/media studies, law (intellectual property rights) ("aesthetics")

As we can see, just a "core" focus like this entails at least a dozen disciplines, all quite different. Still, it might be possible to contain them all in a departmental structure and to let them be part of the same teaching program, as long as the core empirical focus remains stable. However, different game genres will draw attention to and lend themselves to different components, so the success of this three-pronged approach would depend on the empirical balance. Some games, such as strategy games, are clearly more interesting from a rules/structure perspective; others, such as adventure games, are mostly interesting from a game-world point of view; and games such as massively multiplayer online games are most interesting in terms of game-play and player interaction.

As a less ambitious alternative, only one or two of the components/perspectives could be used, but this might create an imbalance that should be compensated by an explicit delimitation of the field. It is hard to understand games without knowledge of how they are constructed, and it is hard to construct them without an understanding of how they are played. A balanced combination of these three elements seems ideal but might be hard to achieve in a real-politics university setting.

We might also be able to learn from the mistakes made in other fields. There are other disciplines that combine user, design/production, and aesthetic perspectives, most notably film/media studies and architecture. The lessons they have learned concerning the combination of these sub-disciplines could prove invaluable for the successful establishment of game studies as an integrated combination of the three elements.

The Game/Story Debate: Do We Have a Field Yet?

Though there is much momentum at the moment toward establishing undergraduate game-development programs and a growing dialogue between industry and academics through channels such as the Game Developers' Conference and the International Game Developers' Association (IGDA), the idea that games are an important area that deserves serious study is not enough to validate game studies as an academic field. If everyone agrees that games are important and should be studied, then all we have is a movement but hardly a field or discipline. A field is a social structure made up of people who produce, validate, and dispute scholarly results, and this is why, until very recently, the field of game studies did not exist, even though there were a fair number of academics who studied games. A field where everyone is in agreement, or not able to formulate differences through a common terminology, is not really a field but at best a special interest group or a thematic network.

In the beginning of the 1980s, games were studied by literary scholars who thought they were watching the birth of a new literary genre, the text-based adventure game, often called interactive fiction. In the early 1990s, games were studied by film scholars who thought they were watching the birth of a new cinematic genre, the interactive movie. Finally, at the start of our present decade, in reaction to these claims, a critical mass of researchers advocated an approach that takes as its point of departure the fact that games are games, not an (inferior) form of storytelling or filmmaking but a genre with its own intrinsic values, goals, and characteristics. This reaction against the application of older media theories has often been identified as "ludology," a term suggested by one of the main advocates, the game designer and theoretician Gonzalo Frasca (1999). From a history-of-science perspective, it is not hard to recognize this pattern as a paradigm shift, characterized by, not least, the average age difference of the participants on each side.

Although lamented by some participants (Jenkins 2002) as a "blood feud," the existence of a crucial debate in the early, formative stages of a new field is not only good but vitalizing and a sign of good health. The exchange of claims and counterclaims early on will only sharpen the participating scholars' senses and help them hone their critical apparatus and ideas. Other "new media" fields, such as the field of literary hypertext, have grown stale partly because of the lack of open disagreement and critical dialogue. For a critique of the concept of "new media," see Aarseth (2003b).

Conclusion: And the Next Big Thing Is . . .

If we regard games like EverQuest, which has evolved into "virtual economies" (Castronova 2001) with real money being made by players, as something more than "just games" and games like South Korea's Lineage, with its four million players, as a radical new form of social practice, it is possible to suggest that games have, indeed, interesting and serious ramifications beyond themselves and that they can well influence and shape the future of our culture and society as the most dominating and creative form of "new" media and cyberculture. Then it becomes obvious that games cannot simply be left to the newborn field of game studies but should also be allowed a place in disciplines such as sociology, architecture and urban planning, and even art history. Game studies may become a viable and critical contribution to the academic world, but games are too important to be confined to any single field.

NOTES

1. Jesper Juul (2001) calls it "the repeatedly lost art of studying games."

REFERENCES

Aarseth, E. (2003a). Playing Research: Methodological Approaches to Game Analysis. Paper presented at the Digital Arts and Culture conference, June, Melbourne. Available at hypertext.rmit.edu.au/dac/papers/Aarseth.pdf.
———. (2003b). We All Want to Change the World: The Ideology of Innovation in Digital Media. In Gunnar Liestøl, Andrew Morrison, and Terje Rasmussen (eds.), *Digital Media Revisited*. Cambridge, MA: MIT Press, 415–439.
Berthelsen, J. (2003). Internet Hacks: Web News Cashes In. *Asia Times,* April 12. Available at http://www.atimes.com/atimes/Global_Economy/ED12Dj01.html.

Castronova, E. (2001). Virtual Worlds: A First-Hand Account of Market and Society on the Cyberian Frontier. CESifo Working Paper Series No. 618. Available at http://papers.ssrn.com/sol3/papers.cfm?abstract_id=294828.

Frasca, G. (1999). Ludology Meets Narratology: Similitude and Differences between (Video)games and Narrative. Available at http://www.ludology.org/articles/ludology.htm.

Jenkins, H. (2002). Game Design as Narrative Architecture. In Pat Harrington and Noah Frup-Waldrop (eds.), *First Person*. Cambridge, MA: MIT Press. Available at http://web.mit.edu/CMS/People/henry3/games&narrative.html.

Juul, J. (2001). The Repeatedly Lost Art of Studying Games. *Game Studies* 1:1. Available at http://www.gamestudies.org/0101/juul-review/.

Chapter 4

Internet Studies in Times of Terror

David Silver and Alice Marwick

Despite the Orwellian memoryhole that infects so much of contemporary American discourse, many of us will remember George W. Bush's *Top Gun*–like landing aboard the USS *Abraham Lincoln* on May 1, 2003. With "Mission Accomplished" as a backdrop, Bush appeared on deck in an outfit heretofore never worn by an American president: a flight suit featuring, among other gadgets, a bulging codpiece. Resembling a *militarized computer game avatar,* Bush praised the troops and declared, "major combat operations have ended in Iraq" (D. Bush 2003).

On the following day, Bush left the USS *Abraham Lincoln* and landed in Silicon Valley, where he would reveal his postwar economic vision for the country. With all major U.S. media outlets in tow, his motorcade ended in Santa Clara, formerly known as the prune capital of America and now a prominent hub of what only a few years ago was called the "new economy." His destination was United Defense Industries, or UDI, a defense contractor specializing in *militarized digital technologies* (DeYoung and Weisman 2003; Sanger 2003).

Like the day before, Bush praised the heroes of the war in Iraq, only this time they included high-tech war machines and the high-profit corporations that build them:

> The new technologies of war help to protect our soldiers and, as importantly, help protect innocent life. You see, new technologies allow us to redefine war on our terms, which makes it more likely the world will be more free and more peaceful. . . . You do a lot to keep the American Armed Forces on the leading edge of technological change here at United Defense. And I want to thank you for that. You not only help save lives, but you're an agent for peace. (G. W. Bush 2003)

Before departing, Bush tried his hand at virtual combat, in what UDI calls its "Combat Simulation and Integration Lab," or what digital culture scholars call a first-person shooter game. The computer game gave Bush trouble, and he was unsuccessful in his first few attempts to blow up enemy tanks and helicopters. According to some reports, he finally made a "tank kill"; other reports left the gamer's fate out of the story (DeYoung and Weisman 2003; H. Kennedy 2003).

Bush's landing, his codpiece, his remarks, and his turn at the console were more than merely performance. They signaled a shift in, and full-throttled return to, the military-industrial complex. In 2003, federal military spending reached an all-time high at $401.7 billion a year. Add to that $36.2 billion pumped annually into the Department of Homeland Security (Schrader 2004; Weisman 2003). Encouraged by Defense Secretary Donald Rumsfeld's call for high-tech military strategies, defense contractors like UDI are reaping the spoils of our current climate of fear and its concomitant federal spending priorities.

Of course, defense contractors like UDI and Boeing and Lockheed and Halliburton are not the only ones who stand to gain financially. Indeed, today's U.S. high-tech industry[1] is scrambling to *militarize the new economy.* Witness Microsoft, who last summer made its biggest sale ever: $470 million worth of software to the U.S. Army (Microsoft Wins Biggest Order 2003). Witness Oracle's Information Assurance Center (ICA), a unit that designs homeland security applications and markets them to the federal government. As current head of ICA and former number-three man at the CIA David Carey remarked, "How do you say this without sounding callous? . . . In some ways, September 11 made business a bit easier. Previous to September 11, you pretty much had to hype the threat and the problem. . . . Now they clamor for it!" (Rosen 2002, p. 49). Witness Jim Opfer, CEO of the Silicon Valley firm LaunchPower, who in 2003 addressed the Tampa Bay Technology Forum. Reminding the audience of the growing budgets of both the Department of Defense and the Department of Homeland Security, Opfer cut to the chase and exclaimed, "Thank God for Osama Bin Laden!" (Leavy 2003).[2]

In a post-9/11, post-dot.com America, high-tech regions like Silicon Valley, Northern Virginia, Redmond/Seattle, and Boston are receiving, once again,[3] major federal funding for their development of *digital technologies for militaristic purposes.* In 2002 alone, over nine hundred Silicon Valley companies received more than $4 billion from the Department of Defense (Baker, Wallack, and Kirby 2003). As the president of the Bay Area Council notes, "What we've seen is a transition from the kind of defense companies we envisioned a decade ago to the new-economy, high-tech applications that are the hallmark of today's military defense" (ibid.). Or, as the publisher of the industry newsletter *Defense Mergers & Acquisitions* explains it, "Just 20 or 30 years ago, the airplane was the thing or the ship was the thing. Now those things are just nodes in the network, and the network is the thing" (Merle 2003).

Along with digital technologies, economies, and geographies, large chunks of *digital culture are being (re)militarized.* In 2003—the year when computer games became a mainstream phenomena and when, for many, especially young Americans, computer games were digital culture—one of the year's most popular games was America's Army, created by the U.S. Army.[4] It was also the year that the U.S. military perfected convergent media strategies. For example, the U.S. Army's "An Army of One" television commercials featured reality-show-like settings starring actual recruits solving military problems; for narrative closure (and recruitment hook), viewers were invited to goarmy.com, where they could take virtual tours of U.S. bases, read Army manuals, and peruse job openings. The same year, the Army instituted its "Taking It to the Streets" recruitment tour, driving spray-painted Hummers with computer games and multimedia sound systems into American "urban" areas (city parks, housing projects, and basketball courts) and events (NAACP events, MTV's Spring Break, and BET's Spring Bling). The tour's cosponsor, *The Source,* the oldest and once countercultural hip-hop magazine, eased entrance into particular communities and secured leading rappers and DJs to accompany the tour (Joiner 2003).

Such convergent branding strategies make the U.S. Army an industry leader in the sphere of digital marketing. In June 2002, the American Marketing Association awarded "An Army of One" its Gold Effie in the category of Recruitment Advertising (Army Public Affairs 2002). The same year, the Army's basic-training Web site was a finalist in the Webbys, the self-declared "leading international honor for the worlds [sic] best web sites," established in 1996 with a hint of countercultural ethos (Singer 2002).[5] With a brilliant campaign that fuses marketing and recruitment, computer game and computer manual, the Internet and television, the U.S. Army pushes the bar on *militarized guerrilla marketing.* Indeed, throughout 2003, Army recruitment goals were easily met (M. J. Kennedy 2003; Melillo and Barr 2003).[6]

And finally, also in 2003, the Electronic Entertainment Exposition (E3) awarded Full Spectrum Warrior, an X-Box training aid for the U.S. Army, top honors in two categories: Best Original Game and Best Simulation Game. Full Spectrum Warrior was also the most nominated title at E3, garnering votes in Best Console Game and Best of Show (Institute for Creative Technologies 2003). Significantly, Full Spectrum Warrior was designed and developed by the Institute for Creative Technologies (ICT) at the University of Southern California. ICT, a cross-disciplinary enterprise involving USC's School of Cinema-TV, the School of Engineering, and the Annenberg School of Communication, was made possible by a $45 million grant awarded by the U.S. Army in 1999 (Pentagon and Hollywood to Work Together 1999).

Conclusion: Resisting InternetStudies.mil

Dot.mil is the result of a militarized state, a militarized economy, and militarized everyday life. Dot.mil can be seen in the president dressing up as an avatar from a shoot-'em-up computer game. It can be seen in defense contractors rebranding themselves as "system integrators" and in dot.bombs morphing corporate strategies from business-to-business software to surveillance applications. Dot.mil can be perceived geographically with Silicon Valley's shift from venture capital to federal funding. Dot.mil is seen in free and commercial computer games, at goarmy.com (that's .com by the way), in the fully decked Hummers in our (poor, black and Latino) parks and streets. It can be seen, like a spectacle, in the U.S. Army's Gold Effie and runner-up Webby. And dot.mil appears in academia, when military field experiments merge with funded research objectives, when goarmy.com avatars are followed by our students via their computers in the dorms.

If some of the most cutting-edge research, and certainly some of the most well-funded research, is taking place with support from the U.S. military, the question *What can we do about it?* certainly arises. As a means to conclude this essay and to jumpstart a new thread, let us suggest five potential strategies.

The first step is to acknowledge, individually and collectively, .mil. By individually, we mean scholars should begin and continue to address such topics in their research and include them in their syllabi. By collectively, we mean scholars should begin and continue to edit anthologies and special issues of journals around the topics, as Cynthia Enloe did for a recent special issue of *Women's Review of Books*, titled "Women, War, and Peace," and as John Armitage did for a special issue of *Body & Society*, titled "Militarized Bodies." We also must work collectively on an organizational level. It is disconcerting that while the American Studies Association selected the theme of "Violence and Belonging" for its 2003 conference and the Association for Cultural Studies chose "Policing the Crisis" for its 2004 event, the Association of Internet Researchers selected the innocuous theme of "Ubiquity?" for its 2004 event.

The second step is to historicize our object of study and teaching. We must remind our colleagues, our students, and ourselves that .mil is not a new development. While Edwards (1996) offers an excellent history of the development of computers within a militaristic, Cold War environment, Abbate (1999) provides us with a superb early history of the Internet, tracing it to its ARPA roots. Moreover, Borsook (2000) and Winner (1992) remind us that Silicon Valley as we know it has always been .mil, with the Department of Defense supplying the necessary investment to transform the agricultural region into a high-tech mecca. These are the histories we must know. These are the histories we must teach our students. And these are the histories within which our organizations could and should situate our conferences.

The third step is, as Steve Jones suggests in the foreword to this book, to theorize our topic of study. Although plenty of theory exists around the military-industrial complex, only recently, perhaps starting with De Landa (1991) and Haraway (1991), have we begun to generate theory revolving around the military-entertainment complex, especially as it relates to digital media and technologies (Lenoir 2000; Wark 2003). Der Derian's recent book, *Virtuous War: Mapping the Military-Industrial-Media-Entertainment Network* (2001), is especially effective in not only collecting relevant theory but also in applying it to contemporary digital developments.

Of course, institutes of higher education have always been part of the complex, which leads to the fourth step: a rigorous examination of the intersections between .com, .mil, and .edu. While corporate investment in digital scholarship has decreased since the .com fallout, federal funding, streamed through the Departments of Defense and Homeland Security, is enjoying a mini-renaissance. This has profound implications for all academic fields but especially ours: young fields need money; young fields are more malleable; and young fields can transform more easily to capitalize on current trends in capital investments. As individual scholars, as collective units working within departments, colleges, and universities, and as individual and collective members of academic organizations, we must demand public discourse about funding priorities and insist that research values have as strong a voice as budgetary woes in determining the field's future directions.

Finally, the fifth, and a more hopeful, strategy is to understand, examine, and help build acts of resistance to .mil. These acts come in various shapes and sizes, but particularly relevant to scholars of Internet studies are works of *digital artivism*. By digital artivism, we refer to massively distributed digital artifacts that creatively and intellectually challenge and subvert hegemonic powers. They incorporate multiple elements of digital technologies—the archive, the database, animation, multiple media—and can be found in Open Secrets (www.opensecrets.org); a voluminous archive that allows users to track financial contributions made to specific industries (say, Iraq contracts) and local and national campaigns; Iraq Body Count (www.iraqbodycount.net), an innovative and collaboratively built database charting the number of reported civilian deaths in Iraq; and Cost of War (www.costofwar.com), a script-run total of the money spent by the United States to finance the war in Iraq, accompanied by speculative scenarios if the funds were to be spent on things like public education, children's health, and public housing.

The boundaries between .edu, .com, and .mil have always been, for better and for worse, leaky. As academics, we must resist marginalizing ourselves solely with the academy. We must foster and sustain alliances across a spectrum of domains and collaborate with individuals and collectives working in .org, .gov, .net, .art, .green, and .labor. This is no easy task, yet our purpose becomes clearer when we acknowledge where we—and our field of study—currently stand.

NOTES

1. We are aware that calling digital/Internet technologies brought to the market by U.S. companies "American" is problematic, especially when considering the current rate of outsourcing, the manual labor of undocumented citizens, and so forth.

2. While we are at it, let's also witness Aanko Technologies, a company that produces digital anthrax detectors, whose CEO recently noted in *Business 2.0* that his company is "turning risk into revenue" (Hitt 2003, p. 106).

3. It is important to note that Silicon Valley as we know it has always already

been dot.mil. For the role of military spending on the development of the high-tech region, see Borsook 2000 and Winner 1992.

4. In 2003, two million users downloaded America's Army, making it the number-one free downloadable game and number-five most popular online game (Wooley 2003).

5. Webby Awards, http://www.webbyawards.com. The Web site for U.S. Army Basic Training was nominated for the Best Practices category alongside Amazon .com, Google, National Geographic, and the Peace Corps. Google won.

6. It must be noted that in 2004, a year in which the war in Iraq raged on, recruitment goals were not met.

REFERENCES

Abbate, J. 1999. *Inventing the Internet*. Cambridge, MA: MIT Press.

Army Public Affairs. 2002. Army "Basic Training" Ads Receive Gold Effie Award. June 26. Available at http://www4.army.mil/ocpa/read.php?story_id_key=1315 (accessed February 14, 2004).

Baker, D. R., Wallack, T., and Kirby, C. 2003. Score of Area Businesses Feed Military Machine's Need for Gear. *San Francisco Chronicle*, March 23, p. I1.

Borsook, P. 2000. *Cyberselfish: A Critical Romp through the Terribly Libertarian Culture of High Tech*. New York: PublicAffairs.

Bush, D. 2003. Bush: Iraq Is One Victory in War on Terror. CNN.com, May 2. Available at http://www.cnn.com/2003/ALLPOLITICS/05/01/sprj.irq.bush.speech.

Bush, G. W. 2003. Remarks to Employees of United Defense Industries in Santa Clara, California. Available at http://frwebgate.access.gpo.gov/cgi-bin/getdoc.cgi?dbname=2003_presidential_documents&docid=pd05my03_txt-28 (accessed September 1, 2003).

De Landa, M. 1991. *War in the Age of Intelligent Machines*. New York: Zone Books.

Der Derian, J. 2001. *Virtuous War: Mapping the Military-Industrial-Media-Entertainment Network*. Boulder, CO: Westview Press.

DeYoung, K., and Weisman, J. 2003. Bush Urges Passage of Tax Plan; President Cites Rising Unemployment in Call for Action. *Washington Post*, May 3, p. A12.

Edwards, P. 1996. *The Closed World: Computers and the Politics of Discourse in Cold War America*. Cambridge, MA: MIT Press.

Haraway, D. J. 1991. *Simians, Cyborgs, and Women: The Reinvention of Nature*. New York: Routledge.

Hitt, J. 2003. The Business of Fear. *Business 2.0*, June, pp. 106–114.

Institute for Creative Technologies. 2003. ICT's New Army Training Aid Wins Best Original Game and Best Simulation Game @ E3. June 10. Available at http://www.ict.usc.edu/content/view/90/2/ (accessed February 14, 2004).

Joiner, W. 2003. The Army Be Thuggin' It. *Salon,* October 17. Available at http://archive.salon.com/mwt/feature/2003/10/17/army/index_np.html (accessed January 10, 2004).

Kennedy, H. 2003. Fired-Up W Gives Tanks for Help. *Daily News,* May 3, p. 9.

Kennedy, M. J. 2003. Wanna Play? Military Recruiters Update Their Arsenals to Reach Kids. *Los Angeles Times,* February 26, p. E1.

Leavy, P. G. 2003. Silicon Valley Leader Assesses IT Defense Spending. *Business Journal of Tampa Bay,* February 27. Available at http://tampabay.bizjournals.com/tampabay/stories/2003/02/24/daily35.html (accessed January 10, 2004).

Lenoir, T. 2000. All but War Is Simulation: The Military-Entertainment Complex. *Configurations* 8, pp. 289–335.

Melillo, W., and Barr, A. 2003. U.S. Army Looks to Next Agency Front. *Adweek,* May 5, p. 6.

Merle, R. 2003. Defense Firms Consolidate as War Goes High-Tech. *Washington Post,* May 27, p. A1.

Microsoft Wins Biggest Order. 2003. *Seattle Post-Intelligencer,* June 25, p. C1.

Pentagon and Hollywood to Work Together. 1999. *Agence France Presse,* August 19. Available at http://www.isi.edu/afp_uarc.html (accessed February 14, 2004).

Rosen, J. 2002. Silicon Valley's Spy Game. *New York Times Magazine,* April 14, pp. 47–51.

Sanger, D. E. 2003. Bush Begins Campaign to Sell His Economic Program. *New York Times,* May 3, p. A13.

Schrader, E. 2004. Bush Seeks 7% Boost in Military Spending. *Los Angeles Times,* January 24. Available at http://www.latimes.com/news/nationworld/nation/la-na-defense24jan24,1,4306122.story?coll=la-home-headlines (accessed January 26, 2004).

Singer, M. 2002. Webby Awards Announces Nominees. Atnewyork.com, April 29. Available at http://www.atnewyork.com/news/article.php/1024441 (accessed January 26, 2004).

Wark, M. 2003. Escape from the Dual Empire. *Rhizomes* 6. Available at http://www.rhizomes.net/issue6/wark.htm (accessed February 9, 2004).

Weisman, J. 2003. Government Outgrows Cap Set by President. *Washington Post,* November 13, p. A01.

Winner, L. 1992. Silicon Valley Mystery House. In *Variations on a Theme Park: The New American City and the End of Public Space,* ed. Michael Sorkin, pp. 31–60. New York: Hill and Wang.

Wooley, W. 2003. Video Game Hits Its Target. *Seattle Times,* September 22, p. E7.

Chapter 5

Catching the Waves
Considering Cyberculture, Technoculture, and Electronic Consumption

Wendy Robinson

There has been talk recently of a "second wave" of cyberculture. What might a second wave entail? How do we define a field that had barely begun to take shape during the first wave? What comes next and where might some intersections and contestations lie? This chapter explores these questions and will hopefully encourage further consideration about border crossings between new and "traditional," or electronic, media and consumer electronics.

The First Wave

David Silver (2000) nicely established the parameters of the first wave of cyberculture—defined here as Internet-centric popular culture—in "Looking Backwards, Looking Forwards." The first wave probably is shaped by the twin peaks of Howard Rheingold's (1993) *The Virtual Community* and Sherry Turkle's (1995) *Life on the Screen*. From that point forward, there undoubtedly are many opinions. Where some might see Donna Haraway's (1991 [1985]) cyborgs, others might see William Gibson's (1984) cyberspace and cyberpunk literature, *Cities of Bits* (Mitchell 1995), *Hamlet on the Holodeck* (Murray 1997), *Burn Rate* (Wolff 1998), *Wired* and the Electronic Frontier Foundation (mid-1990s), *Being Digital* (Negroponte 1996), or *Code and Other Laws in Cyberspace* (Lessig 1999). The first wave was fun. It was active and activist. What happened?

Adoption of the Internet spiked and then slowed. Microsoft's Internet

Explorer happened. E-commerce happened. Y2K didn't happen, although it was an excellent incentive to upgrade. Everyone lost money on the dot-com start-up crash or through blue-chip corporate malfeasance. AOL–Time Warner happened, but then AOL became another Pathfinder. The outcome of the 2000 presidential election erased the popular vote, despite the greater flow of customizable information into American homes. September 11 happened, followed by Afghanistan, Iraq, and rhetorical weapons of mass destruction. If the first wave—called "the second media age" by Mark Poster (1995)—had been teenage and ebullient, ripe with promise, then perhaps the temper of the times today feels resigned to disillusioned middle age.

The Second Wave

However, with the sobering comes an opportunity to take stock. My thoughts on a second wave are clustered around three ideas:

(1) Cyberculture is a continuation of technoculture. There is much to be learned by reconsidering techno-media history and earlier forms of mediated popular culture (see Sterne, in this volume, also 2003) and how they were conceptualized. Often erroneously bookended as "sixties television theory," the complementary contributions of Marshall McLuhan and Raymond Williams have spurred well-worked-out media theory that might be further tapped and developed.

(2) Online life has been materialized in several senses, and we are being mobilized in several senses. Cyberculture always has attracted lifestyle marketing (e.g., *Wired*'s fetishware and glossy advertising and the many sales outlets and publications for electronics). Indeed, purchasing cyber-stuff is a necessary requirement for joining the club. We constantly are mobilized to shop online or at the local brick-and-mortar mall, beckoned with newer, faster, more compact, brighter, shinier, chrome and Plexiglas gizmos (Myerson 2001). We are also mobilized in that we are no longer tied to the wall when connecting to the Internet or talking on the phone. That earlier understanding of usage—immobile, if global, reach—was more about the limitations of the electrical cord at home or in the office than of media programming or hardware distribution channels across the world. Regarding mobilization and materialization, because our bodies may be involved today (carrying the devices on our backs or shoulders, in hand, embedded), our presence is ever more detectable. Therefore,

much of the strangeness of disembodied virtual life has been demystified (e.g., the "Internet dog" is no longer invisible). Our cyberselves have been materialized. The media theory of popular music and television has had much to offer about the processes of materialization and commercial mobilization.

(3) The third thought relates to the first two. Increasingly, I'm interested in the consumer electronics industry. We don't yet have a theoretically satisfying way to discuss the convergence between the computer and the television set, the mouse and the remote control, the MP3 player and the mobile phone, the mobile phone and the computer. By convergence, I don't just intend all-in-one devices and whatever goes on "beneath the hood." I mean a convergence of uses and cultural practices—using a computer while watching television or perhaps a prerecorded show or film (via VCR or DVD), sending text messages or photographs through a hand-set, which is a combination computer–telephone–personal stereo, and synchronization between devices, their importance in our lives, and the technoculture thereof. These devices and their audiences have all been studied but generally separately. Yet we clearly multitask, consuming media in multiples: for example, listening to broadcasts while driving or doing any number of other activities, which is nothing new (see Bull 2001). The device essentialism of distinct scholarly camps (e.g., popular music, film, photography, radio, or television studies; marketing and advertising; computercentric studies or telecommunications) is running out of steam. Second-wave or second-age media studies should reflect our hyperconnected media hybridization and intersections between disciplines and devices.

Technocultural Political Style

A sociopolitical New Age didn't accompany the change of millennium. The utopian pioneer mentality treated by Fred Turner (in this volume) was notably friendly to commodification. The cyberevangelists always preached belonging through electronic consumption, a virtual community of tangible privilege. The sale of *Wired* to Condé Nast in 1998 was not a rupture. Digital devices and the democratizing of information didn't change the world, except in the sense of reaction against the Western, capitalist high regard for material progress and associated globalization. The White House home page today is just another bland governmental site, equivalent to a visitor packet or automated phone tree: the disinformation society. The high bandwidth trumpeted by the telcos and cable companies turned out to be a colonization of the Internet, so that it could be controlled and parceled out through advertising and subscription fees. Slower bandwidth is not in the best interest of the technomedia companies with content and services to sell—with the notable exception of the publishing, entertainment, and recording industries, which inevitably must adapt if they are to survive.

This is not to argue whether, particularly in light of the dot-com bust, the corporate colonization was economically necessary or whether access is or isn't "better" today. The fact is, it happened. But the corporate interests always had been present. Microsoft already was the eight-hundred-pound gorilla when the Macintosh personal computer was introduced two decades ago, synchronous with the release of the original *Revenge of the Nerds* (1984). The Internet is no longer privileged above other media or related services. But the personal computer–Internet–Web revolution didn't emerge from a vacuum. The shift in electronic consumption took place alongside and as an exemplar of the emergence of personal consumer electronics such as VCRs, portable audio (preceded by the transistor radio), portable phones, answering machines, camcorders, disposable wristwatches, and smarter household gadgets (e.g., the Cuisinart and microwave). The technoculture wave of the 1980s coincided with other consumerist, mediated trends—particularly spurred by MTV—to which it is related in terms of popular culture, manufacture, marketing, and corporate confluence.

The lauded digital revolution, therefore, can be seen as the product, a not entirely unintentional product, of evolutionary shifts that are interwoven with politics and commercial interests. The revolution has been shaped by a society that continually must cope with an ever-widening dissemination of electric to electronic devices, introduced within specific contexts of self-perpetuating consumption. The devices often seem to or may actually require periodic reinvestment as older devices become outmoded, batteries must be replaced, and fashions change.

Furthermore, these e-devices are used in ways that are not necessarily value-neutral. Cyberculture is a subset of technoculture, just as atomic-age culture or pro-green counterculture are subsets of technoculture. Cyberculture reflects style and commerce and politics and influences political-commercial style. For or against, it doesn't much matter, since the consumer can have it both ways: cute retro nuclear symbols show up on eco-friendly, limited-edition java mugs. The mass-marketed coffee and its receptacles, branded with a recognizable logo, are intended to keep geeks, or those who affect a geek lifestyle, tied 24/7 to the electronic leash of the keyboard and mobile phone—a "perpetual contact" (Katz and Aakhus 2002) promoted as desirable. Within reach may be a mousepad shaped like a target, featuring the head of Osama bin Laden, the Chairman Mao of contemporary Warholian-Kubrickian pop. As Umberto Eco (1986) has long argued, politics aren't emptied out of such mass consumption but are deeply embedded. The ironic polysemic messages ricochet off each other in a globally connected echo chamber of commodification and political association.

Flowing with the Waves

Cyberculture reflects the ambivalent tugs and accommodations that have gained momentum since the industrial revolution, or Alvin Toffler's (1980) "second wave." The secondary waves of industrialization have affected different cultures at different times in different ways, with ongoing ripple effects that continue to be felt. Cyberculture obviously is buoyed by the assembly-line production and distribution of a prior and current time as much as by revolutionary claims for a different, better world tomorrow— a notion of Western progress redolent with nostalgic sentiment. Meanwhile, in less privileged parts of the world, women wearing hairnets and plastic gloves stuff transistors into plastic cases at minimum wage or less. There is nothing New Age–ish about the conditions of their workplace. There are no trendy mugs or mousepads in sight, nor do they drink overpriced coffee. But the beans may be grown nearby, near where the wood, rubber, silicon, and other raw materials used in the manufacture of consumer electronics are harvested.

Increasingly I glance back at media culture before cyberculture, at the first excitement over Toffler's "third wave," i.e., to the first electronic media age, the prehistory of (and underlying continuation of) the digital age. I think about the advent of broadcast media as trumpeted by McLuhan, *Wired*'s patron saint. The central role of the television set within domestic life is useful to reconsider (Spigel 1992). As first conceptualized by Williams (1974), its episodic flow has been assimilated with other home-based technological consumption. A wonderfully mature body of interdisciplinary study was somewhat abandoned during the cyber excitement of the mid- to late 1990s. Television studies had been considering time-shifting, channel-surfing, and couch commandos, all of which can be drawn on to discuss contemporary wireless access and media customization. As Ellen Seiter (1999) noted, the directions television studies took a decade ago likely will continue to be relevant (see also Ang 1996 and Morley 2000).

What can cyberculture studies learn from television and "traditional" media studies? Or why circumscribe our discipline with reference to the digital? More to the point, what in media isn't digital these days? Why not go further in a mainstream direction and consider what has been left behind to consider where we're headed? Given the convergence between the Web and television, it makes sense that electronic media theories should also converge and that the theory should draw on and adapt insights beyond specific media studies.

The Electronic Hearth, Revisited

I'm interested in the television set—not so much in watching its programming (although I confess, I do) but in observing the practices that have grown up around the set and its marketing, which is to say its cultural consumption. The way some emerging, often portable or environmentally pervasive, devices are positioned in the marketplace leverages the set's centrality in the household, even as those devices encourage greater fragmentation of the family. We are increasingly in touch now, but we spend decreasing unmediated time with one another. Our gadgets may be in better touch with one another than their owners, even among people who share the same living quarters.

In the early twenty-first century, Apple's marketing plan centered on the "digital hub." The iMac was considered the central device, with the iPod, digital cameras, hand-held computers, and other devices in wireless touch through the hub computer. The computer plays the role of the television set. Sony has a similar strategy, but the home entertainment center has pride of place and the universal remote or "air mouse" does much of the connecting between gadgets. The metaphor of the electronic hearth (see Spigel 1992 and Tichi 1991), then, continues. The contestation between domestic practices, theoretical approaches, and audience measurement for commercial purposes, named the "living room wars" by Ien Ang (1992, 1996; see also Arlen [1969], who intended Vietnam as the "living room war"), also will continue, taking on new resonance.

The central unit is a hybrid, not exclusively a television set or a personal computer but with the emphasis leaning toward one side or the other, depending on the manufacturer. The electronic convergence is not hard to understand, since CD and DVD players are small computers. The personal devices long ago crossed over from the office into our living rooms and from there into other rooms of the house and onto our bodies (e.g., Sony's Discman and Apple's iPod). Sony and Apple promote portable audio as the hub's prime modular device. Easy downloads may encourage music fans to develop company identification and brand loyalty, à la Nike or Starbucks, through celebrity association and lifestyle marketing (Klein 1999).

Moreover, our devices may replace us, clustered around the central infotainment unit. We are mobile, experiencing the episodic flow of media; they sit still, pulsing, blinking, and "talking" among themselves. We retire for the evening, but "our toys stay up and play," James Gleick (2001: 64) wrote about wireless communication devices that "recharge their spirits and swap data." They communicate through small-area wireless networks, infrared ports and docking cradles for recharging, later taken away for mobile use. As peripheral devices, they extend the hand-held metaphor within the context of the electronic hearth as well as the McLuhanesque (1964) reach. The devices act as extensions of the animate. They are labor-saving toys with near volition of their own: Sony's AIBO (Artificial Intelligence Robot) dog-toy-servant already has limited autonomy.

Individual family members can tune in and hang out, carrying and zapping and snapping their portable devices wherever they go or getting the AIBO to fetch the media for them. What will matter is less what each device does separately than what they do together as one, how they synchronize with one another and how they reflect and contribute to our increasing mobilization and materialization. If we think of the television-stereo-playback-gaming-box-computer as a Williamsean device with programming or software flow, then we will be carrying its flow and commercial messages, a nonstop corporate-sanctioned soundtrack to Westernized lives. There is resistance, of course, but nonetheless the increased presence of consumer electronics seems unavoidable. Indeed, the resistance can be accommodated—a continuation of the living room wars, flowing through the other environments of our lives, wherever we access the Internet on the fly, talk on mobile phones, or otherwise consume media and electronics. We've been mobilized.

Material Convergence

Consumer electronics is an $85 billion business in the United States alone, according to the Consumer Electronics Association (2003). That's a sizable material reality. Sales of consumer electronics have continued to accelerate, while the rest of the information technology sector has been slow to flat since 1999, albeit with a rebound over the past year or so. But the distinction between electronic devices is of small importance in terms of mass commodification. Whether mobile phones, home entertainment devices, remote control devices, or other personal electronics, including personal computers, they are merchandised together, such as at Best Buy or Circuit City; marketed together, such as through *Rolling Stone* or *Wired*; and likely manufactured through the same plants, with the same raw materials. The smart gear was depicted as elements of the cyberpunk world described by Gibson in the 1980s. Gibson's vision always was more rooted in commercial reality than science fiction.

For two decades—a generation—there hasn't been much difference between technoculture and cyberculture in the material sense. Personal computers have long been used while wearing the headgear of personal audio; the remote control of television and home stereo is reached for much as a mouse or the car keys and garage-door remote. Today's younger adopters are unlikely to differentiate between pre-cyber and high-cyber electronics. Is text-messaging over a mobile phone the same as sending an e-mail or instant message? If not, does the distinction really matter anymore? Cyberculture studies does not yet have a good cultural answer to this question.

But there is another way of considering the problems of consumption in cyberculture, of the omnipresence of corporate giants such as Microsoft, Sony, and Apple (the VW of information technology); their sprawling cousins Best Buy, Circuit City, Nike, and Starbucks; and their house organs MTV, *Rolling Stone, Wired,* and any number of lifestyle vehicles across various media. Throughout this chapter, I've offered McLuhan and Williams as earlier theorists who may be drawn on to consider trends in electronic media from the sixties through the consumer electronics of today. I haven't wanted to suggest your father's McLuhan or Williams, substituting instead McLuhan or Williams 2.0 or 3.0 perhaps. McLuhan and Williams can, indeed, be recycled, much as the cultural practices continue through new iterations of devices that do more or less the same as the old, but "better," faster, with more portability, convergence, and so forth.

Material-culture studies also provide a useful theoretical lever. Better known in Great Britain than elsewhere, material-culture studies generally are associated with Daniel Miller (1987). Material culture is concerned with the ordinary objects of mass consumption and how they are used. Particularly useful is what Miller defines as "appropriation," a concept he arrives at in a way similar to John Fiske's (1987, 1989) discussion of television, that is, by drawing on Pierre Bourdieu, Michel de Certeau, Henri Lefebvre, and the other theorists of everyday life who have followed (see Highmore 2001 and 2002). Our personal devices are often associated with our domestic and personal lives, becoming constant companions, "on" even when we are unavailable, close to our hearts, extensions of our minds, senses, and physicality. Our private lives are played out in public, such as through openly conversing on mobile phones or tapping to the beat of personal audio. It makes sense, then, to consider other areas of scholarly inquiry that have considered our close relationship to objects of consumption and how they become identified with our sense of self.

I can't do justice to Miller's complex argument here, but appropriation suggests that despite corporate ownership and the alienated origins of much of the objects of mass consumption, it is possible to fuse or bond with objects of daily life, imbuing them with our own presence to "appropriate" them for our own ends, which may well be at odds with their original manufacturer's intent (street style, for example, or recycling objects in inventive ways and other found subcultural uses). Therefore, the picture I've sketched here need not be bleak. Through consumption there may be a kind of resistance—or since globalization and commodification is nearly inevitable anyway, don't just relax and enjoy yourselves, *Dr. Strangelove*-style, but find a way to de-alienate the objects of consumption that make up a large part of Westernized lives. Rather than a lament, such as Walter Benjamin (1969 [1936]) offered about mechanical or replicable consumption, appropriation suggests an active way of coping with the electronics we find arrayed around us, that we carry as extensions of our bodies and that are part of our mediated lives, regrettable or not. Miller is an anthropologist, so his concern is more with how people actually live their lives than with being prescriptive. Forget consumerist amnesia, then: we can consciously carve out a space for our personal electronics that at least somewhat undoes their corporate and political context, with which we may be at odds.

Surfing the Distant Shores of the Internet

I would like to suggest some writers who are contributing to a second wave of cyberculture, some of whom made notable contributions to the first wave and its antecedents. Howard Rheingold's (2002) *Smart Mobs: The Next Social Revolution* has been the first widely read text on mobile communication and mobilized political action: Rheingold likes to be first to catch the cyber waves. I particularly have been influenced by David Morley's (2000) *Home Territories: Media, Mobility and Identity,* which should attract much greater attention. *Home Territories* is an impressively scholarly work that takes the television and domestic sphere as a point of departure for considering our dual mobilization and globalization, of which the Internet and its devices have played a key role. Morley largely extends the work of Williams, including his conceptualization of flow and mobile privatization, as well as Morley's own earlier work on television, audiences, and geography (1986, 1992, and, with Robins, 1995). Completing the trilogy begun with *City of Bits,* William J. Mitchell's (2003) *Me++: The Cyborg Self and the Networked City* considers the role of mobile devices, global interconnection, and our incipient cyborgization. Mark Poster hasn't yet published a book on the topic, but his thoughts in recent essays, such as the one on the cyber-performance-artist Stelarc in Joanna Zylinska's anthology *The Cyborg Experiments: The Extensions of the Body in the Media Age* (Poster 2002), which recasts McLuhan's work, and the one on personal devices and postmodernism that was presented at a mobile communication conference in Budapest (Poster 2003), are in accord with the others mentioned here and with my own thoughts.

The Internet became mainstream several years ago. Cyberculture has to deal with grown-up problems now. We can't avoid the messy questions of money and power or our political disappointments much longer, if we want to press deeper and advance the field. The field is still young, but its problems are venerable. We don't need to make a case for the potential audience reach of this or that Web site. We know about all that. Let's get past the dot-com era, American-style euphoria, and its hangover. The situation as presented today is richer, if also darker. Our relationship with our cyber objects is part of our real, material, embodied life, life lived with families, life lived on the move, juggling between our various roles and responsibilities. Virtuality probably was a red herring all along, a byproduct of using systems that had to be plugged into the wall.

So, what do we want to think about next? I strongly agree with Lisa Nakamura (in this volume; see also Kolko, Nakamura, and Rodman 2000 and Nakamura 1999 and 2002) that we have to think outside the box of the privileged white subject or his "identity tourism." I strongly agree with Sterne (in this volume) that reconsidering the media and technologies of the past can help us move past the cyber impasse. I strongly agree with Turner (in this volume) that we need to look at the political and economic connections of the fathers—and they were mostly privileged white guys, weren't they?—of the first wave. What I suggest is watching more TV—or at least thinking about others who do, and have for several generations, and what their theorists have had to say about the accommodation and commodification of media in our everyday lives. What does television have to do with the Internet and mobile phone? This is a riddle I will continue to puzzle out, while paddling out to catch the wave.

Afterword

As this book goes to press, a third wave of cyberculture is washing ashore: blogging, Podcasting, further convergence in ever-smaller devices incorporated within ordinary Westernized everyday life. The consumer electronics business has grown to $110 billion annually in the United States, an increase of $25 billion in the past eighteen months (Consumer Electronics Association 2005), and has grown in importance worldwide. There may be an answer to my last rhetorical question. Television content is being driven to Internet-enabled mobile phones through neotelecommunications companies such as T-Mobile. Computers can be easily connected to television sets for high-resolution output; monitors, portable personal computers, and television sets are converging. At the annual consumer electronics trade show held in Las Vegas in early 2005, television was the "killer app." The vendors' focus of digital interest was centered on the living room and the materialized body electronic, envisioned as rarely offline or inaccessible via telephone or Internet.

REFERENCES

Ang, I. (1992). Living-room wars: New technologies, audience measurement and the tactics of television consumption. In R. Silverstone and E. Hirsch (eds.), *Consuming Technologies: Media and Information in Domestic Spaces.* London: Routledge.

Ang, I. (1996). *Living Room Wars: Rethinking Media Audiences for a Postmodern World.* London: Routledge.

Arlen, M. J. (1969). *Living-Room War.* New York: Viking.

Benjamin, W. (1969 [1936]). The work of art in the age of mechanical reproduction. In H. Arendt (ed.), *Illuminations: Essays and Reflections,* trans. H. Zohn. New York: Schocken.

Bull, M. (2001). Soundscapes of the car: A critical ethnography of automobile habitation. In D. Miller (ed.), *Car Cultures.* Oxford, UK: Berg.

Eco, U. (1986). *Travels in Hyperreality.* Trans. W. Weaver. San Diego: Harcourt Brace.

Consumer Electronics Association. (2003). Press release. Available at http://www.ce.org/press_Room/.

———. (2005). Press release. Available at http://www.ce.org/press_Room/.

Fiske, J. (1987). *Television Culture: Popular Pleasures and Politics.* New York: Routledge.

———. (1989). *Reading the Popular.* Boston: Unwin Hyman.

Gibson, W. (1984). *Neuromancer.* New York: Ace.

Gleick, J. (2001). Inescapably, obsessively, totally connected: Life in the wireless age. *New York Times Magazine,* April 23, 62–67, 101, 108, 112.

Haraway, D. (1991 [1985]). A cyborg manifesto: Science, technology, and socialist-feminism in the late twentieth century. In *Simians, Cyborgs, and Women: The Reinvention of Nature.* New York: Routledge.

Highmore, B. (ed.). (2001). *The Everyday Life Reader.* London: Routledge.

———. (2002). *Everyday Life and Cultural Theory.* London: Routledge.

Katz, J. E., and Aakhus, M. (eds.). (2002). *Perpetual Contact: Mobile Communication, Private Talk, Public Performance.* Cambridge: Cambridge University Press.

Klein, N. (1999). *No Logo: Taking Aim at the Brand Bullies.* New York: Picador.

Kolko, B. E., Nakamura, L., and Rodman, G. B. (eds.). (2000). *Race in Cyberspace.* New York: Routledge.

Lessig, L. (1999). *Code and Other Laws of Cyberspace.* New York: Basic.

McLuhan, M. (1964). *Understanding Media: The Extensions of Man.* New York: McGraw-Hill.

Miller, D. (1987). *Material Culture and Mass Consumption.* Oxford, UK: Basil Blackwell.

Mitchell, W. J. (1995). *City of Bits: Space, Place, and the Infobahn.* Cambridge, MA: MIT Press.

———. (2003). *Me++: The Cyborg Self and the Networked City.* Cambridge, MA: MIT Press.

Morley, D. (1986). *Family Television: Cultural Power and Domestic Leisure.* London: Comedia/Routledge.

———. (1992). *Television, Audiences and Cultural Studies.* London: Routledge.

———. (2000). *Home Territories: Media, Mobility and Identity.* London: Routledge.

Morley, D., and Robins, K. (1995). *Spaces of Identity: Global Media, Electronic Landscapes and Cultural Boundaries*. London: Routledge.

Murray, J. H. (1997). *Hamlet on the Holodeck: The Future of Narrative in Cyberspace*. New York: Free Press.

Myerson, G. (2001). *Heidegger, Habermas and the Mobile Phone*. Cambridge, UK: Icon.

Nakamura, L. (1999). Race in/for cyberspace: Identity tourism and racial passing on the Internet. In V. J. Vitanza (ed.), *CyberReader*, 2nd ed. Boston: Allyn and Bacon.

———. (2002). *Cybertypes: Race, Ethnicity, and Identity on the Internet*. New York: Routledge.

Negroponte, N. (1996). *Being Digital*. New York: Vintage.

Poster, M. (1995). *The Second Media Age*. Cambridge, UK: Polity.

———. (2002). High-tech Frankenstein, or Heidegger meets Stelarc. In J. Zylinska (ed.), *The Cyborg Experiments: The Extensions of the Body in the Media Age*. London: Continuum.

———. (2003). Everyday life and mobile phones. In K. Nyíri (ed.), *Mobile Communication: Social and Political Effects*. Vienna: Passagen Verlag.

Revenge of the Nerds. (1984). Dir. J. Kanew. Interscope.

Rheingold, H. (1993). *The Virtual Community: Homesteading on the Electronic Frontier*. New York: Addison Wesley.

———. (2002). *Smart Mobs: The Next Social Revolution*. Cambridge, MA: Perseus.

Seiter, E. (1999). Television and the Internet. In T. Caldwell (ed.), *Electronic Media and Technoculture*. New Brunswick, NJ: Rutgers University Press.

Silver, D. (2000). Looking backwards, looking forwards: Cyberculture studies. In D. Gauntlett (ed.), *Web.Studies: Rewiring Media Studies for the Digital Age*. London: Arnold.

Spigel, L. (1992). *Make Room for TV: Television and the Family Ideal in Postwar America*. Chicago: University of Chicago Press.

Sterne, J. (2003). *The Audible Past: Cultural Origins of Sound Reproduction*. Durham, NC: Duke University Press.

Tichi, C. (1991). *Electronic Hearth: Creating an American Television Culture*. New York: Oxford University Press.

Toffler, A. (1980). *The Third Wave*. New York: Bantam.

Turkle, S. (1995). *Life on the Screen: Identity in the Age of the Internet*. Cambridge, MA: MIT Press.

Williams, R. (1974). *Television: Technology and Cultural Form*. London: Fontana.

Wolff, M. (1998). *Burn Rate: How I Survived the Gold Rush Years on the Internet*. New York: Simon and Schuster.

Chapter 6

Cyberculture Studies
An Antidisciplinary Approach (version 3.0)

McKenzie Wark

> The work to which the Institute devoted itself before
> the emigration meant something new in comparison to
> the then official education system. The enterprise suc-
> ceeded only because a group interested in social theory
> and from different scholarly backgrounds came together
> with belief that formulating the negative in the epoch of
> transition was more meaningful than academic careers.
> —Max Horkheimer, 1971

01. We are in the midst of a double becoming, a dual appropriation, only one side of which appears at all clearly. On the one side, the media that is the academy appropriates the emergent media vectors of cyberspace to its conventions and genres. Thus, we have cyber-sociology, net-criticism, digital economics, and so on. But the other side of the appropriation proceeds in reverse. Academic media is itself being infiltrated and subtly re-wired by the vector. The possibility of new regimes of knowledge/media appears as the shadow or double of the anxiety of disciplinarity.[1]

02. Knowledge never appears as such. It always takes a historical form as knowledge/media. It is always embedded in a discourse-network that is at once technical and political-economic.[2] We live at a time when the evolution of the technical forces of the media of knowledge outstrips their political-economic relations. The current political-economic forms are a fetter, not just on the technical development of the media of knowledge for

its own sake but also on the transformation of the political-economic relations of knowledge in a more democratic direction. We have the forces,
but not the relations, for a revolution in the form of knowledge/media.[3]

03. At this conjuncture, the fate in store for cyberculture studies is a tragic
one. At worst, it finds itself appropriated by existing disciplines in the current ossified state of knowledge/media. Cyberculture studies becomes just
the latest acquisition that already bankrupt disciplinary forms of knowl-
edge/media might appropriate to stave off foreclosure for a while—until
the next thing comes along. Or in other words, cyberculture studies might
go the way of "postmodernism."[4]

04. A fate not much better would be the assent of cyberculture studies into
the ranks of the disciplines in its own right. The formal attributes of a discipline are not hard to acquire: association, journal, conference, canon.
These external attributes give the semblance of an internal coherence to
all the disciplines, all of which are equally arbitrary. Once it had mim-
icked the formal semblance of a discipline, cyberculture studies would not
merely prop up one particular bankrupt discipline, it would be a legiti-
mating decoration for the whole useless edifice of disciplinary discourse.

05. To see why appropriation by the existing disciplinary apparatus of
knowledge/media would be a calamity, it helps to perceive the state of
knowledge/media in a certain critical light. A critical approach to knowledge turns its tools toward its own conditions of production—toward the
forms of knowledge/media themselves. A critical theory that does not
reflect on its own conditions of existence rapidly becomes hypocritical
theory.[5] To take actual forms of knowledge to be all there is to knowledge
is to lapse into a naturalizing ideology about knowledge. To perceive the
virtual dimension of knowledge as being as real as its actual dimension
opens up the critical perspective within knowledge itself.[6] One sees that
knowledge can be otherwise.

06. The disciplinary structure is not an artifact of nature, although it may
appear so within the current ideologies of the academy—even its "critical"
ones. The disciplines arose as a historical stage in the struggle for knowledge, one determined by the intersection of a given technology of knowledge within a given political-economic regime for maintaining scarcity.
The disciplines arise not as a necessary means of managing the abundance

of knowledge but, to the contrary, as an artificial means of maintaining the scarcity of access within a regime of knowledge/media predicated on a politics of hierarchy and arbitrary division and an economics of exclusion.[7]

07. It is a characteristic of knowledge in the modern era that the technical limits to liberating knowledge from scarcity have consistently declined. From the printing press to the Internet, the material labor of communicating knowledge across time and space becomes ever more efficient. The technical limits of knowledge/media disappear. The regime of scarcity has become overwhelmingly political and economic. The political and economic constraints become a fetter on the free communication of knowledge.

08. It is not by accident that the idea arose that this is a "post-Enlightenment" era. The movement beyond the Enlightenment has less to do, however, with its theoretical overcoming than with the inversion of its practical orientation. The Enlightenment sought both a technics and an economics for the widespread diffusion of knowledge. The post-Enlightenment era seeks an economic and political regime for limiting the diffusion that precisely this technics might enable.[8]

09. Information wants to be free but is everywhere in chains. Not because it has to be. Only on the ideological plane is it natural or necessary that knowledge be restricted or limited in any way. Knowledge is scarce because an artificial regime of scarcity has been imposed on it, by those with an interest in confining knowledge within a regime of identity and property that restricts the authorizing of statements that can be considered knowledge to a restricted set of owners duly licensed.

10. The university was a major site at which the Enlightenment project of expanding the technical means for liberating knowledge from scarcity were invented and perfected—from the printing press to the Internet. And yet the university is also the site at which scarcity is now most vigorously enforced by other means—by the monopoly on the licensing procedure, by the division of knowledge into arbitrary fields.

11. The disciplinary regime of knowledge/media maintains scarcity by dividing knowledge on the field-coverage principle. Knowledge is divided

into plots, which are the property of individual scholars, licensed to trade them. These individual scholars form trade associations—disciplines—to police the boundaries of their holdings.

12. The university has a corporate interest in regulating scarcity of access to knowledge and forms a proprietary system that overlaps that of the disciplines. It rations access to the licensing of ownership to those portions of the fields it chooses to cover.

13. Universities collude and struggle against other entities that would privatize knowledge on a different basis. One obvious example is the publishing conglomerates that seek to monopolize the journals and leverage that monopoly to extract exorbitant fees from university libraries. As the technical form of the vector develops, formerly separate political-economic regimes that managed information are brought into conflict. Nothing but a mere habit of thought now separates knowledge/media from other institutionalized forms of the vector.

14. Cyberculture studies is presented with a problem: it can either collude with the maintenance of this pernicious regime of scarcity—or not. It may be the first kind of knowledge to really possess this antidisciplinary potential. It is the first practice of knowledge/media to confront the privatized forms of disciplinary discourse with not merely a theoretical critique but an alternative practice.

15. Taken together, the tools of cyberculture create a veritable ontological revolution. Information now has a purely abstract relation to materiality. Information always exists within the realm of material form, but its relation to that form has become arbitrary. There is no necessary reason for this bit of data to be encoded on this bit of paper, that hard disk, this screen. There is no longer any material necessity for a scarcity of information. Scarcity is only maintained by repressing this emergent virtuality, by the limiting of knowledge to forms of media based on privatization and exclusion.

16. The arbitrary relation Saussure found between signifier and signified turns out to be just a special case of a larger relation of abstraction that has come into being, in the wake of speech, in the development of the material form of media in history.[9] Just as poststructuralism discovered

the nonidentity of signifier and signified, so too cyberculture studies stands on the brink of the discovery of the nonidentity of information and its material form.

17. Whether it is listservs, blogs, Web sites—these are just particular expressions of a now general relation of abstraction. This abstraction puts an end to the merely technical constraints on scarcity and calls for the creation of new political-economic relations that can release the virtuality of knowledge/media. Cyberculture calls for an immanent procedure of evaluation that works within an unfolding net-time, within a heterogeneous space where concepts encounter percepts and affects.[10] The possibility appears on the horizon of a knowledge/media constrained by nothing not internal to its own immanence, nothing not given in its own free encounter with the world.

18. Cyberculture studies has the potential to be not just another discipline but the end of disciplines as a way of maintaining the scarcity of knowledge. Cyberculture studies can be the point at which the liberation of knowledge from scarcity begins as a self-conscious process. Cyberculture studies can be the critical theory—not the hypocritical theory—of the production of knowledge in itself and for itself.

19. The field-space of the disciplines cuts knowledge off from its own heterogeneous space of virtuality and subordinates it to a transcendental principle of identity and property.[11] Cyberculture studies opens the door to the transformation of the field-space of the disciplines into a net-time, where the communication of affects, percepts, concepts finds its own rhythm.

20. It may not be necessary for cyberculture studies to oppose disciplinary knowledge. A better tactic may be more like the Trojan horse. It may look like an offering to the existing organization of education, while concealing something else.[12] The best tactic may be to escape from the constraints of identity, property, and disciplinarity—which are after all the same thing—from within.

21. A few modest policy decisions may help keep cyberculture studies from collapsing back into the fetters from which it seeks to escape. A refusal to participate in the privatization of knowledge by the major journal-publishing conglomerates would be a start.[13]

22. A more profound challenge is to avoid the disciplinary boundaries that condemn knowledge to live within arbitrary constraints. The disciplinary procedure creates an arbitrary boundary between one discipline and another. This in turn becomes the site of the merely "interdisciplinary"—a sort of trade agreement between two territories. The artifice of a border creates the illusion of a homogenous space thereby enclosed. By diverting anxiety to the border, the empty and incoherent space enclosed goes unexamined. In refusing the arbitrary border, cyberculture studies opens the space of thought to thought itself and, thus, to anxiety. Cyberculture studies requires a certain courage in living without identity.

23. In place of the formal procedures of the exchange of knowledge within a discipline, or the masquerade of the "interdisciplinary," cyberculture studies without identity calls for new protocols of dialogue that are not based on the authority of property or the patrimony of shared ancestors or the policing of proper codes. It calls for a heterogeneous space of exchange and mutual translation.[14]

24. The net-time extends into the past as well as into the future. Once ancestors are decided upon, the future is also set within limits, and its ownership decided. Cyberculture studies would thus call for a permanent suspension of the question of the canon.[15]

25. There is still something to learn from the disciplines, and hence they cannot be abolished overnight. One has to learn from them how their discursive structure and practice impedes knowledge. Indeed, knowledge of the human—formerly known as the humanities and social sciences—may not yet exist. They have lacked the form adequate to their realization.

NOTES

1. The concept of knowledge/media owes something to Foucault's (1980) power/knowledge, but shifts attention to what Foucault neglects, the technical or, rather, "vectoral" dimension to twentieth-century disciplinary formations.

2. While drawing on Foucault, Kittler (1990) shifts attention to the vectoral dimension of disciplinary regimes but gets caught up in the realm of the technical, at the expense of the economic determinants of disciplinary regimes.

3. The shift toward the digital, which frees information from any particular material regime, making possible an abstract relation between information and

materiality, is precisely the sort of abstraction at work in the world on which Marx would have us focus. Property is of central importance in Marx's thought. Drawing on English political economy, Marx saw a progressive abstraction of regimes of property. These nevertheless reach their limit and become a fetter upon the abstraction of information, which in our time threatens to break out of all regimes of scarcity maintained by property. The file-sharing mania and the efforts of the culture industries to shut it down are but a symptom of this. Appropriately, the reader is directed to a free resource for Marx's key texts: The Marx/Engels Library, at http://www.marxists.org/archive/marx/works/.

4. The discourse on the postmodern ground to a halt precisely because of an inability to think through its implications to the very practices of knowledge within which it was discovered. Jameson's (1991) illuminating work relies on rather dated understandings of "late capitalism" and does not think through the symptoms discovered on the surface of culture to mutations in an economic logic beyond capitalism, if as yet still within the longer, overarching history of the commodity abstraction.

5. One easily forgets that critical theory's attack on commodified forms of culture was at the same time an attack on commodified forms of knowledge. The rejection of the former may really be triggered by anxieties about the latter (Adorno 1991).

6. If, as Jameson once remarked, every generation rethinks the dialectic for its own requirements, then the rethinking of the dialectic one might take as central here is the one that takes the most distance from its classical formulation. The categories of the virtual and the actual may have licensed a whole new era of scholastic metaphysics, but it may yet also prove a useful critical tool (Deleuze 1994).

7. If cyberculture studies does indeed turn out to have a critical potential in regard to the organization of knowledge, at the levels of both form and content, then it proceeds best in conjunction with a thorough critical knowledge of actually existing higher education (Aronowitz 2000).

8. Dean (2002) offers a particularly suggestive account of the role of the secret in the construction of the ideology of this postcapitalist era (what I would call the vectoralist era). If one is to avoid merely attaching cyberculture studies to the ideology of cyberspace as "access," then one's critical approach to this discourse is essential.

9. The "semiotic turn" in cultural studies seemed on the surface to be a huge step forward, but we see now that it was a step backward as well. It licensed a disciplinary boundary between culture and economy, each with its own master thinker (Saussure, Marx) and its own formal terms (signifier/signified, use/exchange value). But by tearing language out of its roots in speech acts (and media vectors) and creating a purely formal and homogenous terrain of the sign, cultural analysis cut itself off from history and, most specifically, from the history of the

vectoral form of communication. Saussure's (1983) discovery misidentifies its object as language rather than the abstraction of communication.

10. An example of just such a heterogeneous space, which attempted to both do critical cyberculture studies and to be a critical cyberculture, is net-time. See Bosma et al. 1999.

11. A suggestive work for thinking a practice of knowledge without the a priori of a boundary is Deleuze's (1988) remarkable book on Foucault.

12. For more on the tactics appropriate to critical knowledge within the institution see the section "Education" in Wark 2004.

13. An example of an alternative to the restricted economy of knowledge within the regime of property is the Brisbane-based journal *m/c*: www.media-culture .org.au/.

14. For a theoretical approach to the possibilities of communication, and their pathologies, see Guattari 1995.

15. Eshun's (1998) remarkable book approaches the cultural present not through its past but through its future.

REFERENCES

Adorno, T. (1991). *The Culture Industry: Selected Essays on Mass Culture*, edited by J. M. Bernstein. London: Routledge.

Aronowitz, S. (2000). *Knowledge Factory*. Boston: Beacon.

Bosma, J., et al. (eds.). (1999). *Readme! Filtered by Nettime*. New York: Autonomedia.

Dean, J. (2002). *Publicity's Secret: How Technoculture Capitalizes on Democracy*. Ithaca, NY: Cornell University Press.

Deleuze, G. (1994). *Difference and Repetition*, translated by Paul Patton. New York: Columbia University Press.

————. (1988). *Foucault*, translated by Sean Hand. Minneapolis: University of Minnesota Press.

Eshun, K. (1998). *More Brilliant Than the Sun*. London: Quartet.

Foucault, M. (1980). *Power/Knowledge: Selected Interviews and Other Writings*, edited and translated by Colin Gordon. New York: Pantheon.

Guattari, F. (1995). *Chaosmosis: An Ethico-Aesthetic Paradigm*, translated by Paul Baines and Julian Pefanis. Sydney: Power Publications.

Jameson, F. (1991). *Postmodernism, or, the Cultural Logic of Late Capitalism*. London: Verso.

Kittler, F. (1990). *Discourse Networks 1800/1900*, translated by Michael Metteer. Palo Alto, CA: Stanford University Press.

Saussure, F. D. (1983). *Course in General Linguistics*, translated by Roy Harris. London: Open Court.

Wark, M. (2004). *A Hacker Manifesto*. Cambridge, MA: Harvard University Press.

Part II

Critical Approaches and Methods

Chapter 7

Finding the Quality in Qualitative Research

Nancy K. Baym

From the outset, some of the most important and influential research in this emergent field of "cyberculture studies" or, more broadly, internet research has been qualitative. One of the earliest academic studies was Elizabeth Reid's 1991 thesis, which offered a critical analysis of how Internet Relay Chat represented a postmodern phenomenon. Sherry Turkle's *Life on the Screen* (1996) and Sandy Stone's *The War of Desire and Technology* (1995) both drew on ethnographic participant observation, as did almost all the chapters (including my own) in Steve Jones's 1994 oft-cited collection *Cybersociety*. With its insights into the meanings made in and of the internet, qualitative research has been and continues to be essential in shaping our understanding of the internet, its impact on culture, and culture's impacts on the internet.

On the other hand, I review a lot of journal submissions, most of which are qualitative analyses of online phenomena, and most of which leave a great deal to be desired. There are several reasons for this. As anyone who's heard a significant number of conference papers in most any discipline is all too well aware, research using any method is prone to flaws. However, regardless of its subject, qualitative research is beset by a particular set of problems. These are exacerbated in internet research, which has its own recurrent problems. This chapter briefly outlines these problems and sketches a set of principles for quality in qualitative internet research.

Perhaps the biggest problem facing all qualitative research is that the standards for what makes qualitative research good are very unclear. While quantitative researchers disagree on some topics, there is pretty clear agreement that if p is more than .05, your findings aren't statistically significant, and that an N of 8 is not adequate for making general claims. Qualitative research, in contrast, has no such clear-cut rules, a problem magnified by the sense that the new medium of the internet might bring new rules with it. How are we to determine what evidence is good enough to make a claim or how many subjects are enough?

Perhaps just as important, many fields offer no graduate training in qualitative methods, so that those who choose to use these methods are often forced to learn what they can from textbooks and exemplars and make it up as they go along. I have received many e-mails in the past decade from graduate students trying to teach their committees about both the internet and the methods they were using to examine what interests them about the Net.

There is also a myth that qualitative research is "subjective" and therefore immune to issues of accuracy. At one extreme, some dismiss all qualitative research on the grounds that it is too soft and impressionistic to be of scientific value. At the other extreme, some insist that all qualitative research is valid since nothing subjective can ever be wrong. Although it may be true that subjectivities cannot be false, some are a good deal smarter than others. One result of these problems is that many people who conduct qualitative research are not methodologically prepared to plan and carry out high-quality projects. These are also problems for people who want to read and make sense of qualitative internet research even if they don't intend to conduct any themselves. I've had many a conversation with stellar quantitative researchers or theorists faced with a piece of qualitative research who have no idea whether it is methodologically sound. Being literate internet scholars requires that we be adequately versed in methods other than those we practice ourselves so that we can tell something good from something poor.

Internet research also faces its own challenges. These problems I have just discussed are magnified by the aforementioned sense that perhaps the old rules don't apply in this new medium (most of them do). Furthermore, many internet researchers have a misguided sense that they are the first to have discovered an online phenomenon (a sense so strong that many apparently never bother to search existing literature to see whether this is the case). I would like to think that time and the Association of Internet Researchers have begun to mitigate that problem, but we certainly haven't solved it yet. Furthermore, even when one does search for existing research, it can be hard to find. Internet researchers generally hold their allegiances to their home disciplines above the still-emerging forum of Internet Research, which lacks institutionally recognized disciplinary status or premier journals. As a result, internet research is published in an extraordinary variety of disciplinary forums, most of which will be unfamiliar to even well-read internet researchers.

In the remainder of this chapter, I take a stand on what makes for good qualitative research. I believe that despite the variability in how qualitative studies are done, there are standards for quality practice. I begin with an insight from Sally Jackson (1986), who argued that all research methods are forms of argument rather than recipes for truth. The standards that characterize quantitative methods, she suggested, are conventionalized responses to anticipated counterarguments. For instance, the obvious response to a causal claim (e.g., internet use decreases political engagement) might be "How do you know these results (decreased engagement) were caused by the independent variable (internet use) rather than other variables or chance?" The research practice of using a control group anticipates the first half of this counterargument, and the setting of an alpha level against which to determine the likelihood of chance anticipates the second. Qualitative research is also a means of making an argument. Although counterarguments may be a little harder to predict, high-quality qualitative work should anticipate those counterarguments and provide a persuasive evidence-based case against them both in the structuring of the research design and the presentation of the findings. It is not only fair but also necessary to ask of any qualitative work the simple question "Am I convinced by the evidence?"

Space precludes a thorough consideration of what makes qualitative work convincing, but a brief look at some exemplary qualitative works in contrast to the kinds of flaws one tends to find elsewhere can at least lay the groundwork for thinking about these concerns. Lynn Cherny's (1999) research into a MOO she called "ElseMOO," published as *Conversation and Community,* was a linguistically grounded long-term exploration that explicated the details of the group's interactions in ways that demonstrated and explained the ability of their language use to create online community. In her book *Cyberplay,* Brenda Danet (2001) (who, as David Silver once commented, "puts the funky back in internet research") collects a decade's worth of discourse analyses to examine a variety of online forms of play, including online theater, fonts, e-mail, and graphically oriented chat rooms in which people build identities and community through the construction of elaborate multicolored ASCII images. Annette Markham's (1998) book *Life Online* explores both the experience of "living online" and the methodological challenges of that exploration. Markham used the method of online interviews to grapple with heavy users' experience of being online. Perhaps the best-known qualitative piece of internet research is also one of the best (although only a small part of it is really about the internet, and several criticisms of that section have been appropriately raised). Turkle's (1996) book *Life on the Screen: Identity in the Age of the Internet* was a close examination of how people understand computers and how this then plays out in their interactions with the internet, specifically MUDs. My own research (Baym 2000) into the Usenet discussion group rec.arts.tv.soaps, published in the book *Tune In, Log On*, aimed to elucidate the ways in which participants made soap opera viewing collaborative and how they used this collaboration as a base on which to develop individualized identities, interpersonal relationships, and a rich set of group values and norms, ultimately creating a sense of community. My methods included nearly four years of participant observation, open-ended surveys of group members, face-to-face meetings, and discourse analysis of their messages.

Each of these studies has a different focus and takes different methodological approaches. Each can certainly be faulted for many things that were not considered. I have been criticized for saying too little about gender and/or cultures of consumption and consumerism, criticisms that could be made of most of these works. These books are also apolitical and noncritical, in the sense that they do not have an agenda for world improvement and do not challenge existing power structures. However worthy these purposes may be, and critical research certainly has its place, good qualitative research does not need to be critical. If it is to be taken seriously by those who might make a difference, however, qualitative research that is critical does need to be good.

My discussion here is limited to what makes the arguments in these works compelling. There are, I think, at least six interrelated strengths they share: they are grounded in theory and data, they demonstrate rigor in data collection and analysis, they use multiple strategies to get data, they take into account the perspective of participants, they demonstrate awareness of and self-reflexivity regarding the research process, and they take into consideration interconnections between the internet and the life world within which it is situated.

All of these works are grounded in existing theory and research that concerns the internet and, more important, that does not. Too often internet researchers take the stance that since the internet is new, old theory has nothing to offer its exploration. This assumption is wrong. The theories that we have developed to explain social organization need to be able to address new media. Danet turned to theory and research on the history of typography, aesthetics, and folk art, among other areas, to understand the phenomena she studied. My work adapted practice theory, and both Cherny and I drew on the concept of the "speech community" from the interdisciplinary field known as the ethnography of communication. Existing theories may not be perfect fits. This is, in fact, a way in which internet research can contribute to social theory as well as enhance our understanding of the internet. As internet researchers find the ways in which old theory does and doesn't work, we are able to refine and improve social theory. But new technology does not reinvent the social world. Old structures have not simply collapsed and been replaced by new ones in the wake of the internet. Old ways of relating to others and conducting social life have not been supplanted by e-mail. For example, people may now meet others online before meeting in person. I met all the authors in this collection online before we met face-to-face. Online relationships do develop in ways that are somewhat different from face-to-face relationships, for example, language is privileged over appearance and geographic proximity is not a constraining factor. But as relational theory has held for decades, relationships are still built on attraction created through common interests, ease of interaction, and running into one another in the same public spaces, even if those spaces are now digital rather than terrestrial. Theory may need to be refined, but it does not need to be reinvented.

I have complained already that too many researchers ignore existing internet research, assuming instead that since the internet is relatively new, they must be the first to discover a phenomenon. I saw too many scholars give conference papers in the 1990s proudly claiming the discovery of the smiley face. Good internet researchers do their homework, and when they do, they find that there is, if anything, an overwhelming amount of existing work on which they can build. Grounding in existing research makes the work more solid because it allows the scholar to assess what is already known and to sharpen the tools of the current inquiry. Just as important, with regard to making a compelling argument, a grounding in existing work allows the scholar to show how the work tells us something we did not know before. High-quality qualitative research makes its unique contribution clear.

Rigor in data collection is also essential. I have seen too many works that were highly selective in the data they collected. One researcher who was interested in online sexism, for instance, collected examples of online sexism. Although the author was able to demonstrate that sexism happens online, that was hardly an earth-shaking claim, and its force was seriously undermined by the author's inability to address whether such instances were common or rare and how they were handled when they occurred. I have also seen papers in which people analyze very brief time periods, which may be appropriate if one is looking for immediate reaction to an event, say, September 11, but which is highly problematic if one is seeking to describe an online group or phenomenon that is not so temporally bound. I have also seen Web analyses that focus only on the most accessible parts of a site, front pages for instance, without any examination of what goes on a few clicks in, where, one presumes, most of the users are actually engaging the site. One cannot make claims about what is frequent, rare, important, or irrelevant unless one has spent considerable time with the phenomenon in its ever-changing natural state. The authors I have chosen as exemplars all spent a long time, often years, collecting the data for their projects. They collected data in a range of areas of their online spaces or in a range of situations both online and off. As a result, they are able to situate the examples they discuss against a broader backdrop of data that they do not detail but that nonetheless clarifies the significance of their findings. One of the best tests of whether an analysis holds is to offer a counterexample and see what happens. In my work, for instance, I argued that soap opera viewers were constructed within the group as intelligent, clever, and extremely witty people. I was able to present many messages that demonstrated this implicitly. However, I believe my argument was strongest when I was able to show that, when someone did violate this norm by telling the group that soaps were for idiots and that they should all "get a life," the articulation of the positive view of soap opera fans was made explicit in response after response.

Related to this is that most good qualitative work uses multiple strategies to get at the phenomena that interest them. Researchers may look at multiple forms of online discourse, they may conduct interviews, and they may complement online data collection with offline encounters with participants. To some extent, this is the qualitative tact known as "triangulation." Triangulation has been criticized for suggesting that one will get at Truth with a capital T if one takes multiple perspectives, but it is undeniable that two or more routes into a phenomenon will provide more insight than one. One will certainly be able to build a better argument when claims can be supported with more than one kind of evidence. For instance, in my own work, the surveys repeatedly emphasized the group's friendliness, and the discourse analyses allowed me to unpack how that friendliness was accomplished through examination of the participants' actual practices. I am always wary of qualitative research that asks a question and then offers only one route to an answer, regardless of what that route may be.

Another strength of the exemplars I have cited is that their claims about user experience were grounded in discussion with users. Too many researchers analyze Web sites, online discussions, or other cybertexts and, based on textual analyses, make claims about the users. For instance, one Web site analysis I read argued that because the link to discussion spaces on the main page was small, users were discouraged from engaging in discussion. In contrast, I'd (counter)argue that regular users (and there were many) probably went straight to the discussion sections, skipping the top level of the site altogether. Though it is by no means always the case, critical research seems particularly prone to this error, moving from critical readings of texts to assumptions about how those texts empower or disempower their readers or how they are experienced by their readers. This is true not just of internet research but of all media research. As I review elsewhere (Baym 2000), soap opera research contains many of the most egregious examples of this imaginable. I cannot say this too strongly: if researchers do not interview participants or have other access to their points of view, they have no grounds for claims about how online phenomena are understood or how they influence those who engage in and encounter those phenomena. Researchers can talk about the possibilities the text constructs but not about what real people do within or around those possibilities.

Markham's work is a wonderful example of reflexivity in qualitative research. She set out to discover "heavy user experience" only to find that there didn't seem to be any such thing. Heavy users had experiences that differed from one another. Rather than give up on the project, she modified its aims. She does a favor to all researchers by discussing this process explicitly in her book. Danet also offers a great example of reflexivity in action when she describes searching her saved screenshots trying to find a user's image that was not interrupted by another user's text (they were created on synchronous and interactive Internet Relay Chat). As she did this, she realized that almost all the illustrations contained interruptions. This led her to the insight that part of becoming a competent member of these groups is learning how to see the images as uninterrupted wholes even when they have been disrupted by others' comments during their transmission. Qualitative research is ongoing and dynamic and requires that researchers be aware of how they are influencing data and interpretation and how initial questions may need to be adjusted as the data roll in.

My final point is that really good internet research, be it qualitative or not, does not really believe in cyberspace in the sense of a distinct place that stands in contrast to the earth-bound world. How online spaces are constructed and the activities that people do online are intimately inter-woven with the construction of the offline world and the activities and structures in which we participate, whether we are using the internet or not. Offline contexts always permeate and influence online situations, and online situations and experiences always feed back into offline experience. The best work recognizes that the internet is woven into the fabric of the rest of life and seeks to better understand the weaving.

Much of the appeal of qualitative methods is their openness. They can be used in as many combinations and adjusted in as many ways as there are phenomena worthy of inquiry. It is a mistake, however, to equate this flexibility with ease or simplicity. Doing good qualitative research is hard. In this essay I have made explicit the primary criteria I apply as I read and review internet research. I anticipate that some will argue against some or even all of my criteria. I encourage them to let that argument begin. It's through such explicit discussion of the expectations and standards we hold implicitly that we will develop the clear principles that allow re-searchers to produce work that is credible not just to those who produce it but also to those who read it.

REFERENCES

Baym, N. (2000). *Tune in, log on: Soaps, fandom, and online community.* Thousand Oaks, CA: Sage.

Cherny, L. (1999). *Conversation and Community: Chat in a virtual world.* Stanford, CA: CSLI Publications.

Danet, B. (2001). *Cyberplay: Communicating online.* Oxford, UK: Berg.

Jackson, S. (1986). Building a case for claims about discourse structure. In D. G. Ellis and W. A. Donohue (eds.), *Contemporary issues in language and discourse processes* (pp. 129–147). Hillsdale, NJ: Erlbaum.

Jones, S. (ed.). (1994). *Cybersociety.* Thousand Oaks, CA: Sage.

Markham, A. (1998). *Life online: Researching real experience in virtual space.* Walnut Creek, CA: AltaMira.

Reid, E. M. (1991). Electropolis: Communication and community on Internet Relay Chat. Master's thesis, University of Melbourne, Australia.

Stone, A. R. (1995). *The war of desire and technology at the close of the mechanical age.* Cambridge, MA: MIT Press.

Turkle, S. (1996). *Life on the screen: Identity in the age of the internet.* New York: Simon and Schuster.

Chapter 8

Web Sphere Analysis and Cybercultural Studies

Kirsten Foot

One way of approaching cybercultural studies is to focus on the relations and patterns, means and artifacts of cultural production and exchange online. Viewed as an evolving set of structures that enable and manifest the production of cyberculture, the hyperlinked, coproduced, and ephemeral nature of the Web challenges traditional approaches to research of social, political, and cultural interchange. Cultural studies of the Web may benefit from new methods of analyzing Web form and content, along with processes and patterns of production, distribution, usage, and interpretation of Web-based phenomena. In this chapter, I propose the concept of a *Web sphere* as a unit of analysis for cybercultural studies, explain the value of Web archives, and discuss methods of Web sphere analysis that may be useful for understanding cybercultural phenomena. I illustrate these methodological reflections through two studies of personal expression on the Web in the wake of the attacks of September 11, 2001.

Borrowing a concept from the work of Taylor and van Every (2000) on the relationship between communication and organizing, we can view the Web as both a "site and surface" for communicative action. In order to conduct an analysis of both the "site" and "surface" of the Web, it is helpful to create and analyze an archive not just of Web sites but of a Web sphere. A Web sphere is a collection of dynamically defined digital resources spanning multiple Web sites deemed relevant or related to a central theme or object, in the sense of the *gegenstand* concept from classical German philosophy (Foot and Schneider 2002). The *gegenstand* notion of an object as a focal point embedded-in-activity (see Foot 2002; Leont'ev 1978) enables the identification of a Web sphere as a collaborative production. As a unit of analysis, a Web sphere is boundable by time and object-orientation, and it is sensitive to developmental changes. Within the sphere social, political, and cultural relations can be analyzed in a variety of ways.

The most crucial element in this definition of a Web sphere is the dynamic nature of the sites to be included. This dynamism comes from two sources. First, the researchers involved in identifying the boundaries of the sphere are likely to continuously find new sites to be included within it. Second, as will be discussed below, the notion of defining a Web sphere is recursive, in that pages that are referenced by other included sites, as well as pages that reference included sites, are considered part of the sphere under evaluation. Thus, as a Web sphere is archived and analyzed over time, it boundaries are dynamically reestablished by both the researchers and the sites themselves. The Web sphere can function as a macro unit of analysis, by which historical and/or intersphere comparisons can be made. For example, the Web sphere of the 2000 elections in the United States can be comparatively analyzed with the U.S. electoral Web sphere of 2002, as well as with electoral Web spheres in other countries. Alternatively and/or simultaneously, other, more micro units, such as features, links, or textual elements, can be employed in analyses of a Web sphere, as I explain below.

Web sphere analysis is an analytic strategy that, fully implemented, includes analysis of the relations between producers and users of Web materials, as potentiated and mediated by the structural and feature elements of Web sites, hypertexts, and the links between them (Schneider and Foot 2004, 2005). In a nutshell, the multimethod approach of Web sphere analysis consists of the following elements: Web sites related to the object or theme of the sphere are identified, captured in their hyperlinked context, and archived with some periodicity for contemporaneous and retrospective analyses. The archived sites are annotated with human and/or computer-generated "notes" of various kinds, which creates a set of metadata. These metadata correspond to the unit(s) and level(s) of analysis anticipated by the researcher(s). Sorting and retrieving the integrated metadata and URL files is accomplished through several computer-assisted techniques. Interviews of various kinds are conducted with producers and users of the Web sites in the identified sphere, to be triangulated with Web media data in the interpretation of the sphere.

From the perspective of Web sphere analysis, the essence of the Web is the link (Foot et al. 2003). Links provide the nutrients that give the Web the energy and nourishment necessary for growth and development. Links serve as the neural pathways through which the collective intelligences and performances of Web producers and users are created, displayed, and distributed. Several approaches have emerged that take hyperlink relationality into account in more nuanced ways. Lindlof and Shatzer (1998) point in this direction in their article calling for new strategies of media ethnography in "virtual space." Hine (2000) presents a good example of sociocultural analysis of cross-site action on the Web. Similarly, Howard's (2002) conceptualization of network ethnography reflects methodological sensitivity to processes of Web production. In these examples and in Web sphere analysis, attention is given to the hyperlinked context(s) and situatedness of Web sites, as well as to the aims, strategies, and identity-construction processes of Web site producers, as they are produced, maintained, and/or mediated through links.

In order to engage in any kind of developmental or retrospective study of cyberculture on the Web, it is helpful to capture Web materials in a time-sensitive way. The ongoing evolution of the Web poses challenges for scholars as they seek to develop methodological approaches permitting robust examination of Web phenomena. Some of these challenges stem from the nature of the Web, which is a unique mixture of the ephemeral and the permanent. There are two aspects to the ephemerality of Web content: First, Web content is ephemeral in its transience, as it can be expected to last for only a relatively brief time. From the perspective of the user or visitor (or researcher), specialized tools and techniques are required to ensure that content can be viewed again at a later time. Second, Web content is ephemeral in its construction—like television, radio, theater, and other "performance media" (Hecht, Corman, and Miller-Rassulo 1993; Stowkowski 2002). Web content, once presented, needs to be reconstructed or re-presented in order for others to experience it. Although Web pages are routinely reconstructed by computers without human intervention (when a request is forwarded to a Web server), it nevertheless requires some action by the producer (or the producer's server) in order for the content to be viewed again. In other words, the experience of the Web, as well as the bits used to produce the content, must be intentionally preserved in order for it to be reproduced (Arms et al. 2001). Older media —including printed materials, film, and sound recordings, for example— can be archived in the form in which they are presented; no additional steps are needed to re-create the experience of the original.

At the same time, the Web has a sense of permanence that clearly distinguishes it from performance media. Unlike theater or live television or radio, Web content must exist in a permanent form in order to be transmitted. The Web shares this characteristic with other forms of media such as film, print, and sound recordings. The permanence of the Web, however, is somewhat fleeting. Unlike any other permanent media, a Web site may regularly and procedurally destroy its predecessor each time it is updated by its producer. That is, absent specific arrangements to the contrary, each previous edition of a Web site may be erased as a new version is produced. By analogy, it would be as if each day's newspaper was printed on the same piece of paper, obliterating yesterday's news to produce today's.

The ephemerality of the Web requires that proactive steps be taken in order to allow a re-creation of Web experience for future analyses. The permanence of the Web makes this eminently possible. Although saving Web sites is not as easy as, say, saving editions of a magazine, archiving techniques are evolving in such a way to facilitate scholarly research of Web sites. In distinction to other ephemeral media, the Web can be preserved in nearly the same form as it was originally "performed" (Kahle 1997; Lyman 2002; Lyman and Kahle 1998) and analyzed at a later time. Web archiving enables more rigorous and verifiable research, as well as developmental analyses that are time sensitive (e.g., Foot et al. 2003).

Robust Web sphere analysis benefits from robust Web archives. Going further, I suggest that Web archives enable an expanded range of investigable questions and greater analytical rigor for social research on Web-based phenomena. In the remainder of this essay I illustrate the potential benefits of Web archiving and Web sphere analysis for cybercultural studies through a brief overview of the September 11 Web Archive project in general and two studies of personal expression in the post–September 11 Web sphere that exemplify some of quantitative and qualitative methods of analysis enabled by a Web sphere/Web archive approach.

The September 11 Web Archive consists of Web sites related to the airliner attacks in the United States on September 11, 2001, and archived between September 11, 2001, and December 1, 2001. During this period, Steve Schneider and I worked with the Pew Internet and American Life Project, the U.S. Library of Congress, the Internet Archive, and volunteers from around the world to identify and archive URLs that were likely to be relevant to the question of how Web site producers were reacting to the events of September 11. Twelve basic categories of site producers were identified that were expected to be responding to the attacks on the Web. The findings for the studies on personal expression summarized below were based on an examination of Web sites produced by nine of these: news organizations such as CNN, the *New York Times,* and Salon.com; federal, state, and local government entities; corporations and other commercial organizations; advocacy groups; religious groups, including denominations and congregations; individuals acting on their own behalf; educational institutions; portals; and charity and relief organizations.

To build the archive, systematic searches were conducted for URLs produced by these sets of actors, and links to other URLs were followed to find more sites with relevant content. In most cases, the salient feature of these sites was content referring to the attacks and/or their aftermath. In some cases, the absence or removal of such content was salient. These collection efforts identified nearly twenty-nine thousand different sites. Each site was archived on a daily basis from initial identification to the end of the collection period. The objective of the archiving activity was to preserve not only the bits and the content but also the experiential dimensions of this rapidly emerging Web sphere. By capturing pages and sites in their hyperlinked context, the archiving tools preserved not just the collection of Web pages but also an interlinked Web sphere, characterized and bounded by a shared object orientation or reference point, in this case, the September 11 attacks.

The first study on expression as one form of sociopolitical action (Foot and Schneider 2004) included analysis of the types of site producers that enabled Web users to contribute personal expression or access expression posted by others on their sites, as well as whether mechanisms of expression were produced autonomously on a site (onsite) or jointly across sites (coproduced). For this analysis, a sample of 247 sites was generated from the September 11 Web Archive. The sampling strategy, designed to include a broad representation of site producers and to focus on those sites that were captured closest to September 11, yielded a sample of three "impressions" or site captures of the different Web sites. A preliminary analysis of the site pages eliminated those without content relevant to the September 11 events, as well as those not captured in a readable format by the archiving tools. The refined sample of Web sites was then closely examined by trained observers for the range of social and political actions made possible by site producers, including personal expression.

Not surprisingly, we found that personal Web sites produced by individuals were most likely to both give Web users access to others' expression (typically the personal reactions of the site producers) and enable them to provide their own expression to the site (see table 8.1). More interesting was that at least a quarter of all sites and over 40 percent of sites in our sample produced by news organizations, government entities,

TABLE 8.1
Percent of Sites, by Producer Type Enabling Expression

Action Enabled	Type of Site Producer									All Sites
	News	Government	Business	Charity	Advocacy	Religious	Personal	Educational	Portal	
Get Expression	54%	16%	47%	50%	55%	53%	86%	76%	37%	55%
Provide Expression	50%	42%	23%	44%	32%	26%	69%	47%	26%	44%
Number of Sites	24	38	30	18	22	19	59	17	19	247

TABLE 8.2
Mode of Production in Enabling Expression

Mode of Production	Action Enabled	
	Get Expression	Provide Expression
On-site	80%	75%
On-site and coproduced	13%	15%
Coproduced only	8%	11%

Based on analysis of 247 sites

charities, and educational institutions enabled the provision of personal expression by Web users. We interpreted these findings as suggesting an increased willingness in facilitating multivoiced discourse if not dialogue on the part of site producers who might normally have a vested interest in maintaining content control and a more singular voice on their sites.

In this study we also took note of the mode of production employed in enabling expression. We defined an autonomous or onsite mode of production as one in which the site producer provides the content directly. In contrast, a joint or coproduction mode is evidenced when a site producer links to another site to facilitate the user action, in this case accessing or providing personal expression. As table 8.2 illustrates, many site producers combined these modes of production, providing some of the content themselves and linking to another site for additional content or functionality.

Of those site producers whose sites enabled access to or provided personal expression by Web users, a strong majority did so autonomously. Most site producers who engaged in coproduction in enabling expression did so in addition to providing onsite access to expression and/or mechanisms for users to express themselves.

In the second study of online expression my coauthor and I employed textual analysis to explore the particular forms of expression manifested on the Web (Siegl and Foot 2004). This study shed light on the types of public expression evoked by personal or mediated exposure to a crisis and posted on the Internet, and it served as a case study in collective mourning on the Internet. The research questions guiding this analysis included: (1) What kinds of expression were posted on the Web after 9/11? and (2) How do these forms of online expression compare with public mourning and bereavement? Using the same sample of daily impressions of 247 sites from the September 11 Web Archive described above, we identified 84 sites that enabled site visitors to post their own textual expression and/or access the textual expression of others. As in the previous study, these Web sites represented a broad cross-section of Web site producers, including personal or individual sites, charity or civic organizations, businesses, and governments, as well as Web sites constructed for the sole purpose of memorializing the attacks. Due to the large variety of the Web sites, it was necessary to standardize the portion of expression observed on each site. This was accomplished by analyzing the first five discrete units of textual expression; a discrete unit was defined as a temporally bounded entry posted to the Web by an author.

Through close readings of the selected units of textual expression from archived impressions of each site, we identified nine forms of expression manifested on the Web in the three weeks following September 11 (September 11, 2001–October 2, 2001) and noted the changes in dominant forms of expression during that period that deserved further study. We then compared the post-9/11 Web expression with emotional phases identified in the literature on public mourning and bereavement, such as shock, anger, and grief. We demonstrated that post–September 11 Web expression included more than these emotions, suggesting that the functions of the Web-based post-9/11 expression went beyond public mourning and bereavement and included attempts at analysis, sense-making, and advocacy. We concluded by arguing that the broader range of expression on the Web after September 11 (in contrast with expression documented from offline/non-Web contexts in the public mourning and bereavement literature) is at least partially due to characteristics of the Web and processes/practices of Web production that distinguish it from traditional broadcast and print media.

The September 11 Web Archive and the two studies on post-9/11 online expression described here illustrate the usefulness of thematic Web archives and Web sphere analysis in facilitating investigations of some kinds of cybercultural phenomena. The demarcation of a Web sphere requires systematic identification of Web site producers as well as particular sites, which in turn creates a strong base for analyzing patterns and modes of Web (co)production, as demonstrated in the first study. An archive of the Web sphere, collected at regular intervals during a specific period, enables retrospective and developmental analyses of many aspects of online relations, as well as the means and artifacts of cybercultural production and exchange. Web sphere analysis can function as a framework for research on sociocultural phenomena manifested in Web texts, features, or links, at a micro or macro level, and employing a diverse range of methods. As scholars of cyberculture undertake broader and deeper studies of Web form and content, as well as processes and patterns of production, distribution, usage, and interpretation of Web-based phenomena, archive-based Web sphere analysis may provide a helpful foundation.

REFERENCES

Arms, W., Adkins, R., Ammen, C.. and Hayes, A. (2001) Collecting and preserving the Web. The Minerva prototype. *RLG DigiNews,* 5 (2) (April 15). Available at http://www.rlg.org/preserv/diginews/diginews5-2.html.

Foot, K. A. (2002) Pursuing an evolving object: Object formation and identification in a conflict monitoring network. *Mind, Culture and Activity,* 9 (2): 132–149.

Foot, K. A., and Schneider, S. M. (2002) Online action in campaign 2000: An exploratory analysis of the U.S. political Web sphere. *Journal of Broadcasting & Electronic Media,* 46 (2): 222–244. Available at http://politicalweb.info/preElection.html.

Foot, K. A., and Schneider, S. M. (2004) Online structure for civic engagement in the post-9/11 Web sphere. *Electronic Journal of Communication,* 14 (3/4).

Foot, K. A., Schneider, S. M., Dougherty, M., Xenos, M., and Larsen, E. (2003) Analyzing linking practices: Candidate sites in the 2002 U.S. electoral Web sphere. *Journal of Computer-Mediated Communication,* 8 (4). Available at http://www.ascusc.org/jcmc/vol8/issue4/foot.html.

Hecht, M. L., Corman, S. R., and Miller-Rassulo, M. (1993) An evaluation of the drug resistance project: A comparison of film versus live performance media. *Health Communication,* 5 (2): 75–88.

Hine, C. (2000) *Virtual ethnography.* Thousand Oaks, CA: Sage.

Howard, P. (2002) Network ethnography and hypermedia organization: New organizations, new media, new myths. *New Media & Society,* 4 (4): 550–574.

Kahle, B. (1997) Preserving the Internet. *Scientific American,* 276 (3): 82–83.

Leont'ev, A. N. (1978) *Activity, consciousness, and personality.* Englewood Cliffs, NJ: Prentice-Hall.

Lindlof, T. R., and Shatzer, M. J. (1998) Media ethnography in virtual space: Strategies, limits, and possibilities. *Journal of Broadcasting and Electronic Media*, 42 (2): 170–189.

Lyman, P. (2002) Archiving the World Wide Web. *Building a National Strategy for Digital Preservation*, April. Available at http://www.clir.org/pubs/reports/pub106/web.html.

Lyman, P., and Kahle, B. (1998) Archiving digital cultural artifacts: Organizing an agenda for action. *D-Lib Magazine*, July. Available at http://www.dlib.org/dlib/july98/07lyman.html.

Schneider, S. M., and Foot, K. A. (2004) The Web as an object of study. *New Media & Society*, 6 (1): 114–122.

Schneider, S. M., and Foot, K. A. (2005) Web Sphere Analysis: An Approach to Studying Online Action. In *Virtual methods: Issues in social research on the Internet* (ed. C. Hine). Oxford, UK: Berg, 157–170.

Siegl, E., and Foot, K. A. (2004) Expression in the post–September 11th Web sphere. *Electronic Journal of Communication*, 14 (1/2).

Stowkowski, P. A. (2002) Languages of place and discourses of power: Constructing new senses of place. *Journal of Leisure Research*, 34 (4): 368–382.

Taylor, J. R., and van Every, E. J. (2000) *The emergent organization: Communication as its site and surface*. Mahwah, NJ: Lawrence Erlbaum.

Chapter 9

Connecting the Selves
Computer-Mediated Identification Processes

Heidi J. Figueroa Sarriera

Subjectivity is not one of the favorite themes of cyberculture studies. Most of the so-called cyberpsychology trend applies traditional psychology categories, especially those that pathologize users' behaviors. Even if the analysis does not get seduced by the pathology discourse, it tends to focus on identity formation without questioning the conceptual premises behind psychological discourses. Personal-identity formation theories found in any traditional psychology textbook have in common the premise that identity is forged in social relations, that is, through contact with the other. Taking part in the semiotic exchanges of communication is the basic requirement for the formation and transformation of personal identity as an integrated and coherent entity. (The Latin root of the word "identity" is *idem,* "the same," the same entity.)

However, poststructuralist approaches shake the ground of such premises. Contemporary deconstructionist theory reminds us of the ways in which language simultaneously includes presence and absence. The conflicting relations between the *self* and the *other* have an important position in contemporary sociopolitical discourses as well. Michel Foucault (1980a, 1980b, 1985) has documented that the asymmetrical relationships between the *self* and the *other* produce technologies of power. The main purpose of these technologies is the objectification of the subject in order to subjugate it to specific assumptions of what is considered *normal.* The discourses of politics presuppose a rational subject as a psychological self, whose boundaries warrant an observable and measurable identity more or less fixed to fit social order and regulations.

From another perspective, current theorization has raised doubts about how coherent and stable that identity is, given that the subject is able to exhibit multiple self portrayals when interacting with the other in cyberspace or virtual space. Research has been developed to acknowledge that these self portrayals may be different from, or even in conflict with, the way the person presents himself or herself in "real life" (that is, in face-to-face communicative relations). Many metaphors have been used to describe the appearance of these multiplicities of selves in online interactions: *protean self, saturated self, flexible self, virtual self,* and so on. In contrast, the issues surrounding how connections are built to inform new identity processes and their relation with the body politics have not been addressed as frequently.

What are the central issues engaged in relationships, if any, between identity construction, body constraints, agency, and "the social"? This chapter addresses some of the basic assumptions regarding these concepts found in current research on technology and subjectivity and presents Actor Network Theory (ANT) as an alternative framework. In doing so, the focus will be placed on the *semiotic ontology of narratives* as an important strategy to assume responsibility for the politics of construction of boundaries.

When we examine several ethnographic studies of cyberspace or virtual space experience, we find that there is an exchange of agencies, in the sense in which Stone (1995, p. 96) uses the term as a "politically authorized personae." This implies a particular relationship between the possible horizons of agency and the authorizing body in the social act. It is very common to see quotes of different fragments of Stone's book *The War of Desire and Technology at the Close of the Mechanical Age* in writings and lectures discussing issues about the self as a body and/or the *self* and the *other* in computer-mediated communication, particularly in the synchronic mode. Stone especially emphasizes the *embodied* character of online communication. Communication is conceived "in terms of an imagined physical locus within which an exchange of information took place between physical entities" (Stone 1995, pp. 110–11).

Notwithstanding that this kind of work questions differences between *disembodied* experience and *embodied* experience, it still does not grasp the emergent forms of subject locations in the grid of complex human-machine network. Many of these arguments still sustain rigid boundaries around the self or deploy a more imaginative construction of boundaries in an attempt to portray the cyborgian self. Both perspectives appeal to the provocative and seductive image of the singular; whether this singular is conceptualized as a boring unity or a hybrid unity, both perspectives rely on the general premise of identity as an entity. This assumption is very pervasive in social psychology discourse too. To claim, then, that subjectivity is not one of the favorite themes in cyberculture studies is not to say that cyberculture studies do not use traditional psychological premises in their analyses of the user as a subject.

Martín Baró (1985) sums up social psychology's assumptions associated with the concept of personal identity in four statements: (1) identity exists in reference to a world; (2) it asserts itself in the interpersonal relationship; (3) it is relatively stable; and (4) it is a product as much of society as of the individual's actions. I have elsewhere examined this set of assumptions to stress inconsistencies between them and the concept of self as a consistent singular entity (Figueroa Sarriera 1999). The core of that argument is that these assumptions about identity formation presuppose that the individual's context—and, in particular, the most immediate interpersonal relationships, those that link the self to a *nonself* (that is, to the *other*)—reveals itself as a reality of meaning. That reality of meaning is necessarily plural (ethnic groups, the individual's position within the family configuration, gender and class differences, and so on). However, it is assumed that within that reality—in spite of its plurality—the person's self is consistent. We might think that given the uniqueness of personal formation, transformations in the context will be accompanied by variations in the self throughout its existence, to the point of questioning the singularity premise. But this is not the case. There is an insistence that these changes do not negate the continuity of the self, nor do they contradict the assertion that the self is stable. How can this be possible?

Social psychologists emphasize the self-referentiality capacity of the subject. Even though the embodied subject is constructed within a frame of multireferential semiotic markers, it remains a subject as long as he or she retains a capacity for reflexivity or self-referentiality. The interior boundary makes self-reference or reflection possible. From the psychoanalytic perspective, the subject is lost in this game of reflections and becomes the object of desire of the other/Other, Father, or Symbolic Order, in symbolic identifications. The subject can be found oscillating in the contradictory stance, keeping distance and at the same time going along with the order. The subject oscillates between desire and self-interest, if she or he accepts castration and at the same time becomes committed to a transfinite process of going beyond the exterior and interior boundaries that castration imposes (Ibáñez 1985). Social psychology research on stereotyping and prejudice also points to the separation between *self* and *other* as a primary factor in these behaviors, whether the theoretical approach of this research is sociocultural, cognitive, psychoanalytical, etc.

From this common ground, self-reference makes possible the so-called agency of the subject, an agency filled with value judgments. Precisely the question that arises is where the boundary is constructed, because this brings up ethical issues about barriers between the *self* and the *other*. The construction of the self is definitely bound to power devices that discursively construct materiality. This is what has been called *semiotic ontology.*[1]

Harré (1983) reminds us that our personal being is the product of appropriations and transformations from social sources, including local theories regarding the self. Identity-formational projects are aimed at the production of uniqueness. This process requires cognitive reflection, or self-knowledge, and reflexive action, or self-control, depending on the assumptions of local knowledge as to what *self* is. This means that the psychological conditions for the development of the subject must be provided by self-reference apparatus, which can only be given in social relationships (whether *real* or *virtual*) during the semiotic discursive processes. Therefore, self-reference is tightly bound to the subject agency that is related to others, but the subject maintains a deep egotistic individuality. On the other hand, self-reference is also bound to the concept of rational intentionality.

But what would happen if we complicate the ratio of agency to include artifacts and other beings? Techno and cybercultural studies have demonstrated the ways in which machines and other beings play an important part in the process of configuring social intentions and desires. One classic statement related to this idea is Haraway's (1991, p. 180) discussion of the machine: "The machine is not an *it* to be animated, worshiped and dominated. The machine is us, our processes, an aspect of our embodiment. We can be responsible for machines; *they* do not dominate or threaten us. We are responsible for boundaries; we are they." This is the basic aim that animated, for example, such works as the *Cyborg Handbook* (Gray 1995) and its proposition of cyborgologies as a process of constructing the knowledge of cybernetic organisms.

How can we speak about self-referentiality when faced with processes that unfold on a computer screen, processes in which the embodied subject is said to transmute? In its transit, the transmuting subject changes into a disembodied or virtual subject in ways that are particular to computer-mediated communication. Ethnographic research states that this disembodied subject can take on multiple representations. The well-known research of Turkle (1995) has fluently described the ways in which in the virtual setting the subject reproduces not only what she or he is but also what she or he would like to be and what she or he would not want to be in the real physical world. Turkle described the various ways in which a person interprets his or her life in MUDs. In short, there are three uses for the virtual experience: (1) as an escape; (2) as a way of attaining a degree of social mobility; and (3) as a means of resistance. Some people have revealed that in their virtual lives they can escape from a stifling reality, albeit only temporarily. Others talk about the possibility of experiencing a degree of social mobility that is part of the *imaginaire* of the American Dream but that is not accessible to all in real life. In the MUD, a person can create objects, turn them into possessions, and develop a representation of her- or himself with a higher social status. Likewise, the subject can gain privileges while developing and demonstrating his or her programming talents. In addition, there are those who see their virtual life as a way of resisting the conventional organization and significance of social life, in that they are able to construct alternative worlds.

But there are many ways in which users interact with computer devices, each of them generating a different space of and for significations. There is a wide array of interfaces and transmutation between humans and machines; synchronic communication is just one of them. A common concern, though, is the problem of agency in human-machine interaction. The positive valorization of interactivity in contemporary Web design, for example, acknowledges the production of space over territories. At the same time, it poses the ultimate challenge to technological systems: the emergence of activities that were not initially contemplated in the design. Furthermore, Suchman (2001) reminds us of the ways in which the growth of the Internet has strengthened the idea of personified computational artifacts attributed through interactive behavior. She also argues that "while the language of interactivity and the dynamics of computational artifacts obscure enduring asymmetries of person and machine, people inevitably rediscover those differences in practice" (p. 4). In her critique of the usages of the term *agency,* she adds, "The problem is less that we attribute agency to computational artifacts, than [that] our language of talking about agency, whether for persons or artifacts, presupposes a field of discrete, self-standing individuals" (p. 6). This notion of agency corresponds to the notion of *self* as a singular entity, and complexity emerges when other entities are brought in for interaction.

The notion of the self as an agent presupposes a singularity within a frame of interrelated parts, but in the Actor Network Theory (ANT)—proposed and debated by Bruno Latour (1993, 1996a, 1996b) and Michel Callon and John Law (Callon and Law 1997; Law 1992, 2001; Law and Hassard 1999), among others[2]—*agency* is conceived as a relational effect. *Agency* is a semiotic attribute where "the natural" and "the cultural" are intertwined. Therefore, in the communication network, the subject sitting before a screen travels around within different boundaries, as does the so-called reality. From this perspective, *agency* must be seen as a network where there is no differentiation between subjects and objects. This is one of the most controversial arguments of ANT, because it triggers a humanistic panic. Law (1992) clarifies this assertion by saying that although in the analytical stance there is no fundamental difference between people and objects, we must use this assertion to sharpen ethical questions about the special character of the human effect. From this point of view, *agency* emerges because the subject inhabits a set of elements—the body being one of them—that extend into a network of other objects and subjects. Law adds that "social agents are never located in bodies and bodies alone, but rather . . . an actor is a patterned network of heterogeneous relation, or an effect produced by such a network. The argument is that thinking, acting, writing, loving, earning—all the attributes that we normally ascribe to human beings—are generated in networks that pass through and ramify both within and beyond the body. Hence the term actor-network—an actor is also, always, a network" (p. 4). Identity is like a byproduct of the network in a very specific moment.

Maybe it is more productive to talk about *identifications* than to speak in terms of *identity*. If *identity formation* operates in a mode of exclusion, then the *identification process* operates in a mode of inclusion, connectivity within ruptures. Connecting the *selves* supposes the messy and problematic incorporation of technological networks into *bodyness,* in many cases flesh together with prosthetic devices. There is a wide variety of relationships between the subject and its prostheses. If we approach the *self* as a network of connectivity, these prosthetic devices cannot easily be ignored or disposed of. They are prostheses we live by, and we should claim responsibility and ethical positioning for what they—we—are.

Assuming a particular identity requires taking on at the same time a universe of meaning. This, then, implies an ethics and aesthetics of the social relationships that have shaped that identity, through multiple identification processes. Self-referentiality then expands inside and outside the screen, inside and outside what we generally call "the person."

I have stated that the relationship between the *virtual personae* and the *real person* could be represented as a sort of heteronomous-autonomous self. Each virtual self has its own logic of organization and reflexivity yet maintains another level of organization with the "real self," the demographical-embodied self. The virtual selves somehow interrogate and simultaneously explain their identity-formational projects to the *embodied self*, and vice versa. In short, as *disembodied subjects*, we represent ourselves in various ways in virtual space, but at the same time, this virtual experience continues to interrogate the territorialized (*embodied*) subject, keeping up a sort of extended conversation through the self-reflection that is now unfolding or transmuting from the open space to the territory (Figueroa Sarriera 1999). These self-reflection processes construct a subject and a body that cannot be reduced to an entity, where even such distinctions as *embodied* and *disembodied* do not have any sense. This body invites us as researchers to take account of a complex multireferential context. I believe this approach has an affinity to ANT, yet ANT provides a conceptual frame to address the politics of the network as an actor without reducing agency to a singular entity (human or machine).

Indeed, there still is a question that has to be addressed: How does this process develop? Although this is an open question, ethnographic studies in this area show that people are able to re-create their experiences narratively, putting into words what they like or do not like about their virtual identities and the relationships they establish with the other in virtual space. Narratives about new technologies are situated at the center of these analyses.

What types of narratives related to the subject have been privileged in cyberculture studies? We can present these in eight groups that address different types of texts: advertisements, science fiction, technoscientific texts, technology policies, social engineering processes, systems designs, cyberpunk, and transhumanist narratives. Some of these construct the subject as a user within the metaphor of the computer as an instrument, while others construct the subject as an actor within the metaphor of the computer as a theater, and so on. The voyager metaphor is very common in some of these narratives. Moravec (1988)—a well-known robotician—speaks about a consciousness that could migrate to a robot's location, and we speak in terms of *navigating* cyberspace. The metaphor is also present in the slippery notions of *final frontier* and *Internet highway.* The navigation metaphor assumes multiple forms: participants are *cybernauts,* we talk about *immersion* in very interactive environments, and the goal is to reach *new worlds.* These discursive forms reflect echoes of past and present feats of annihilation, extermination, and genocide in the history of our so-called third world countries, as well as echoes of mastery, wealth, and life in other countries' official histories (Figueroa Sarriera 1996).

For centuries, this will to cross over boundaries has played an important role in technological development in modern Western culture. It seems that within the context of asymmetric social relations, the struggle to control space or territories (conventional or electrodigitized) works as an indisputable trigger for attempts at systematic hegemony, not to mention the indomitable resentment of those who are displaced, occluded, and/or reduced to silence. In science fiction narratives, the game played out over the definition of frontiers always threatens by its reverse: Dr. Frankenstein's monster, Rossum's robot, Roy the replicant—like the scene in *Blade Runner* in which Roy's pursuit by Deckard is quickly reversed into the hunted pursuing the hunter—or Godzilla, the mutant. But we might also think of the nightmare of Chernobyl, the final frontier of *Challenger* and *Columbia,* the warfare of bodies with suicide prosthetic devices, and others. This means that the openness of the techno sensibilities bring to the forefront more than ever the importance of the ethical dimensions of our techno choices, especially if we want to inhabit a world in which those who are alive are something more than mere survivors within predator networks. In this kind of analysis, we can speculate about the subject position within power relations in the social grid, which implicates ethnicity and gender issues, class and geopolitical struggles.

Less considered are the narratives linked to the subject as a complex unity. Some cognitive science authors such as Frawley (1999) argue that the linguistic construction of the metaconsciousness can be found in those features of language that permit self-reference. The concept of private language as language for thinking, formulated by Vygotsky (1986), has special relevance as a basic level of narrative structure. The study of private language could be added to the list of narratives analyzed by cyberculture studies because it is relevant to the process of subject construction and self-referentiality not as a single entity but as a complex connection of multiple communicational entities organized in a heterarchical network.

Private language emerges from the subject position in social networks. The language for thinking is at the same time private and public language.

From this point of view, the private language is objective and subjective, public and private at the same time, and it is the vehicle permitting subject autoregulation and positioning within the limits of possible beliefs and inferences available at a given time. Departing from an instrumental perspective, the private language of the computer user is an important node for connectivity in the human-machine network. It is also important for the recognition of the socially constructed frontiers and their questioning. Linked to this argument, the subject position must be conceived within the network, and the positioning could be plural. In other words, we could have multiple selves—even in conflict with one another but, at the same time, unified in the language for thinking. Narratives about technological systems always imply a subject, but at the same time, the subject is constructed in multilevel narratives about connected selves and machines. The ethics and aesthetics of these connections and their frontiers should be the focus of psychosocial and political debates.

NOTES

1. The concept of *semiotic ontology* as well as *discursive ontology* and some others gained currency in psychology research within the framework of the second cognitive revolution. From this point of view "the subject matter of psychology has to take account of discourses, significations, subjectivities and positionings, for it is in these that psychological phenomena actually exist" (Harré and Gillet 1994, p. 22).

2. Visit the Web site of the Actor Network Resource: Thematic List of Publications (http://www.lancs.ac.uk/fss/sociology/css/antres/ant.htm) for a great compilation of working papers and other resources on this subject. See also the anthology edited by Law and Hassard (1999).

REFERENCES

Callon, M., and Law, J. (1997). L'Irruption des Non-Humains dans les Sciences Humaines: quelques leçons tirées de la sociologie des sciences et des techniques. In J.-P. Dupuy, P. Livet, and B. Reynaud (eds.), *Les Limites de la Rationalité: Tome 2, Les Figures du Collectif.* Paris: La Découverte. 99–118.

Figueroa Sarriera, H. (1996). Some Body Fantasies in Cyberspace Texts: A View from Its Exclusions. In C. H. Gray (ed.), *Technohistory: Using the History of American Technology in Interdisciplinary Research.* Melbourne, FL: Krieger.

———. (1999). In and Out of the Digital Closet. In A. J. Gordo-López and I. Parker (eds.), *Cyberpsychology.* New York: Routledge.

Foucault, M. (1980a). *Microfísica del Poder.* España: Ediciones de la Piqueta.

———. (1980b). *Historia de la Sexualidad.* Vol I. Mexico: Siglo XXI.

———. (1985). *Vigilar y Castigar.* Mexico: Siglo XXI.

Frawley, W. (1999). *Vygotsky y la Ciencia Cognitiva: Cognición y Desarrollo Humano,* trans. V. M. Arnáiz Adrián Barcelona. Buenos Aires: Editorial Paidós.

Gray, C. H. (ed.). (1995). *Cyborg Handbook.* London: Routledge.

Haraway, D. (1991). A Cyborg Manifesto: Science, Technology, and Socialist-Feminism in the Late Twentieth Century. In *Simians, Cyborgs, and Women: The Reinvention of Nature.* New York: Routledge.

Harré, R. (1983). *Personal Being: A Theory of Individual Psychology.* Oxford, UK: Blackwell.

Harré, R., and Gillet, G. (1994). *The Discursive Mind.* London: Sage.

Ibáñez, I. (1985). *Del Algoritmo al Sujeto: Perspectivas de la Investigación Social.* Mexico: Siglo XXI.

Latour, B. (1993). *We Have Never Been Modern.* Cambridge, MA: Harvard University Press.

———. (1996a). *Aramis, or the Love of Technology.* Cambridge, MA: MIT Press.

———. (1996b). Social Theory and the Study of Computerized Work Sites. In W. J. Orlikowski, G. Walsham, M. R. Jones, and J. DeGros (eds.), *Information Technology and Changes in Organizational Work.* London: Chapman and Hall. 295–307.

Law, J. (1992). Notes on the Theory of the Actor-Network: Ordering, Strategy and Heterogeneity. *Systems Practice* 5: 379–393.

———. (1994). *Organizing Modernity.* Oxford, UK: Blackwell.

———. (2001). *Aircraft Stories: Decentering the Object in Technoscience.* Durham, NC: Duke University Press.

Law, J., and Hassard J. (eds.). (1999). Actor Network Theory and After. Oxford, UK: Blackwell/Sociological Review.

Martín Baró, I. (1985). *Acción e Ideología. Psicología Social desde Centroamérica.* El Salvador: UCA.

Moravec, H. (1988). *M.I.N.D. Children: The Future of Robot and Human Intelligence.* Cambridge, MA: Harvard University Press.

Stone A. R. (1995). *The War of Desire and Technology at the Close of the Mechanical Age.* Cambridge, MA: MIT Press.

Suchman, L. (2001). Human/Machine Reconsidered. Department of Sociology, Lancaster University. Available at http://www.comp.lancs.ac.uk/sociology/soc040ls .html (accessed 4 January 2003).

Turkle, S. (1995). *Life on the Screen: Identity in the Age of the Internet.* New York: Simon and Schuster.

Vygotsky, L. S. (1986). *Thought and Language,* rev. ed. Cambridge, MA: Harvard University Press.

Chapter 10

The Structural Problems of the
Internet for Cultural Policy

Christian Sandvig

When we are concerned about cultural production, we think chiefly of content. We search for more money for our artists; we seek the preservation of artifacts; we organize exhibits, outreach, and public education programs; and we encourage treatises that explain whichever fading heritage or tradition worries us. This essay argues that at the present moment, the Internet sorely needs the attention of established advocates for culture and expression. But not their concern for content.

At first blush, the Internet seems a boon to culture—it doesn't need our help; it is a great gift. From the outset the network appeared to realize Stewart Brand's (1987) mantra that "information wants to be free." Anyone with an Internet connection can both send and receive: the depressing trend that each new form of communication from antiquity to the present has allowed a smaller number of people to speak to a greater number is now finally reversed.[1] We are free from the awkward prefix "mass" that has plagued "communication" since the introduction of broadcasting (Peters 1996). In some respects, the costs of cultural production have fallen and the hoped-for diversity of voices has materialized. Any Internet user can start a blog, make a Web page, share unpublished writing, or distribute music that would not otherwise be heard. We even have before us the tantalizing prospect of digitizing the public domain and offering it in an instant, for free.[2] The Internet seems, at first glance, to deliver the whole of human creativity to us and to open avenues of expression that were formerly closed.

Yet the same structures of the Internet that grant these new ways to speak also ensure that no one will ever hear you. This new medium is not the participatory turn in the production of culture that it seems to be. It is true that most of the Internet's users prefer a few familiar sources of information—that is, the most popular .01 percent of the Web accounts for about 50 percent of all traffic.[3] But even more important is that we can't write a ratio that is very different from .01:50 without a very different Internet. We will never hear those prophesied new voices, exercising their digital freedoms with new contributions to culture, because the Internet is designed to keep them silent. People who are concerned about cultural production are powerless because by and large they cannot see inside the Internet's design. We must address this problem, as this essay will explain by example.

A Problem: The Slashdot Effect

Let us consider a specific new voice. In a corner of the Web, nerds and geeks banded together to create what they thought might be a new form of journalism: the self-reported electronic newspaper (Baoill 2000). The newspaper existed before the professional reporter, they might have reasoned, and when reporting "news for nerds" (their motto) only the real nerds can be trusted to get the details just right.[4] They started *Slashdot* to report "news for nerds, stuff that matters"—a news service about technology, but a news service run like a bulletin board, where the reporters were readers and the readers were editors. Contributors to *Slashdot* received "points" from other readers for having interesting things to say. First-hand accounts and diverse sources were encouraged. *Slashdot*'s users trawled the Web seeking news for nerds, but as the site increased in popularity, they encountered an unexpected problem.

When *Slashdot* readers/contributors stumble upon a juicy photo, story, or comment tucked away on a personal Web server (a bona fide unconventional news source) and then share their prize on *Slashdot,* the clicks of *Slashdot* readers overwhelm the bandwidth available to the target site. That is, the act of promoting unusual content to even *Slashdot*'s modest audience causes that content to become instantly inaccessible. This phenomenon is common enough that they named it "the Slashdot effect."[5] The Web's eye, in the act of looking, destroys the object of its gaze. But this doesn't happen for the more traditional Web destinations that we visit every day.

Two Solutions to "Delivering a Better Internet"

The *New York Times* never suffers from the Slashdot effect, partly because when you click on a link to nytimes.com, your bits don't really come from New York, as will be explained. The Slashdot effect cripples Web servers because of the way that communication from one to many—broadcasting —is implemented on the Internet (or, rather, the way that it isn't). The Internet's original architecture was built so that when five computers in the same house request the home page of the *New York Times,* five identical copies of the page are sent all the way from the Web server, wherever in the world that may be, to each machine. Since we are dealing with electrons and not broadsheet, it would make more sense to send just one copy. Copying the electrons is cheap, but the bandwidth across the world is expensive. So instead of sending five duplicates around the world, a single copy could be quickly duplicated as close to the house as possible. Sending all five copies the whole distance only congests long Internet pipelines with five times more traffic than necessary.

With the *New York Times* homepage this effect might be trivial, but with the large files required by streaming multimedia the consequences are profound—today's Internet sends two (or ten or a hundred) copies when one will do because the way it delivers traffic is typically not sophisticated enough to realize that the identical requests are related. This is the reason why multimedia streaming on the Internet does not work very well, and it also explains the Slashdot effect: the network near a source of very popular content becomes overwhelmed as duplicate requests proliferate.

So far, this sounds like an arcane technical problem, at best a tangent to cultural production. But for this problem there are solutions, and then there are *solutions.* One approach proposes modifying the Internet's basic protocols to reduce the duplicate transmission of multiple streams. This solution is called "multicasting," and it is being advanced and refined in an open, deliberative process in the standards bodies of the Internet world. These proposed changes to the Internet's protocols have not yet succeeded, and the multicast backbone, or "MBONE," remains experimental (Eriksson 1994).[6] A second approach is called "content caching."[7] Like a guarded cache of pirate treasure, this approach involves employing a third party to store and copy your traffic at some intermediate point between source and destination, but as close as possible to the people that want it. The private company Akamai is the overwhelming leader in the obscure content-caching market.[8] Content-caching systems are both proprietary and expensive.

When you request a Web page from the *New York Times,* Akamai (the *Times*'s content-caching supplier) intercepts your request. Your rough geographical location is traced—this is called geolocation. The page is then dispatched to you from a high-capacity Akamai data center as close to your computer as possible. The technology involved is a trade secret, and this service is available only to Akamai subscribers (the Akamai motto: "Delivering a better Internet"). As a result, when *Slashdot* readers repost links to mainstream news from the *New York Times,* these links never suffer from the Slashdot effect.

The Capital Requirements for Cultural Products to Be Popular

In the example above, the most important difference between the proprietary, private solution to our arcane technical problem and an open, deliberative solution is simple: who pays? Multicasting is a collective solution deep in the guts of the infrastructure—it requires each Internet user to pay for the cost of delivering content from anywhere to anywhere, though with flat-fee Internet pricing the user will never know it. Streaming and broadcasting from anywhere would simply *work.* Content caching—the solution we have today—requires the provider of content to pay for an expensive add-on service, costs that they must recoup through advertising, subscription, or some other source of revenue. Streaming and broadcasting simply work, but only from the *New York Times.*

Therefore, although the fact is unknown to most users, the present Internet requires those who produce popular content to be well capitalized. Companies pay for their own Web hosting, and at anything other than small rates of traffic they pay for the bandwidth their visitors generate. The infrastructure for popularity is available, but it is expensive. The difference between the solutions of content caching and multicasting is nothing less than the decision between an Internet where only capitalized producers of culture can be popular versus one where anyone can.

Even leaving diversity of expression aside, there are other benefits to the multicasting approach. Changing the Internet's fundamental protocols is now accomplished through a public process negotiated in international standards bodies, and the resulting solutions are published and available for free to anyone, as is the specification for the Internet's protocols.[9] This means simply that challenging "technical" problems for the production of culture, or any human value, can be unearthed in these public documents and addressed. In contrast, proprietary solutions like content caching may function in ways that raise privacy concerns (as geolocation might), but we must guess at how these systems function by snooping: peeking at traffic, interpreting sales brochures, and reading annual reports of the companies involved.[10]

This does not mean that we should value open processes in and of themselves. There is no reason to assume that an open solution to a knotty problem of Internet architecture will be more likely to lead to freedom (or any positive normative value) in the long run than a secret solution. In fact, the present dilemma of multicasting versus content caching presents us with a case in which an open process that has produced a flawed solution. That is, our Internet architecture debates are currently open, but multicasting has not (yet) been incorporated into the Internet protocols.

Why Not the MBONE? General Problems for the Public Interest

The preceding summary may suggest a conspiracy to the conspiracy-minded. If one solution (multicasting) is so clearly beneficial, why isn't it yet the standard? One set of answers is clearly related to *process*: even if we prefer open deliberation and public results, open deliberation about complicated issues is hard work. As each new group of interested parties joins the debate about the future of the Internet, consensus becomes even more elusive. In addition, the solution becomes ever more complex to accommodate each new set of interests. Worse, even the long and contentious debates we have today may involve the wrong people. No group of advocates has stepped forward to agitate that multicasting deployment is crucial for freedom of expression; such a group of advocates does not exist because people who concern themselves with freedom of expression typically don't participate in Internet standards debates.

The second set of answers is clearly related to *incentives*: Some multicast functionality has been available in the off-the-shelf equipment used by your Internet Service Provider (ISP) for the past few years, but your provider likely has no interest in using these features. Simply put, "Receivers do not care whether they receive their . . . streams from unicast or multicast" (Diot et al. 2000, p. 81). It doesn't matter to you how the *New*

York Times arrives on your screen. It *does* matter to the sender who wishes to provide multimedia content and has no access to the *New York Times*'s expensive private content-caching supplier, and it does matter to society that successful Internet speech carries a requirement that the speaker be well capitalized. But these concerns are not immediately felt by the users that click on Web links to the *Times*. So to implement a collective solution to broadcasting on the Internet that would let anyone be a sender, we would need to secure the cooperation of the ISPs, who gain their revenue from receivers: the people that click on these links. Implementing multicasting is an additional cost for providers, but there will be no demand from users.[11]

If we had the answers to these normative problems of Internet architecture in our pocket, it would still be unclear what exactly we should do with them. These problems of process and incentive arise in a context where the Internet is thought to be free of anyone's control. In reality, the Internet is at most an uneven anarchy—aside from pockets of ungovernability, the inability of governments to regulate cyberspace has been greatly exaggerated. For instance, the Domain Name System is effectively under centralized control, and this control is a direct delegation of authority from the U.S. government, although the U.S. government hopes that this situation is perceived as a product of international cooperation (see Froomkin 2000).[12] Yet no such governmental relationship exists with Internet architecture, where a jumble of overlapping standards bodies mostly continue to operate under David Clark's credo that "We don't believe in kings, presidents, or voting. We believe in rough consensus and running code."[13]

Although this essay has focused on this problem of broadcasting on the Internet in order to illustrate the structural problems of the Internet for cultural policy, it is important to note that this problem for freedom of expression is only one problem from an infinite series. Even in the realm of the distribution of content there are many more: widespread deployment of filters and caches in firewalls by ISPs have other worrying structural effects on content.[14] Problematic biases also exist in search and directory services (Introna and Nissenbaum 2000; Rogers 2000). The phenomenal success of Google's revolutionary PageRank algorithm makes it much easier to locate the most popular Web content and much harder to locate unpopular content that uses the same words as popular content. Preferred-placement services on search engines and portals also reward capitalized content providers. Concern about the Internet's structure must also encompass complicated overlaps between the legal and the technical.[15] The lack of any legal nondiscrimination requirement for ISPs (unlike, say, telephone companies) means that they can turn away content they disagree with. The Internet's vulnerability to some very specific forms of hacking combine with the nondiscrimination problem to make unpopular content a pariah: Aljazeera, the controversial media network of the Arab world, initially could not find a hosting provider for its English-language Internet site, in part because the site would attract hackers to any provider that hosted it.[16] The legal and technical conspire to make unpopular views a "poisoned chalice" for skittish ISPs.[17] This essay, then, is not meant to highlight the specific problem of broadcasting on the Internet but to raise the problem of a continuing series of technical decisions that need attention from people concerned about the public interest and the role of communication systems in society.

Pragmatic Steps toward the Techno-Socio-Legal

After outlining a number of obstacles that presently exist between us and the Internet we hope for, we must turn to strategy. Yes, the situation is difficult, but it is not hopeless. If we can articulate our normative goals for the Internet's development, a course of action suggests itself. Our situation is far from unprecedented and, indeed, not a surprise. As the scholarly literature on technology predicts, "technical" questions about how a particular function should be realized in technology mask assumptions, interests, and political bargains.[18] The egalitarian potential of new communication technologies like the Internet, then, is lost or gained in a series of early implementation decisions that are debated solely in technical terms, despite their political character and cultural import.

It is true that we are presently faced with a messy, semianarchic Internet that we want to change (but we aren't sure how). But the birth of the Internet was just as messy, and the early stages of other communication technologies may have been even be messier.[19] Even those who pine for the clearer jurisdictional frame of other media are remembering an imagined past.

First, the easy answer: to advance normative goals such as freedom of expression, a straightforward strategy is to continue the successful government policy of funding applied networking research projects. The projects that produced the Internet provided a development environment that (although not neutral) at least developed standards and software under pressures that were orthogonal to the insistent and competing factions of commerce. The keystone of this policy was public ownership of the results. Investment in these protocols should be a priority for technology policy in the United States and elsewhere.

Second, and most important, the situation argues for an infrastructural cultural policy, one in which structural, technical decisions about the development of society's communication system require direct involvement by public-interest advocates charged to give voice to the voiceless. To succeed, this requires an awkward combination of technical, social, and legal expertise. It requires skilled engineers whose technical acumen is matched by an understanding of the place of technology in society and of the normative issues raised by engineering work. It requires scholars who study the political economy of communication systems but who change their research agendas to better embrace the minefield of the technical. The best current researchers have recognized this need and are moving toward a techno-socio-legal convergence, from both inside and outside of engineering (e.g., Clark et al. 2002; Shah and Kesan 2003).

Institutional structures still need to change course to encourage the fusion of this necessary triad. Foundation programs that deliver more money for our artists, the preservation of cultural artifacts, and public-education programs need to be reconsidered to include the structural problems of the Internet. A successful program of philanthropic investment to change these Internet fundamentals will provide a ten- or hundredfold return when compared to more traditional, narrowly defined giving for the purpose of cultural diversity. Similarly, rethinking educational programs as fusions of what is now found in communication, science and technology studies, law, and computer science will directly prepare a new generation of students with the skills to navigate the entangled current landscape of communication technology. Finally, academic institutions and national research councils need to encourage and recognize inter- and multidisciplinary work—not as a general good but as a collaboration across this specific gulf to face these problems.

Toward an Infrastructural Cultural Policy

The future of broadcasting on the Internet may yet be resolved in favor of diversity in cultural production: we can hope for the smooth introduction and adoption of multicasting in the Internet's core. This will render Akamai's private pay-to-speak services unnecessary, and Internet popularity will become affordable. Still, the resolution of this one problem is no answer for the larger problem for cultural policy: a communication system's "plumbing" presently seems irrelevant to people concerned about cultural production, and this must change.

It is true that attention to these problems requires an unusual combination of expertise: this situation begs people who care about culture, society, and the law to care about technology at a level of detail where few outside computer labs are comfortable. But if the history of other media is any guide, the structural decisions made in the early decades of the Internet—these decisions, made these days—have the potential to endure for years to come. After these decisions are made, it will be very costly to change our minds when we realize we are unhappy with the Internet we have built. To care usefully about the freedom of expression and the production of culture on the Internet, we must care about the "plumbing." An attention to infrastructural cultural policy may be a lot to ask, but it is the least that is required. The unsettled character of today's advanced communication systems is not our burden; it is our chance to act.

NOTES

This research was kindly supported by a visiting fellowship from the Oxford Internet Institute at Oxford University. The author thanks Rajiv Shah for his helpful comments on an earlier draft of this essay.

1. This compelling though debatable trend was expressed by Innis (1964).

2. This possibility is similar to the promise now offered by Project Gutenberg after the concept of charging for content was dropped. See http://gutenberg.net/.

3. Statistics on the concentration of Web use among a few sites are notoriously unstable. This estimate is based on data from 2001, combined from market research and academic data (Information Technology Association of America 2001; Online Computer Library Center 2001). Although the numbers given in other estimates vary, the general trend of concentrated attention is clear across a wide variety of studies and methods (e.g., Barabási, Albert, and Jeong 2002; Hindman, Tsioutsiouliklis, and Johnson 2003).

4. For the history of newspapers, objectivity, and reporters, see Schudson 1981.

5. An excellent overview of the Slashdot effect can be found in the Wikipedia. See http://www.wikipedia.org/wiki/Slashdot_effect.

6. For a history and overview of multicasting, see Almeroth 2000.

7. The content-caching market was worth about $430 million in 2001; see Vichare 2002. Participants included the private companies Akamai, Inktomi, and Cable & Wireless.

8. See http://www.akamai.com/.

9. This openness at the basic level of architecture is an often-overlooked benefit that came from the Internet's origins as a government project. The original contractor, BBN, was ordered by DARPA to make its technical specifications freely available, and the home of the early Internet in the academic culture of computer science departments promoted an openness that led to the present public "Request for Comments" system that explains the core of the Internet. For more, see Abbate 1999.

10. Closed systems also raise technical concerns. For example, how do engineers design and plan the future Internet if they cannot determine how applications and protocols will behave? In this section, however, I mean to highlight the problems for human values.

11. This is not to say that multicasting carries a fee to providers but only that the configuration and support for a new feature like multicasting entails some effort. For a discussion of this infrastructure-migration problem in the context of innovation, see David 2001 or, more generally, the economic literature on network externalities.

12. This comment does not mean to endorse the governance of the Domain Name System but simply to point out that control is centralized and effectively under the control of one government.

13. David Clark is now a Senior Research Scientist at the MIT Computer Science and Artificial Intelligence Laboratory, and he is an undisputed leader of the development of the Internet's architecture. Several versions of this comment have been attributed to him at various times, most famously in an address to the Internet Engineering Task Force.

14. This argument has been framed by others in terms of the end-to-end argument in Internet system design, but the end-to-end argument is a technical gloss further obscuring the familiar debates about mediation that occur in all communication systems, as I argue elsewhere (Sandvig, forthcoming).

15. To be fair, though, *every* example in this essay can be conceptualized as a complicated overlap between the legal and the technical. The legal components of a problem are, however, less obvious for some of the more arcane examples.

16. For instance, the provider would be vulnerable to the distributed denial of service (DDoS) attack.

17. The phrase "poisoned chalice" has been used in exactly this way in trade publications catering to ISPs (Lettice 2003).

18. See, e.g., Bijker, Hughes, and Pinch 1987; Winner 1980.

19. See, e.g., McChesney 1993.

REFERENCES

Abbate, J. (1999) *Inventing the Internet.* Cambridge, MA: MIT Press.

Almeroth, K. C. (2000) The Evolution of Multicast: From the MBONE to Inter-Domain Multicast to Internet2 Deployment. *IEEE Network,* 14.1: 10–20.

Baoill, A. Ó. (2000) Slashdot and the Public Sphere. *First Monday,* 5.9. Available at http://www.firstmonday.org/issues/issue5_9/baoill/index.html.

Barabási, A., Albert, R., and Jeong, H. (2002) Scale-Free Characteristics of Random Networks. *Physica A,* 281: 69–77.

Bijker, W. E., Hughes, T. P., and Pinch, T. J. (eds.). (1987) *The Social Construction of Technological Systems: New Directions in the Sociology and History of Technology.* Cambridge, MA: MIT Press.

Brand, S. (1987) *The Media Lab: Inventing the Future at MIT.* New York: Viking.

Clark, D. D., Wroclawski, J., Sollins, K., and Braden, R. (2002) Tussle in Cyberspace: Defining Tomorrow's Internet. *Proceedings of the ACM SIGCOMM,* 222.

David, P. A. (2001) The Evolving Accidental Information Super-Highway. *Oxford Review of Economic Policy,* 17.2: 159–187.

Diot, C., Levine, B. N., Lyles, B., Kassem, H., and Balensiefen, D. (2000) Deployment Issues for the IP Multicast Service and Architecture. *IEEE Network,* 14.1: 78–88.

Eriksson, H. (1994) MBONE: The Multicast Backbone. *Communications of the ACM,* 37.8: 54–60.

Froomkin, M. (2000) Wrong Turn in Cyberspace: Using ICANN to Route around the APA and the Constitution. *Duke Law Journal,* 50.17: 17–184.

Hindman, M., Tsioutsiouliklis, K., and Johnson, J. A. (2003) "Googlearchy": How a Few Heavily-Linked Sites Dominate Politics on the Web. Unpublished manuscript, Princeton University, July 28. Available at http://www.princeton.edu/~mhindman/googlearchy—hindman.pdf (accessed 5 October 2003).

Information Technology Association of America (2001) Alexa Research Finds the 50 Leading Sites Account for More Than 25% of Traffic. Arlington, VA: ITAA. Available at http://www.itaa.org/isec/pubs/e20013-13.pdf (accessed 6 October 2003).

Innis, H. A. (1964) *The Bias of Communication.* Toronto: University of Toronto Press.

Introna, L. D., and Nissenbaum, H. (2000) Shaping the Web: Why the Politics of Search Engines Matters. *Information Society,* 16.3: 169–85.

Lettice, J. (2003) Al Jazeera's Web Site: Ddosed or Unplugged? *The Register* (London), March 27. Available at http://www.theregister.co.uk/2003/03/27/al_jazeeras _web_site_ddosed/.

McChesney, R. (1993) *Telecommunications, Mass Media, and Democracy: The Battle for the Control of U.S. Broadcasting, 1928–1935.* New York: Oxford University Press.

Online Computer Library Center. (2001) Web Characterization Project. Dublin, Ohio: OCLC. Available at http://wcp.oclc.org/ (accessed 7 October 2003).

Peters, J. D. (1996) The Uncanniness of Mass Communication in Interwar Social Thought. *Journal of Communication,* 46.3: 108–23.

Rogers, R. (ed.). (2000) *Preferred Placement: Knowledge Politics on the Web.* Maastricht, The Netherlands: Jan van Eyck Akademie.

Sandvig, C. (forthcoming) Shaping Communication Infrastructure and Innovation: The End-to-End Network That Isn't. In D. Guston and D. Sarewitz (eds.), *Shaping Science and Technology Policy: The Next Generation of Research.* Madison: University of Wisconsin Press.

Schudson, M. (1981) *Discovering the News: A Social History of American Newspapers.* New York: Basic.

Shah, R., and Kesan, J. (2003) Manipulating the Governance Characteristics of Code. *Info* 5.4: 3–9.

Vichare, R. (2002) Content Caching Vendor Market Share. Research report, International Data Corporation.

Winner, L. (1980) Do Artifacts Have Politics? *Daedalus,* 109.1: 121–35.

Chapter 11

Cultural Considerations in Internet Policy and Design
A Case Study from Central Asia

Beth E. Kolko

Discussions of policy with respect to the Internet tend to focus mostly on matters of law and regulation. At times matters of infrastructure may enter into the discussion, and ancillary topics such as economics might also be raised. Rarely, however, do considerations of technology policy focus on cultural factors and their influence on both implementation and the preceding steps of design. Indeed, what remains unstated in much of the work regarding the effect of technology on culture is the effect culture has on technology. But the act of design is as political as the act of regulation. Keeping attention on the question of how to legislate technology misses the possibility of intervening earlier and in ways that can fundamentally transform how technology evolves, how it is implemented, and how it ultimately affects the lives of those who use it.

There is no shortage of academic research that performs cultural studies of technology (Bertolotti 1984; Stabile 1994; Winner 1988). There is also no shortage of studies about policy and regulation (Cavazos and Morin 1994; Frissen 1997; Katsh 1995; Lenk 1997; Lessig 1999; Tang 1997). What such cultural studies of technology do not emphasize, however, is that simply examining the effect of technology upon society circumvents a powerful avenue for intervention. Reception studies of new technologies or readings of digital texts or wider considerations of political issues leave out the valuable cultural studies angle of production. In so doing, such work ignores a crucial avenue for exploration; the design of new media is a pivotal yet unexamined step in the technological transformation of culture.

The goal of this chapter is to open a conversation about design and highlight its importance as a determining force in how technology gets implemented and regulated. I believe that such discussions are essential to any attempt to go beyond an analysis of systems in place and, instead, to influence the capabilities of such systems. Although policy is a crucial element in equitable and just implementations of technology, it is not very productive to consider how to nurture the diffusion of a technology that is framed for a specific and exclusionary worldview. Indeed, framing just policies would be easier were technological artifacts themselves designed with equity in mind.

In these pages, I would like to provide an introduction to a project in progress as a way of framing the argument about design. The case study discussed is part of an ongoing research project in Central Asia; that project is most easily seen as a diffusion study, but the ultimate goal of the research is to question the very foundations of information and communication technology (ICT) design. Defamiliarizing the basic elements of ICT design such as user-interface elements and metaphors raises the possibility of radical reinterpretation of ICTs as an element of everyday life. New media increasingly transform how people get information, communicate, and entertain themselves; interrogating the bases of those transformations seems essential, particularly as new media become reified as both artifact and delivery mechanism. Rather than a purely theoretical reconsideration, the project adds fieldwork to theory in order to craft a thorough argument regarding design.

It is important to note that the goal of interrogating design is not an end in itself. Rather, the argument here is presented as a way to bring designers and policymakers into conversation, for each to see the importance the other has at a structural level, and to recognize that equitable implementation of technology relies on conscientious attention by both parties.

Culture and Technology

A premise of this argument is that ICT is embedded in the culture in which it is created. Scholars increasingly acknowledge that technology recapitulates the values and norms of the culture in which it is created, whether in terms of interface design (the white-collar business environment of the Windows desktop), at the level of code (assumptions of identity or intellectual property prescribed by program configurations), or, more subtly, with the metaphors used to describe the capabilities of technology (the Internet as an online yellow pages). Studies that interpret racial representation or gender stereotypes within digital media have opened the crucial conversation with respect to technology as not value-neutral, and it is important to additionally investigate how gaps between the artifact and actual users affect implementation projects (Day 1996; Kolko 2000; Selfe and Selfe 1994).

For example, Cynthia Selfe and Richard Selfe (1994, p. 481) point toward the "political and ideological boundary lands associated with computer interfaces" that are contained within the office metaphor that dominates the Windows interface. The filing cabinet, trashcan, and filing structure of the operating system all perpetuate a way of understanding the world that is sensible to vast numbers of users in countries like the United States. However, such metaphors are not meaningful to all users in such countries, nor are they meaningful to the vast majority of users in other countries. Selfe and Selfe discuss the impact such interface elements have on their role as teachers trying to reach diverse groups of students, and they conclude that such a narrow channel of meaning embedded within the interface interferes with principles of universal usability. In many respects, their argument has preceded a sea change in digital-divide scholarship, as researchers have gradually come to realize that patterns of technology use are not simply ascribable to infrastructure elements.

Indeed, the studies that examine a persistent digital divide seem increasingly preoccupied with understanding how cultural elements affect usage patterns. And although I would argue that this is an improvement from conversations that hinged solely on the availability of cable, such discussions manage to overlook the structural, design-related elements that help to perpetuate assumptions about who should and who should not be considered an "appropriate" user for a particular system. Or, as Selfe and Selfe illustrate, the Windows interface is notable for what it does not show about American culture as well as what it does show. In other words, through the Windows interface, the notion of a formal, efficient, hierarchical office environment is disseminated as the dominant trope of American culture. What is left out of that picture is all the myriad ways people live and work that do not fall into the narrow channel of white-collar work. One could argue that the Windows interface projects a subtle sense of illegitimation of pursuits outside the office; one might also argue that these design choices tie the technology to office labor, consequently downgrading the relevance of a desktop computer to the meaningful labor of other types of workers—or individuals.

Selfe and Selfe provide some alternative interface metaphors in an attempt to illustrate how constrained the desktop imagery can be:

> We can grasp the power of this ideological orientation—and thus sense its implications—by shifting our perspective to what it does *not* include, what it leaves unstated. The interface does not, for example, represent the world in terms of a kitchen counter top, a mechanics workbench, or a fast-food restaurant—each of which would constitute the virtual world in different terms according to the values and orientations of, respectively, women in the home, skilled laborers, or the rapidly increasing numbers of employees in the fast-food industry. (1994, 486–497)

If we extend Selfe and Selfe's argument to the global society, we see profound implications for potential users on all continents, particularly for users at the bottom of the pyramid (Prahalad 2005). We also see emerge a possible and poignant explanation for why access is not the only relevant variable that determines whether potential users adopt new media technology.

I do not mean to give short shrift to considerations of culture as a determinant of technology use. Indeed, such arguments are politically crucial. However, I would like to draw attention to the ways such discussions can be articulated as an intervention, with the hope of having as significant an impact as possible. Recent research argues, for example, that distance-education initiatives in impoverished regions must meet local conditions (Damatin 2000; Rubens and Southard 2000) or that e-health initiatives must provide flexible modes of Internet access (McCloskey 2000; Peterson-Bishop et al. 2001) or that conceptual levels of infrastructure—such as whether content is locally generated or locally meaningful—impinge on a user population's willingness to use content (Carvin 2000; Chon 2001; Davis and Trebian 2001; Peterson-Bishop et al. 2001; White and Lester 2001). But the emphasis of this research is on how culture affects *usage* and, thus, how we can modify implementation efforts to accommodate local needs. I argue, rather, that we must place importance on how we can modify processes of initial *design* so as to generate technological artifacts that appeal to wider user populations.

As mentioned above, numerous studies seek to examine what factors influence whether a population demonstrates a willingness to adopt ICTs. An increasing number of authors do acknowledge that accommodating a diverse population requires an understanding of local needs. Whether for distance education, community technology centers, or small-scale e-government initiatives, policymakers are beginning to acknowledge that cross-cultural implementation of ICTs requires attention to culture and that policy must accommodate social differences. This realization is a significant move past the point that infrastructure was the pivotal element in technology adoption. However, acknowledging the importance of local culture in how policies are formed and technology implemented does not acknowledge the role design plays in making the case for the relevance of the technology to a proposed user population.

There are clearly those who follow the "if you build it, they will come" model of ICT adoption. Such proponents use the rapid diffusion of ICTs as proof that imperfect technologies will still manage to find a substantial user base. Although in many respects this is true, it also remains to be seen whether the parts of the world that are far from where the designers of those technologies live will mimic the diffusion patterns seen in the West. It is true that, given enough time, many users will be able to find a filing-cabinet-driven operating system usable. However, that does not mean such a desktop metaphor is the best design effort we can muster. My argument here is that we have a responsibility to make technology as accessible as possible and that this means rethinking design as a culturally coded act. Although some people will clearly overcome barriers to use and persist until they become adept at the clunkiest technologies (remember Wordstar?), the majority of users require something more. We should not gauge the effectiveness of design by the willingness of a minority population to overcome barriers to entry.

Everett Rogers (1995) described the patterns by which new technologies are adopted by a population by highlighting the varying pace with which distinct groups will make the leap to become users. He outlines several categories of users and illustrates how these potential users come to embrace a new technology, forming its overall pattern of diffusion. The first batch of users he labels as innovators, who make up about 2.5 percent of the population. The next group is known as early adopters, then the early majority, then the late majority, followed finally by the laggards. One of Everett's most interesting points has to do with the characteristics of each group: the innovators, he describes, are risk takers who are drawn to the daring and who are comfortable with venturing outside their established social networks; later adopters illustrate different and potentially more conservative characteristics. Although Rogers's research demonstrates that design issues such as usability and cultural assumptions are not crucial for all users, his work also points to the demands that culturally coded design makes upon some users. If using the Internet means one must be a risk taker who happily operates outside one's social network, what does that mean about the potential of the Internet to deliver vital medical information to rural populations, educational resources to impoverished schools, or government information to those living precariously under authoritarian rule? Good design is not created with innovators in mind; good design is created for the later stages of adopters, up through so-called laggards, who do not want to be forced to take risks in order to make use of a purportedly beneficial technology.

Internet Adoption in Central Asia

Central Asia is a region that is in the early stages of ICT adoption. It is also a region that until recently has remained, for both geographical and political reasons, uniquely isolated from Western cultural models. For the past several years I have been involved with a project investigating Internet development in Central Asia (Uzbekistan, Kazakhstan, Kyrgyzstan, Turkmenistan, and Tajikistan), with a particular focus on Uzbekistan (Kolko 2002; Kolko and Thayer 2003; Kolko, Wei, and Spyridakis 2003). This project grows out of years of previous research projects that have included analyses of gender issues in virtual world and avatar design, of racial assumptions in interface design, and of community configurations prescribed by computer-mediated communication systems. In other words, I have arrived at this project because it provides a mechanism for exploring on a wide scale how diversity issues affect technology use.

As information and communication technologies become integrated into lived experience, increasingly affecting how people learn, work, and play, it becomes imperative to develop a comprehensive understanding of how difference and diversity affect the ways in which technology is adopted and adapted by diverse populations. For example, the Central Asia project demonstrates that cultural and policy issues dramatically affect how a population envisions ICTs, whether they are willing to overcome barriers to entry, whether a technology appears relevant or useful, how users balance risks associated with usage, and so on. This ethnographic and survey research provides a case study of how technology differentially operates as a cultural force in diverse contexts. As this project demonstrates, a persistent digital divide is less about economics than it is about a complex matrix of culture and policy played out within preexisting infrastructures. Such findings can provide key insight into how appropriate ICT-related policies can be created and, ultimately, how design processes can be altered so that the narrow cultural channel that currently informs technology development can be broadened to include diverse cultural perspectives.

The research project itself is a mix of qualitative and quantitative work. It has included extensive on-site research (five months spent in Uzbekistan in 2000 as a Fulbright Scholar; short research trips to Kazakhstan and Turkmenistan in 2000; follow-up work on National Science Foundation grants, including five research trips to Uzbekistan, Kyrgyzstan, and Kazakhstan in 2002–2004; and ongoing work through 2008) and interdisciplinary background research that spans work in development studies to post-Soviet methodology. Central Asia is a promising site for such research because the region is in the early stages of technology adoption. Furthermore, because of the area's historical isolation and minimal exposure to Western cultural influences, an examination of the region holds the additional promise of providing information on how communities distinct from those within which ICT was created react to the metaphors and other cultural elements embedded within the technology. That is, Central Asia traditionally has drawn from the East and the Soviet Union for cultural models; thus, the Western cultural assumptions embedded within ICT stand in stark contrast to local cultural traditions.

Project findings thus far raise a number of provocative issues relating to what motivates a population to adopt a technology. One of the most intriguing findings thus far concerns the role information plays within the culture. The yellow-pages metaphor of the Internet, for example, relies on patterns of information seeking that embrace the appropriateness of disembodied information resources. By contrast, as interview and survey data from the region has demonstrated, people in Uzbekistan rely primarily on personal networks as sources of information. Traditional institutions such as reciprocal networks dominate everyday life, and the *mahalla,* or neighborhood, structure of Uzbekistan is a social structure that exercises a great deal of influence over information networks, serving as a significant disseminator of news items, small and large. Other news sources, such as newspapers, radio, and television, are viewed skeptically by people, raising the issue of how useful it is to discuss the Internet as primarily an information medium. These findings have significant implications for both design and implementation policies for ICT. Confronted with extensive information that is separate from the social network, users in Uzbekistan demonstrate a reluctance to engage with the resources. However, there are alternative ways to present an ICT network like the Internet, one that highlights the social situatedness of resources and that prioritizes, in design elements, how sources are connected to one another and, ultimately, connected to personal network elements in the offline world. Incorporating such design elements, however, requires a conscious consideration of how extensively cultural difference affects usage patterns. The stakes can be quite high when one considers the potential of ICT as a provider of health information, educational resources, and community-building communication opportunities.

Conclusion

Ultimately, research on ICT development and usage patterns in Central Asia is about both how to implement ICT effectively in the area and what the experience of the region with technology can teach us about ICT in general. There are increasing numbers of scholars writing about how technology and cyberculture reflect and reinscribe cultural patterns; it is essential at this point to take the results of this intellectual work and bring it to bear on the decisions made by designers of both technologies and public policies. Such a shift allows us to move beyond assessments of technological artifacts and consider how to alter, ultimately, both policies and practices. Diverse groups of people use technologies differently, and understanding those varying patterns holds the key to designing technology that is universally usable. It does not seem very momentous to argue that technology can be changed to meet the needs of people rather than expecting people to adapt to technology. And although the radical rethinking of design called for by such an argument is no small task, it holds out the possibility of allowing a transformation that works in conjunction with policy to redraw the boundaries of cyberculture and its inhabitants.

REFERENCES

Bertolotti, D. S. (1984). *Culture and Technology.* Bowling Green, OH: Bowling Green State University Popular Press.

Carvin, A. (2000). More than Just Access: Fitting Literacy and Content into the Digital Divide Equation. *EDUCAUSE-Review, 35*(6), 38–47.

Cavazos, E., and Morin, G. (1994). *Cyberspace and the Law.* Cambridge, MA: MIT Press.

Chon, K. (2001). The Future of the Internet Digital Divide. *Communications of the ACM, 44*(3), 116–117.

Damatin, S. K. (2000). The "Digital Divide" versus Digital Differences: Principles for Equitable Use of Technology in Education. *Educational Technology, 40*(4), 17–22.

Davis, T., and Trebian, M. (2001). Shaping the Destiny of Native American People by Ending the Digital Divide. *EDUCAUSE-Review, 36*(1), 38–46.

Day, D. (1996). Cultural Bases of Interface Acceptance: Foundations. In M. A. Sasse, R. J. Cunningham, and R. J. Winder (eds.), *People and Computers XI: Proceedings of HCI '96* (pp. 354–357). London: Springer Verlag.

Frissen, P. (1997). The Virtual State: Postmodernisation, Informatisation, and Public Administration. In B. Loader (ed.), *The Governance of Cyberspace* (pp. 111–125). New York: Routledge.

Katsh, M. E. (1995). *Law in a Digital World.* New York: Oxford University Press.

Kolko, B. E. (2002). International IT Implementation Projects: Policy and Cultural Considerations. *Proceedings from the Annual IEEE IPCC Conference,* Portland, OR, pp. 352–359.

Kolko, B. E. (2000). Erasing @race. In B. E. Kolko, L. Nakamura, and G. B. Rodman (eds.), *Race in Cyberspace* (pp. 213–232). New York: Routledge.

Kolko, B. E., and Thayer, A. (2003). Games as Technological Entry Point: A Case Study of Uzbekistan. *Proceedings of the Digital Games Research Association,* Utrecht University.

Kolko, B. E., Wei, C., and J. H. Spyridakis. (2003). Internet Use in Uzbekistan: Developing a Methodology for Tracking Information Technology Implementation Success. *Information Technologies and International Development, 1*:2, 1–19.

Lenk, K. (1997). The Challenge of Cyberspatial Forms of Human Interaction to Territorial Governance and Policing. In B. Loader (ed.), *The Governance of Cyberspace* (pp. 126–135). New York: Routledge.

Lessig, L. (1999). *Code and Other Laws of Cyberspace.* New York: Basic.

McCloskey, K. M. (2000). Library Outreach: Addressing Utah's "Digital Divide." *Bulletin of the Medical Library Association, 88*(4), 367–373.

Peterson-Bishop, A., Bazzell, I., Mehra, B., and Smith, C. (2001). Afya: Social and Digital Technologies That Reach across the Digital Divide. *First Monday, 6*(4). Available at http://www.firstmonday.dk/issues/issue6_4/bishop/index.html (accessed February 7, 2003).

Prahalad, C. K. (2005). *The Fortune at the Bottom of the Pyramid: Eradicating Poverty through Profits.* Philadelphia: Wharton School Publishing.

Rogers, E. (1995). *Diffusion of Innovations.* New York: Free Press.

Rubens, P., and Southard, S. (2000). Using New Technologies for Communication and Learning. In *Proceedings of the IEEE IPCC and ACM SIGDOC Conference: Technology and Teamwork, September 24–27* (pp. 185–189). Piscataway, NJ: IEEE Educational Activities Department.

Selfe, C., and Selfe, R. (1994). The Politics of the Interface: Power and Its Exercise in Electronic Contact Zones. *College Composition and Communication, 45*(4), 480–504.

Stabile, C. (1994). *Feminism and the Technological Fix.* Manchester: Manchester University Press.

Tang, P. (1997). Multimedia Information Products and Services: A Need for "Cybercops"? In B. Loader (ed.), *The Governance of Cyberspace* (pp. 190–208). New York: Routledge.

White, S. D., and Lester, W. F. (2001). Cultural Relevance: Hip-Hop Music as a Bridge to the Digital Divide. In *Proceedings of the 34th Annual Hawaii International Conference on System Sciences, January 3–6* (p. 1024). Los Alamitos, CA: IEEE Computer Society.

Winner, L. (1988). *The Whale and the Reactor.* Chicago: University of Chicago Press.

Chapter 12

Bridging Cyberlife and Real Life
A Study of Online Communities in Hong Kong

Anthony Fung

Why are city dwellers nostalgic for community life? Why do Internet users form online communities? A possible reason is a desire for a sense of belonging, security, and identity, feelings that we have lost in our contemporary technological world. Assuming that this is true, could online communities become a nook that substitutes for a geographically bounded community? Does the emergence of the former mitigate the death of the latter?

Being a Chinese Canadian who returned to Asia after years of study in the United States, I have found that the "weird" cybercultural phenomenon in Asia suggests an answer to these questions. In major Asian cities, and increasingly in Western cities, active online communities coexist with many formal and informal social groups. Real-life communities have not faded away, and there is no sign that online communities are about to replace them. There are, however, two paradoxes related to this Internet activity: First, given that real-life communities have continued to exist, why do Internet users build alternative communities? Second, some Asian cities are highly urbanized and metropolitan—the urban area of Hong Kong, for example, is around one-third the size of New York City but accommodates 6.9 million people.[1] When people interact in small, hectic, and crowded environments at home, work, and school, why do they bother creating other locales to provide them with additional interactions?

These paradoxes seem to suggest that even after a number of years of cyberculture study we continue to have an incomplete picture. An insight into the "extreme development" of the Internet in Asia can assist in answering these questions. Asia is extreme in the sense that although it came late to the Internet, the government and private sectors injected huge resources into the telecommunication infrastructure, and they did so in a way that was somewhat independent of consumer behavior. This resulted in massive growth. For example, as a byproduct of this government push, South Korea has a broadband penetration rate of 50 percent, the highest in the world. Aspiring to be the Asian information hub, Hong Kong has a broadband penetration of 45 percent, the second-highest in the world.[2] According to the China Internet Network Information Center, in 2003 China had 80 million households with access to the Internet, second to the United States (166 million) in terms of number of home Internet users. This accelerated development has provided a testing ground for the development of global cyberculture.

The Study of Chinese Online Communities

In this chapter, I look at Hong Kong as a case study to examine why cyberlife and real life exist simultaneously and how and in what forms they interact. Specifically, I examine how youth in Hong Kong have explored the online space to create their own community via online games, while at the same time these activities have to be located in real locales such as Internet cafés, schools, and home settings (with broadband services as the basic technical requirement for these online games). Although the current literature on cyberculture argues for the formation of imagined communities, this study illustrates that the communities of online users— connected with and by the availability of hardware but geographically colocated—are not purely virtual, unreal, and imagined but are often actually closely connected to one another through real-life identities. In this case, cyberculture is constituted by and interwoven with daily life.

The real geographical setting and context that molds the online culture in this case is important. Cyberculture flourishes in an environment with well-connected broadband service at home and school and with 290 cybercafés—mostly unregulated by any government ordinance.[3] This networked society provides the prerequisite infrastructure for youth to form communities via online network gaming.

To locate these communities, between August 2002 and March 2003 I became a researcher, as well as a game player, engaged in ethnographic observations and interviews in two Internet cafés, in a high school, and with three families. My aim was to understand the relationship between daily life and cyberlife by scrutinizing the diverse uses of games for different youth groupings.[4] One of my concerns was how youths travel back and forth between the real world and the cyberworld. I noted that the most popular online game among Chinese communities (Taiwan, the People's Republic of China, and Hong Kong, as well as Japan) is called Online Jinyong (in Chinese, Jinyong Qun Xia Zhuan), a network odyssey based on the fictional epic and kung fu novels of Hong Kong writer Jinyong.[5] Players role-play specific characters from the novels, wandering and combating in the "lifeworld" (jianghu) within a virtual map of ancient China. The game integrates elements of chatting, cheating, warfare, trades, camaraderie, and self-development, which are also indispensable elements in real life. By rough estimation there were already 240,000 players at the end of 2001. Much of the analytical examination in this chapter is drawn from the interpretation and study of the formation of the online communities, or what the players called "gamelife," under the auspices of Online Jinyong.

Gamelife = Online Community

As in society, isolation is a disadvantage in Online Jinyong, and individual gamers are thus encouraged to join tribes or branches of triads (conceptually known as "gamelife"). As written in one of the online Jinyong discussion groups, apart from "trusting your intuition and fulfilling your desires," Jinyong is a "community game" for performing roles using division of labor, strategic combating, affinity, and solidarity. The regulations of some tribes (posted on Web sites) even stress the avoidance of brutal killings in the game, and precise punishments (e.g., boycott or isolation) are laid down for "PKs," or "player killers" (PK is also roughly how the Chinese word is pronounced), whose notorious identities are usually circulated and publicly condemned.

By way of summary, the cybercommunities formed in these online games display characteristics of imagined communities or groupings that participants belong to while they are online. Regarding the relationship between the cyberlife and real life of these communities, two questions are worth investigating: (1) Are cyberlife and real life connected, and, if so, what is the impact of these communities on the real social life of the gamers? (2) In what forms and contexts is the real life of the communities connected to the cyberlife of online communities? The context of cybercafés and that of the online game provide rich data for the answers.

Cyberlife has evolved into a vital part of the real life to the extent that real social relationships have become inseparable with cyberlife. Contrary to studies that support a weakening of the relationship between Internet use and social relationships (Kraut et al. 1998), a questionnaire I used to survey 476 students from two high schools suggests that gamers who spend more time visiting Internet café actually have a stronger attachment and more-intimate relationship with their peers. It also appears that the sense of alienation that the cafégoers perceive is lower. The discrepancies between my observations and the previous studies might have two interpretations. First, in previous studies of online communities, the measurement of time spent on the Internet only accounts for the actual time online, without consideration of the real offline moments and activities that may connect to cyber activity. The very presence of the person in a cybercafé or any consumption activity, like purchasing computer games, in fact has direct or indirect influence and implications for subsequent online activities. Second, since the life of an Internet user has extended from the daily peer or family relationship to cyberlife, virtual social networks can be equivalent to social relationships in everyday life. Despite the possibility of a displacement effect with the time spent on the Internet, online gaming can create an extended social network, which may or may not overlap with the real groupings in existing communities. On the one hand, an extended brotherhood or sisterhood is developed through the networking activities of the fictional characters with other players on the Jinyong game, taking the form of chatting, trading, or going on group missions to fight a common enemy in order to share the treasures left by rivals. In fact, many of the group missions (e.g., killing a giant) are pre-set by the game developer (with new ones added occasionally) to increase the number of participants and enhance the cohesiveness of the gamelife. On the other hand, the practical need for coalition (e.g., to reduce danger by exploring in groups) necessitates offline discussion among the players sitting in close proximity in a cybercafé or school's computer lab or at home communing via telephone. Such communication also enhances social relationships in real life.

These various communications are the breeding ground for the formation of online communities. In the past, studies in this area tended to argue that the Internet constitutes a new frontier and social space pointing toward individual satisfaction and sustenance of relationships (Baym 1993) or public deliberation (Wilhelm 2000). For some scholars (Mitra 1997), this leads to a discussion about ideal imagined communities or cyberculture in which subjects are imagined as people sharing and experiencing the same concerns, identity, and interests. These scholars thus attempt to reorganize our space and dissolve the boundaries of the subjects. The concept of imagined communities (Anderson 1983) foregrounds the fact that the participants are not sure how and in what ways belonging matters, if at all. However, given that the Internet has produced possibilities for the creation of virtual communities that reproduce relations similar to traditional real-life communities (Baym 1995) and that the interests of the communities might conflict with real-life interests (Carnevale and Probst 1997), an imagined life independent and disconnected from real life becomes questionable. In light of the fact that real life can also be changed, distorted, or merged with the cyberlife, studies of online communities should examine whether the remote and virtual interests of subjects realized in online space is linked to the everyday sense and complexity of human nature. When Steve Jones (1997, p. 18) proposed the question "Who do we think we are when we are online, and who do we want to be there?" it already implied that the mere investigation of cyberlife does not adequately answer the question. While "who do we think we are when are online" refers to users' search for self-identity, "who do we want to be there" reflects the desire to communicate to others who share the same identities and, more important, to do so regardless of whether the others are on- or offline.

The Connection between Cyberlife and Real Life

The previous studies on online communities focus on the practices, contents, commitment (Rheingold 1993), forms of interaction, and communicative barriers and politics (Fung 2002) of these Internet users without further relating actions of the communities to subsequent actions and network formations. This study further investigates how the communities develop and cultivate relationships and reveals the need for the groups to consolidate opinions for action, to confirm the status of the users, and even to engage in consumption and exchange activities among users. Table 12.1 illustrates a framework for how we can understand the interactions between cyber and real life.

Game and Web developers have been building an online gaming environment similar to the real-life environment, with all sorts of conflicts, chaos, pressures, and problems, as well as the positive potentials, of real life replicated in cyberlife. Although this environment can be frustrating

TABLE 12.1
Cyberlife and Real Life in Gaming

Online Activities	Tasks Accomplished	Relationship between Real Life and Cyberlife
Communication	imagined community formation	mere imagination of unknown others online
Consolidation	building rapport and alliance	the need for tribalization online and offline
Confirmation	verification of status	real personal info for online territorialization
Consumption	exchange of goods	virtual and real transaction for self-fulfillment and satisfaction

and depleting of youths' energy and time to tackle these extra vicissitudes, under certain conditions it can compensate for a real life in which a participant feels powerless and at risk. There are demonstrated cases in which cyberlife has helped restore participants' lost confidence and given them a second chance to develop a new (virtual) life in which they learn to train the strength of the virtual body, personality, and mind of a fictional character to accomplish pre-set linear goals.

Communication for Imagined Communities

Online game players must learn to join communities, make friends, deal with other players, and cultivate a socially acceptable virtual character because there are informal tribal rules in the game, as well as strategic methods for characters to "raise their levels" within the game. As gamers have indicated, it is not a game that celebrates individuality but a game of community. This cultivation of community is not only instrumental online but is also beneficial to players in daily life and in further extending their social lives. Language and textual communication via some form of chatting activities are perhaps prerequisite for developing and maintaining relationships with the tribe and with friends. Quite often, game players use ICQ, Yahoo!, or MSN Messenger while playing the game, or they simply chat on the chat board built into the game. It seems that for most users, the game becomes a platform for the players to communicate and interact with others who they think share the same values and beliefs. In this sense, the players act like imagined communities, and the bonds that tie these gamers together are essentially communicative acts. These bonds dissolve quickly when someone cuts off his or her communication, often due to a busy schedule during examination time or when he or she moves to a new stage of life, for instance, entering university.

Consolidation for Support

A community that exists for a long period gradually seeks to chart and fix an identity. This is a period of inclusion and exclusion. The act of unanimously deciding to unite for joint missions is a means to strengthen internal cohesion. Although online communities might break from geographical and racial, generational, and class boundaries, the cohesion of the group is stronger if it faces a common enemy and maintains the exclusivity of the group or tribe. Such refencing of walls against the others, or tribalization, in the game necessitates virtual contacts that are usually followed up by communications exterior to the virtual settings. Tribalization as a gaming strategy therefore cannot be completed without the networking strategies that operate in real life. "Underground" networking, grouping, and strategizing discussed in a system other than the game setting (e.g., via telephone conference or ICQ) is common. With a diversity of players from different geographical locations, Internet cafés also become the most convenient physical meeting venues for players to organize combat, evaluate collective resources, divide labor, and crystallize leadership. Finding consensus seems more successful when users meet face-to-face, and in particular, players find themselves more similar in terms of outlook, lifestyle, or personality when they actually meet.

Apart from direct communication, message boards or notices in Internet cafés have served as real channels for virtual game information (e.g., availability of weapons). Interviewed owners and workers of a small Internet café actually acted as the ombudsman for different groups to exchange virtual warfare information. Besides acting from the profit motive, owners and workers are also amateur users, becoming part of these communities and serving as the bonds among users. In practice, the owners and workers can arrange group seating for users to facilitate their communication. Thus, what we called "support" among the online communities is not a natural phenomenon, in which users crystallize, consolidate, and recognize one another's position. Rather, the community requires facilitators or moderators who initiate and allow deliberate and overt negotiation, compromise, and grouping, as well as providing active, real-life platforms in which such communication takes place.

Confirmation of Status

It is true that real-life identity in many online discussion groups is unknown, which creates skepticism among members of the tribes. Exposing real-life identity in the gaming environment not only helps build companionship in and outside cyberlife but also makes it possible to gain confidence in collective actions. Many tribal formations or territorialization in virtual space involve stringent evaluation of the identity of the individuals for membership. Such territorialization of gamers in virtual space can be informal or formal. Increasing empathy (and addiction), the game has preestablished tribes or branches (the names of which come from names that actually existed in ancient China) for any game members to join or start with, and each tribe has a virtual locale in which they can communicate and engage one another.

Subgroups of tribe members also cluster among themselves and set up Web sites for their own membership. Not all players have the "privileges" to log on to the private Web site of the group, which facilitates access to tricks of the game, discusses the function of new weapons, and provides collective activities advantageous to the group. Many groups compel those who aspire to membership to contact the captain of the tribe outside the game environment by supplying ICQ contacts, through which confirmation, evaluation, and scrutinization of the identity and philosophy of the members are made before formal inclusion in the group. This illustrates real-life problematics: exclusion and inclusion take place in people's real lives and are brought into the cyberworld. For both realms, the exclusion/inclusion stems from the socioeconomic, psychological, and cultural backgrounds of the individuals. When gamers travel back and forth from the real to the cyberworld, this background can be diluted or hidden, but it cannot be destroyed. Occasionally this background has value in the game. For someone to be included in the community, gamers contact group members online at the expense of revealing one's real-life identity. This is in stark contrast to discussions of online communities that prioritize the imagined identity and dilute the real socioeconomic and cultural components of the membership.

Consumption for Self-Fulfillment

Apart from the satisfaction of gamelife, online games like Jinyong also stress the self-fulfillment of the fictional character: friendliness, wisdom, and various other strengths. Going beyond self-development, which can be done in private, players can train and improve combating skills by practicing with companions or, more directly, by acquiring weapons. The tactic of exchanging and purchasing weapons is common, and in extreme cases, some gamers even sell the entire fictional body to others in the online games. There are reported cases of some "professional" trainers who earned their livings by selling these fictional bodies. The transaction, however, is not accomplished entirely in virtual space. Although they tend to meet in online space to negotiate the deal, for the monetary transaction they go to a real geographical locale (for example, a subway station) and return to virtual world to complete the exchange of virtual weapons.

The fact that Internet users have to consume resources and that there is a conversion of virtual capital to real capital in daily life illustrates the inseparable linkage between the online identity and real-life resources. There is no difference between the cyberworld and the real capitalistic world in terms of "living." To survive, to sustain one's lifestyle, career, or ties, and to advance oneself, one has to garner resources and, through various transactional activities, to accumulate more wealth or resources. Money is the basic unit of capital, and it links both worlds and makes them inseparable. Were it a one-way exchange—that is, real capital exchangeable to virtual capital—other values, lifestyles, and norms might flourish in the online community, provided that the resources are abundant and that users give up competing with one another for self-interest. However, the mechanism, which allows virtual capital and real capital to be exchanged, has essentially announced the death of the ideal and paved the way for real-life intervention of the virtual.

What Links the Cyberworld and the Real World?

Because the setting of online game environments replicates real life, online communities cannot exist without referencing and anchoring some aspects within real daily life. Based on examples of the Jinyong gaming communities in different networked locales, my study conceptualizes the link of the online communities to real-life channels, identities, and resources. The 3Cs, or the process of formation of communities—verification of identity, consolidation for action, and virtual consumption—all require that participants' cyberlife extends into their real life. This does not necessarily mean that all online communities reproduce the same real-life relations or that they simply replicate all the dynamics of traditional communities. Rather, with imagined communities as a departure for inquiry, this study argues for the impossibility of disconnecting the cyberworld from the real world when the online setting (e.g., gaming) is basically dictated by, delimited by, or modeled from real-world settings.

I am both supportive and skeptical about the cyberlife–real life connection. The discovery of the connection reveals the pervasiveness of capitalist and competitive life and its ability to penetrate into the new promised land—the Internet. The phenomenon is discouraging because it suggests a future that will reflect the commercial past. On the other hand, were the connection between real life and cyberlife suggestive of the impossibility of cyberlife's constructing an ideal humanistic and communicative environment, imagined communities would have long ago lost their appeal. I believe there must be some means to fight evil, protect the cyberworld, and save ourselves within it. On an optimistic note, I suggest that we refocus on how to enrich our cyberlife with the communication channels, commonalities, and resources from our real life and that we do so by means of engaging a new arena of normative research.

NOTES

1. The urban area of Hong Kong, namely the Hong Kong Island and Kowloon, is about 127 square kilometers, whereas New York City is close to 946.9 square kilometers. The population of Hong Kong is around 6.9 million, whereas New York City's is 18 million.

2. According to the Office of the Telecommunications Authority, in Hong Kong in October 2004, out of a population of 6.8 million, there were 1,458,110 broadband users, who constituted 60.3 percent of Internet subscribers (see http://www.ofta.gov.hk).

3. This figure represents registrations at the end of 2002. In general, these cafés are unregulated, with the exception that they still have to conform to fire and hygiene regulations. Charging US$1–1.25 for students (and up to US$2 for nonstudents) per hour, the cybercafés, open twenty-four hours a day, serve as social gathering spots for youngsters.

4. These particular sites were chosen because I was able to get access to them with approval.

5. War games (e.g., Solider of Fortune) and shooting games (e.g., Rogue Spear) are popular among youth in Internet cafés and in home settings, but they are less popular than online games.

REFERENCES

Anderson, B. (1983) *Imagined Communities: Reflections on the Origin and Spread of Nationalism.* London: Verso.

Baym, N. K. (1993) Interpreting Soap Operas and Creating Community: Inside a Computer-Mediated Fan Culture. *Journal of Folklore Research* 30, 143–176.

Baym, N. K. (1995) The Emergence of Community in Computer-Mediated Communication. In S. G. Jones (ed.), *Cybersociety: Computer-Mediated Communication and Community.* Thousand Oaks, CA: Sage, pp. 138–163.

Carnevale, P. J., and Probst, T. M. (1997) Conflict on the Internet. In S. Kiesler (ed.), *Culture of the Internet.* Mahwah, NJ: Lawrence Erlbaum, pp. 233–255.

Fung, A. (2002) Identity Politics, Resistance and New Media Technologies: A Foucauldian Approach to the Study of HKnet. *New Media and Society* 4(2): 185–204.

Jones, S. (1997) The Internet and Its Social Landscape. In S. Jones (ed.), *Virtual Culture: Identity and Communication in Cybersociety.* Thousand Oaks, CA: Sage, pp. 1–27.

Kraut, R. E. Patterson, M., Lundmark, V., Kiesler, S., Mukhopadhyay, T., and Scherlis, W. (1998) Internet Paradox: A Social Technology That Reduces Social Involvement and Psychological Well-Being? *American Psychologist* 53(9): 1017–1031.

Mitra, A. (1997) Virtual Commonality: Looking for India on the Internet. In S. Jones (ed.), *Virtual Culture: Identity and Communication in Cybersociety.* Thousand Oaks, CA: Sage, pp. 55–79.

Rheingold, H. (1993) *The Virtual Community: Homesteading on the Electronic Frontier.* Reading, MA: Addison-Wesley.

Wilhelm, A. (2000) *Democracy in the Digital Age: Challenges to the Political Life in Cyberspace.* New York: Routledge.

Chapter 13

Overcoming Institutional Marginalization

Blanca Gordo

Under what conditions and through which social processes do community-based organizations that provide direct support to low-income populations' social and economic development benefit from the use of network technology?[1] This question remains unanswered and is strongly debated among public-policy representatives and community technology advocates who address the negative consequences of the "digital divide," referred to in this chapter as "digital destitution." The digital divide reflects the gap between institutional Web sites and those individuals who are excluded from opportunities to participate, compete, and prosper in today's knowledge-based economies.

Community technology activists argue that the ability to manipulate information technology's features is a necessary (but insufficient) prerequisite for participation in the labor-market force, for online communication with public institutions, and for political participation through the interface. These activists argue that policy makers should assist them in modernizing community organizations to reverse digital destitution, a process of technology-based alienation and deprivation from the productive functions of society.[2] Digital destitution is a negative consequence of not preparing populations to participate in the net process illustrated in figure 13.1.

In general, supporters of community technology are asking institutions to invest in the restructuring of economic development organizations at the community level by integrating information technology into work processes and social service delivery systems. However, facing competing demands and a decline in public funds, public policy makers are asking how technology generates social benefit or facilitates efficiency by reducing transaction costs. The debate continues without a clear theoretical framework and social technical metrics to address the problem. But most

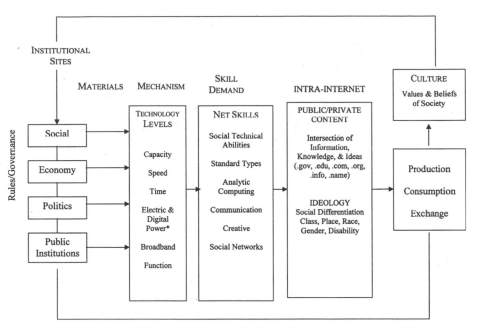

* Digital Power, a concept created by John Seely Brown and Paul Duguid (2002) to measure the pace of change of the digital infrastructure, is a function of computing, communication, storage, and content.

Figure 13.1. The Net Process: Technology as a Social Process

public policy makers agree with the community technology advocates that community-based organizations need the same IT resources that most institutions and firms can take for granted.

Using a case study grounded in these ideas, this chapter begins by suggesting that current conceptions of the organizational divide are flawed in that they do not take account of the ways in which network technology is incorporated into the net process. In order to find ways for community-based organizations to serve the poor using technology, then, one needs greater understanding of the functions of new IT in society. Viewing technology as part of an institutional and productive process, as in figure 13.1, locates these productive functions in an "Intra-Internet," a new technology that is a social service extension of society that operates both within its institutional work processes and as a mechanism regulated by the state. The recognition of this net process highlights that the two-tier social service delivery system is a net loss to American society, which is already generating inefficiency and increasing transaction costs for the poor.

The second part of this chapter suggests the need for a comprehensive discipline of organizational divide studies that takes account of institutional structures. It focuses on a direct service provider of a community technology development program in practice: Plugged In, located in East Palo Alto, California. If anything can be learned about the function of technology for community-based organizations under conditions of extreme disparity between wealth and poverty, it will be from this well-structured experiment within Silicon Valley.[3] Plugged In is recognized as perhaps the most innovative and cutting-edge Community Technology Center (CTC) in the country. This case, then, provides an information-rich example of an attempt to support community economic development goals, serving a population that is diverse in economics and ethnicity and providing technical assistance to community-based organizations.[4] This project has been selected out of a pool of 350 CTCs throughout the country because it meets several important criteria:[5]

1. *Beneficiaries in extreme poverty.* This organization is serving urban residents and community partners in areas high in poverty and unemployment.[6]
2. *Uniqueness.* This project uses novel and innovative approaches applicable in other communities.[7]
3. *Measurable community outcomes.* The project has delineated community outcomes that are tangible, attainable, and novel.
4. *Longevity and size.* Plugged In has over ten years in operation, and it has leveraged ample matching funds. Since its inception, this agency has used technology in its work to provide social services.
5. *Diversity of Staff.* Ethnically and socially diverse personnel have governed Plugged In. The agency has been led by two very strong and charismatic executive directors with close ties to each other.
6. *Public and Private Support.* Plugged In has formal relations with institutions. The organization has a track record of attaining contracts with government agencies, civic institutions, and corporate firms and has embedded itself into the community social service network.[8]

To discover which factors affect Plugged In's ability to accomplish its goals during economic recession, inductive process-oriented research and the use of the qualitative and explanatory case study method were triangulated using different sources of evidence, data, and information gathered through interviews and focus groups with the CTC's staff, participants, and partners. Respondents were chosen by "snowball sampling" of current and past participants and program affiliates. Site visits for field observation and searches of public documents (e.g., annual reports, archival e-mail documents, Web pages, video, TV clips, internal organizational plans) and related literature were also conducted.

The purpose of this research was to explore in greater detail the experience of community technology projects that implement potentially promising practices. The case study is designed to provide information about (1) the specific problems the center is designed to address; (2) the technical approach that is used to ameliorate these problems; (3) the way in which services are created, delivered, and accessed.

Process-oriented research over a period of time gives insight into how the organization works.[9] Theme analysis provides meaningful insights and allows one to build a qualitative model to address research question about the process by which the community organization can benefit from the use of IT. This chapter will conclude with the argument that this case study shows that CTCs have the potential to compete and benefit from network technology by applying it into their work process and innovating productive social service delivery systems for and at the community grassroots level, under extreme competition for public resources and during economic recession. The competitive edge of Plugged In reflects the culture of innovation embedded in the region, a culture that sustains program development.

The Conception of the Organizational Divide Is Simplistic

Community technology agents are limited by the weak theoretical conception of the organizational divide problem. The general definition of the organizational divide is "lack of technology capacity among CBOs" (Servon 2002).[10] According to this view, building the technological capacity of social organizations will make possible the generation of relevant content and help CBOs achieve their mission.

However, this framework presents an overly simplistic assessment of a complex social situation. First, the analysis presumes that simply having a computer and an online connection is an opportunity that makes possible the creation of valued content and the achievement of organizational goals. Yet the problems that face nonprofit community organizations are greater than those of mere connection or access; they are, rather, grounded in social institutional practice. We must change the way technology is integrated into our institutional operational work processes and social-service delivery systems to the public and the ways in which technology is integrated within poor communities.[11] The current lack of technology integration came about because legislators and the state planning administration by and large did not plan or prepare to link community organizations into larger socioeconomic plans based on high-level network technology until President Bill Clinton's administration responded to an internal request to so. For instance, pilot projects such as the Technology Opportunities Project (TOP) and Community Technology Center's Project are the first public-access experiments undertaken by the executive national policy planning administration to research and develop solutions to the imbalance in technology ownership in society in the 1990s.[12]

The new ways in which our society is interconnected and part of a global system in transition has had a major impact on community-based organizations working to support community economic development. To deal with uncertain conditions, keep up with the fast changes of the economy, and adjust to evolving complex structures, organizations are now forced to develop new ideas about how the organization and its programs can adapt and sustain themselves through constantly changing conditions. At the same time, these nonprofits are faced with a multiplier effect on the ongoing crisis due to a combination of (1) new dilemmas related to addressing a negative imbalance of ownership of standard quality technology levels and net skill demands to participate and benefit in the net process (as illustrated in figure 13.1); (2) old obstacles facing their constituency such as (a) disorder in the means of production, consumption, and exchange, (b) bottlenecks in technology markets of consumption among low-income and ethnic populations, (c) illegitimate social institutions, (d) unprepared labor markets, and (e) a dependent and institutionalized (prison) populace. All these problems must be faced while functioning under a traditional and outdated form of operation, which may prove to be unsustainable. The organizational divide conception must take account of the imbalance in the ability to restructure and innovate work and social service delivery systems efficiently at reduced operational transaction costs—a key demand in knowledge-based economies.

There is an opportunity to contribute to the empirical record of long-standing traditions in social theory, organizations, and institutional literature by examining change in structures and mechanisms that generate inequality during transformation and by examining how organizations integrate new technologies. We can also examine how lack of or limited opportunity for community organizations to manipulate technology to innovate internally may refuel institutional marginalization, which can be seen in relations of difference in the exchange of public materials, interaction, and communication through digitally based social structures in place. Research should take into account the institutional structures and rules in flux.[13]

In time, a knowledge of new governance structures and systemic rule adjustments will inform policy communities struggling to help community organizations left out of the institutional process. For instance, in 2001 the U.S. Congress enacted the Children's Internet Protection Act (CIPA), which implements filters or firewalls to protect children from viewing pornography. Although such filters often block valuable knowledge that has nothing to do with pornography, the federal E-rate program gives discounts to public institutions that meet CIPA certification requirements. In this system, CTCs associated with a public library or public school that depend on public E-rate program resources to maintain service are limited in the type of service they can provide. This obstructs the transmission to their populations of valuable knowledge that has nothing to do with pornography.

Building a Discipline of Organizational Divide Studies

Developing scholarship on the organizational divide is complicated by missing or limited databases. In general, comprehensive longitudinal surveys have yet to collect data on how technology factors affect community organizations. The most comprehensive data sets in the subject come from a Census Abstract, collected by the Department of Commerce, that asked respondents about their access to public services. One consistent finding in the Department of Commerce's annual National Telecommunications and Information Administration (NTIA) reports is that black and Latino populations with low income and educational attainment who live in poverty tend to depend on community technology service twice the amount of their counterparts, whites and Asians, except in the Southeast (U.S. Department of Commerce 2000, 2002). But we do not know about the structure of these programs, how they are using technology, for what purpose, and with what outcomes.

Furthermore, it is not clear how or whether community technology organizations are organized to meet community demands or requests at standard quality levels in the society because we do not have a solid theoretical framework with organizational indicators to collect data for numeric measurement. Identifying baseline indicators that capture whether or how the community organization has integrated technology into work processes and is developing social service delivery systems to serve the public is crucial to assess institutional marginalization.

We may be able to build a field of organizational divide studies by identifying a set of core intellectual questions rich in theoretical importance and empirical relevance. In developing this field, one cannot ignore regional economic dynamics; development trajectories and plans must take into account national and global forces and spatial socioeconomic conditions and on-top regulation. Furthermore, we need to understand community organizations within their local environments and how they fit (or do not fit) into wider economic and institutional contexts and growth patterns. A knowledge of the rules, cultural practices, relationships with institutions and market firms, private/public investment levels, types of economic development strategies and trajectories, and political climate by place could provide insight into the sustainability (or lack thereof) of the community organization during competition or recession, which may give us insight into its potential for success.

Social disinvestment in addressing poverty conditions continues and is intensified during times of social transition, economic recession, and institutional crisis, when institutions are unable to predict and design solutions to social problems. We cannot ignore imbalances in the pool of available public resources to help the poor survive during hard economic times, as social disinvestment is layered onto uneven public finance tax systems with place and population imbalances and uneven intra- and interregional development at a global scale. Furthermore, the negative shock in the stock market with redistributive investment into the war on terrorism and reconstruction and homeland security contributes to rapid declines in public money that drain already diminishing social funds— with a negative impact on the poor at a global scale.

To understand the cost savings to organizations of online transactions, we have to be rigorous in our selection of a case study and of the unit of analysis. Important here is to control for place-related factors and socioeconomic conditions under which the community organization functions. Organizations for community technology service function at different levels and under different institutional governance structures and regulations. For example, the Community Technology Foundation of California focuses on raising and retaining private funding streams to support direct service providers. PolicyLink and the California Community Technology Policy Group focus on advocating for legislative policies that support direct social service at the community level.

Furthermore, we have yet to examine how the integration of technology into work processes and social service delivery systems is developed to be (or not to be) efficient. Also, what long-standing constraints are relaxed with technology? We know programs often fail to achieve positive ends against material poverty, but we know less about the causal factors that impede the process in the road to development. Following the actions of influential actors, what decision-makers do—and when and why—could lead to more insight.

Institutions are integrating technology into work, redesigning social service delivery systems, and automating material exchange in an attempt to maximize efficiency, reduce transaction costs, and save time. Thus, it is an important question whether community organizations have the ability to manipulate the productive function of technology to interrelate with institutions through automated operation systems to serve their community constituency. By and large, competitive pressures have driven businesses and public institutions to adopt a wide range of network technology and computer systems to improve productivity, maintain both internal and external communications, manage production, and offer customers new services (Castells 1996). Today's IT represents some of the most important enabling tools to build new jobs with social technical abilities, including low-wage occupations. Across industrial sectors, the ability to use technology is a prerequisite for attaining and retaining employment. Krueger (1993) argues that workers who use computers on the job (other characteristics held constant) have higher earnings than those who do not. His estimates suggest that workers who use computers on the job earn 10 to 15 percent higher wages. Moreover, Krueger argues that the expansion in computer use in the 1980s can account for one-third to one-half of the increase in the rate of return to education.

Governments, public and private institutions, and learning structures are also adjusting their service delivery arrangements and rules of engagement to require such skills. Governments are integrating technology to provide constituents with convenient service. Educational institutions are using technologies to enhance learning. Political processes provide new ways of representation, participation, transfer of voice, and election through network technology. Cities are creating development strategies based on new technology. People in the social arena are using technology for social engagement to maintain ties. Because of the inability of community organizations to connect to and adjust their work process and service through new digitally based institutional forms of communication for transaction within the net process, one can expect a high percentage of institutional marginalization in poor communities. If this situation continues, society will continue to maintain a two-tier social service public system where the poor pay more for less. The community organization will continue to struggle to meet the needs of the deprived, who continue to face unemployment and be subjected to informal networks that often take advantage or manipulate them.

This refuels an "opportunity divide," the imbalance in benefits and the continued disadvantage of ethnic groups residing in poor communities with unskilled populations. One cannot assume that social organizations at the community level are able to accomplish their missions when they are not structured to prepare the poor to become innovators and producers on their own without institutional support in order to gain entrance into the modern institutional systems of operation.

More rigorous study of the impact of the net process on community organizations that serve the poor is needed. To discern the severity of this institutional problem, one needs to develop sophisticated socioeconomic metrics that consider technology levels, institutional regulation, governance structures, and the social technical skills needed. The ability to abstract public content within the net process and interact with institutions online is a necessary (but insufficient) prerequisite to deliver social service to the public and communicate about regulation of these systems.

Culture of Innovation Sustains Program Development

In the growing literature of "local technology development," attention is given to nonprofit organizations committed to (1) economic development; (2) social engagement; (3) political participation and representation; (4) reorganization and restructuring of failing institutions; (5) cultural preservation; and (6) the use of network technologies to aid development. However, this field of study is new and unpaved, and it has not uncovered the utility of or the extent to which use of network technology affects CTCs' ability to accomplish their goals and sustain service during times of economic recession and public social disinvestment. Studies must distinguish cultural practices, internal dynamics and work processes, inputs, rules, strategic approaches, and external factors that influence or determine certain positive outcomes.

While there is little question that community organizations need social technical infrastructures, the crucial question remains how we can develop institutional and social processes to facilitate interaction and transaction of public service with community organizations in a way that benefits the development needs of the poor. To address this question, we turn to the work processes and social production of community programs of one of the most influential and technically wired community technology programs in the country, Plugged In.

Plugged In has a one-million-dollar budget to support strategic network partnerships of corporate, university, nonprofit, government, and community partners, with experiments to uncover and create institutional processes that could reverse exclusion and poverty. Its mission is to assist populations living in poor communities to participate in knowledge-based economies through the development of human capital and place-based development.

Plugged In claims that East Palo Alto residents do not benefit from the use of technology in large part because they do not own the mechanisms of technology at the level of quality available, they lack institutional preparation to meet high skill demand, and with low incomes they do not have the money to pay for interfaces that facilitate access to valuable public and private content made available online by institutions such as .gov, .org, .com, .edu, and so on. This situation makes it difficult for community clients to meet competitive learning objectives and to meet the labor-market skill demands for good paying jobs in Silicon Valley's service- and knowledge-based economy. To support the community's learning objectives and work-skill development to retain employment, the Plugged In directorate works to create technology markets for development.

Accomplishments of Plugged In

To interconnect its constituency internally and externally, this community-based organization has developed experiments that have evolved into structured programs for children, youth, adults, organizations, and the collective community. The main services are (1) public access to the Internet; (2) training for individuals and groups; and (3) support for community

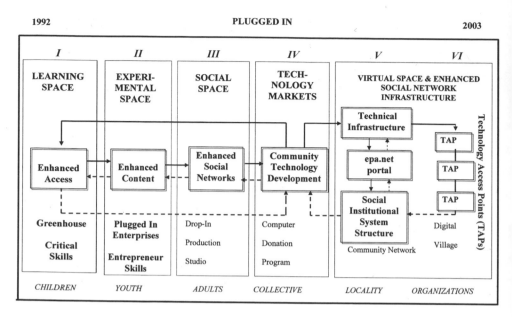

Figure 13.2. Community Technology Development in Practice

agencies to integrate telecommunications into their programs, as illustrated in figure 13.2. This CTC has established an Internet presence (epa.net), labs for community partners, and seven Technology Access Points.[14]

Over a ten-year period, Plugged In has continuously improved social service delivery and kept quality program standards by employing the cycle of innovation illustrated in figure 13.2. This has sustained program development and the competitive edge seen in the agency's global recognition and social benefits. The agency works to innovate and develop new ideas about how to design programs that adapt to the changing structure of the economy and that simultaneously meet the needs of the local community it serves. The strategic network partnerships address needs identified by the community in the areas of social engagement, economic benefit, political participation, and the restructuring of community-based organizations on the basis of technology. Every program now delivered is an outcome of a series of connected social ideas with variable high-value inputs. The agency takes advantage of and strategizes to attain the rich resources Silicon Valley offers: (1) seed funding for trial experiments; (2) expert knowledge and research; (3) the latest network technology; and (4) human capital support. The support offered is input into figuring out potentially productive processes that could solve the socioeconomic challenges the poor face. The organization mainly focuses on improving and developing organizational structures, social programs, and forms of service delivery at the grassroots level. Competition and innovation take place in integrating these developments with technical infrastructures such as systems based on network technology. Once ideas become tangible material products, Plugged In pilots and brings to the public its creations. Thereafter, programs are open for community feedback. The agency continuously goes through this social cycle and incorporates lessons learned from community feedback. Once community outcomes are assessed and lessons are incorporated, the agency undertakes new courses of action. The feedback loop can be found at many levels of the organization. Through this working process, new social services with structured curricula for the community, such as the CTD program illustrated in figure 13.2, have matured.

Community materials such as EPA.net came about through continual progression and refinement. This portal was first conceptualized by teens who came into the center to play or study with computers. The experiments that have led to a mature EPA.net have been supported by NTIA and a Hewlett Packard Digital Village Fund. EPA.net is the first portal to bring e-mail to the city, and it is now an institutionalized program directed and sustained by Plugged In partners. Lastly, the organization has been able to assist in the organizational restructuring and development of community-based organizations in EPA and with global influence, as seen in the creation of TAPs.

The innovation process includes the community organization learning and constantly innovating to sustain program development and keep competitive edge. The cycle is an organic process but holds vital components, as illustrated in figure 13.2. Competition and innovation take place in integrating productive community processes with technical infrastructures to create new community technology devices. Through the assistance of partners with material support in the form of seed funding for trials, expert knowledge and research, network technology application, and human capital support, Plugged In identifies productive processes and integrates technical infrastructures to create community technology innovation. The intent is to deliver quality service for the interest and development of community.

Plugged In works in an iterative process, constantly working to perfect programs and follow a learning curve. The application of knowledge to the process of knowledge generation and information processing devices in a feedback loop leads to innovations that customize and (re)configure community plans and strategies. Shared resources such as information, knowledge, skills, and expertise of associate partners are key. The added value is the information, knowledge, and skills of the community.

This process involves a diverse complex network of contributors who operate at various levels and across space. Specific activities include providing technical assistance, developing local empowerment strategies, providing research, reformulating programs, providing information, assisting in the development of services, and increasing access to valuable information. Partners facilitate innovation and transition efforts and support a path to sustainability for flexible fast-paced knowledge economies. This process requires an open discussion and understanding of community goals as defined by the community organization. Foremost is the ability to provide technical assistance and expertise in an array of specialties, thus providing a range of resources to address community needs. This cycle generates energy and vigor that is realized in community service projects as well as in action research and technical assistance. Adjustments are made where necessary, and proposed ongoing projects are clearly articulated, discussed, and negotiated around the CTC goals. This happens through continuous feedback from community technology providers, who redesign the structure and mission of the project accordingly. This type of collaboration is horizontal, meaning that each partner is viewed to be on parallel and equal ground in terms of the scope of each partner's interest and understanding of the problem and solution being envisaged. The highest level of education does not supersede the ground level of information embodied by the community provider. He or she is accepted as a person who embodies knowledge of practice that is rooted in practical and communal experience.

Crucial to this cooperation and interchange of the innovation process is the recognition that nontraditional community providers who implement and manage the program hold valuable information that leads to new community devices and technologies. They use knowledge to specify ways of doing things in a reproducible manner within a given context. Hence, it is the community that often identifies the problems and challenges of meeting the envisioned goals of a particular project. This level of cooperation fuels a more informed discussion about opportunities for the development of well-designed, well-structured programs.

*

In general, ongoing creative teams are diverse in ethnicity, social background, educational attainment, income levels, and occupation. This Plugged In team, however, comes together around shared cultural values; they have a mutual interest and engagement in social innovation and a joint belief that positive social change can arise when programs meet the needs and interests of the community it serves. For the most part, the culture of innovation is sustained by a network of relationships that are less hierarchical, more horizontal, more flexible, and more specialized. The shared interest and value is to explore, learn, experiment, innovate, and have fun. No prescribed or specified rules constrain available resources for each player. The rules are decided on and created by the group of partners. In this way, Plugged In receives solid knowledge as to what, where, how, when, and why a program can and should be created or (re)structured to sustain a particular project.

While innovation is created through a set of social relationships, information and telecommunications technology is used to communicate and sustain relationships with contributors. Contributors can exchange information and provide services to the community agency via the wires of IT.

Plugged In advances through an information network of experts on theory and professional and practical community work. Practice informs theory and knowledge informs practice. The outcome is innovation. Ideas generated through this process are then implemented, creating a space for more learning through experimentation. Thus, the (in)formal social relationship between partners is based on and sustained by a mutual respect for innovation as defined by the network team. For these partners, mistakes are lessons, part of the process of recognizing the challenges and opportunities that they face and that are worthy of investment. This cycle of innovation is in line with the complex changes, uncertainty, and innovation that occur and characterize the information- and knowledge-based economy.

How the culture of innovation benefits community organizations and low-income communities still needs to be studied. It is important to recognize that technology has different effects in different organizational conditions and contexts. The focus of research should be on how these contexts interrelate and how they are affected by the way technology is used and implemented. It is important to understand how or whether these developments can lead to more effective work within and between other partners. The challenge is to recognize the critical importance of how problems facing the community agency are being framed and constructed. This determines policy solutions. Now research should center on work processes to outline potential outcome measures.

Conclusion

Without public access to technology and training to manipulate technology, poor ethnic populations will be systematically prevented from participating in the political sphere, will be unfavorably positioned to receive economic benefit, will face limits in keeping valuable social ties without interaction via new modes of telecommunication, will lack the materials that are extended online by our institutions, and will be unable to communicate and exchange necessary information with institutions. All of these outcomes come from a lack of available sociotechnical structures that train for development at the community level and in ways that could meet the needs of the poor as the rest of society has gained. This situation would result in exclusion from voting processes of political election and, thus, a political underrepresentation that could lead to a three-tier public service system: (1) high-quality information exchange of materials through efficient digitally based social structures at reduced transaction costs; (2) limited low-rate public service; and (3) no service at all for some Americans, a system that could prove to be unconstitutional for failing to meet requirements for universal-access service.

Today there is an opportunity and challenge for thinking about what purpose community organizations that are focused on technology and economic development can and should serve. Perhaps we can reflect not only on how technology can make these organizations more efficient or better but also on what a community means by "better." It is imperative to conduct serious research and abstract valuable lessons that could advance our knowledge field and inform community technology organizations about their work in progress. Without a change in the rules governing innovation, it will not be possible to advance the organizational mission to support social development for the poor.

NOTES

1. Network technology includes external technology artifacts that facilitate voice, print, and visual communication or representation to produce, consume,

and exchange material products or public/private content. This includes technologies that facilitate social engagement, economic benefit, institutional exchange and collaboration, and the interface that makes possible the transfer of political voice and vote—for example, computers, the Internet, the Intranet, cell phones, online radios, hand-held computer digital devices, and various organizational forms such as listservs, e-mail, Web pages, online postings and transactions, and so on.

2. There are various dimensions or degrees to digital deprivation. For example, alienation can occur at the level of the creation of new technologies (and the social processes that sustain or develop them), at the level of consumption, or as a complete separation from the technology process. One indicator of being a creator of technology is holding a computer science degree. Breaking down federal statistics by undergraduate degrees shows that ethnic social groups that reside in poor communities are underrepresented in the pool of higher education; even fewer are found in computer or information-management science departments in graduate schools. An indicator of complete separation is not owning any kind of network technology.

3. It is possible that Community Technology Centers may claim to provide a new service for the poor only to attain new funding streams. It is also possible that with the integration of technology into work processes and the changing set of skill demands in service knowledge economies, the poor may face a new or more complex set of obstacles and that new forms of social organization are arising to address this problem. A case study is an appropriate method of analysis when we do not have but need to develop a theoretical platform to identify social and economic indicators by which institutions can collect data to measure community technology interventions.

4. Key characteristics of CTCs that are organized to support community economic development include mission, partnerships, networks, institutional collaboration, and community base. Mission determines which individuals, groups, and institutions will support a CTC and establishes a particular development strategy. Institutional collaborations and partnerships determine the ability of staff members and partners to engage in planning, community organizing, fundraising, and implementing programs. Networks are reflected in the links that CTC service providers and board members have with other community-based organizations (CBOs), institutions, and employers. Community base is determined by whether the CTC is based in the community being served and whether the agency works with other CBOs.

5. This list of criteria is adopted from Westat's (1999) case study evaluations of the Telecommunications and Information Infrastructure Assistance Program for the U.S. Department of Commerce.

6. Inequality in East Palo Alto (EPA) can be striking. The economic boom that transformed neighboring communities in the past decade bypassed this pocket of poverty. While Palo Alto could not meet the demand for labor during the digital

economy boom, EPA was faced with a number of serious economic challenges, including a bleak job market. In 2001, there were only nine hundred jobs available for a population of twenty-five thousand people. This small city has four times the unemployment rate of Palo Alto. While $70,000 is the median family income in Palo Alto, 80 percent of the population in East Palo Alto depends on some source of public assistance. Sixteen percent of the total EPA population and 19 percent of the children live under the designated poverty line. According to the California Employment Development Department, EPA has an 11 percent rate of unemployment; this was almost double the rate for the County of San Mateo (4.1 percent) or the State of California (6.1 percent) in September 2002. Furthermore, the majority of the unemployed are considered to be "digital divide" populations—Black, Latino, urban, low-income, women, in poor communities. While Silicon Valley has played a leading role in fostering the digital revolution that is sweeping the globe, East Palo Alto has missed out on much of this prosperity. There is only one computer for every twenty-eight students in East Palo Alto schools, as compared to the one-to-nine ratio for the entire state of California.

7. Enhanced access—the ability to manipulate the productive function of technology to meet personal, political, economic, and social goals—is an indicator of novel and innovative service.

8. From the literature on economic development in communities, we know that well-structured programs need what Plugged In has attained: (1) corporate sponsorship from technology companies such as Cisco Systems, Intel, Sun Microsystems, and Hewlett Packard; (2) government support from as high as the presidency (in 1995 Plugged In was one of the first Community Technology Centers to receive a Telecommunications and Information Infrastructure Assistance Program Award; (3) a history of collaborating with representatives from schools, the city, and community-based organizations; and (4) private investment.

9. To gain more understanding about the work process, I followed and examined the ongoing activity of Plugged In over a five-year period, 1998–2003. This allowed me to identify and analyze the actions and interrelations of the influential members who are actively engaged in the decision making and direction of the project. I examined their activity on and off site, with particular focus on the ways in which they used technology to create and maintain professional ties across space. Off-site activities included attending meetings with funding agents, with the board of directors, and with potential partners and attending professional conferences or conventions, fundraising events, ribbon-cutting ceremonies, and formal or informal gatherings with civic and community agencies.

10. For a more detailed discussion, see the chapter titled "The Organizational Divide" in Servon 2002.

11. Technology goes through a cycle of innovation. One way to break this cycle into phases of development or evolution is, in order, creation, adoption, use, and integration. Society is at the stage of integration, in which technology is merging

into institutional productive processes that sustain systems of operation. But there are still debates about whether it is necessary to diffuse technology to community organizations to meet the needs of the poor. While upper-end public institutions and organizations are rapidly approaching the next stage in the cycle of technology innovation (e.g., Wi-Fi or Internet), technology of the previous generation has already bypassed community organizations in the inner city. Community organizations that serve the grassroots have little exposure even to earlier generation of commercial tools such as laser scanners at supermarkets and bank automatic teller machines, facsimiles, computerization, and telecommunications, and mass media applications are dramatically underrepresented in economically distressed areas.

12. This program has roots in South-Central Los Angeles. The idea that led to the building of pilot programs to serve poor populations at the community level —according to Thomas Kalil, who served as a special assistant to the president for economic policy and was the National Economic Council's "point person" on a wide range of technology and telecommunications issues under President Clinton —came from congresswoman Maxine Waters of Los Angeles's Thirty-fifth District. Her request was based on the concern that without establishing public access to network technology with training, populations in poor communities would be underserved by public social service systems (interview with Kalil, 2003).

13. New governance structures, such as the Internet Corporation for Assigned Names and Numbers (ICANN), are making crucial decisions on Internet policy that affect the public interest and determine the type of service CBOs can offer. ICANN, a global organization, manages the Internet's Domain Name System (DNS) and is developing accreditation guideline standards for obtaining certified domain license names. Legislators and administrative agencies are also passing laws or modifying the old rules of engagement, competition, and ownership. For instance, the Federal Communications Commission (FCC) is devising ways to further deregulate the structure of the broadcast and cable television industries by revising ownership rules to allow greater ownership of frequency airwaves by traditional networks. Furthermore, new institutional processes under the Department of Homeland Security (DHS) are expected to influence an array of technology issues, such as "protecting the nation's online infrastructure, directing the development of new surveillance and defense technology, and preserving the privacy right of ordinary citizens." The Bush administration is establishing a National Strategy to Secure Cyberspace under the rubric of the DHS. On a more local level, law enforcement agencies such as police departments are using the Internet or cell phones for surveillance. Courts of law are accepting content in e-mail or Web site documents as lawful evidence of a crime to prosecute citizens. Increasingly, Internet providers and telephone companies are facing requests from law enforcement for the names of subscribers and their e-mail accounts. Privacy laws are being contested and negotiated in policy circles.

14. For a more detailed discussion about the structure of the community technology development program, see Gordo 2003.

REFERENCES

Brown, J. S., and P. Duguid. 2002. *The Social Life of Information.* Boston: Harvard Business School Press.

Castells, M. 1996. *Rise of the Network Society.* Cambridge, MA: Blackwell.

Gordo, B. 2002. "What Planning Crisis? Reflections on the 'Digital Divide' and the Persistence of Unequal Opportunity." *Berkeley Planning Journal* 6.

Gordo, B. 2003. "Overcoming Digital Deprivation." *IT&Society* 1:5 (Summer): 166–180. Available at http://www.stanford.edu/group/siqss/itandsociety/v01i05/v01i05a08.pdf.

Kalil, T. Community Technology Programs and Policy: Interview with Thomas Kalil. By Blanca Gordo. UC Berkeley, 2003.

Krueger, A. B. 1993. "How Computers Have Changed the Wage Structure: Evidence from Micro Data." *Quarterly Journal of Economics* 107:1: 35–78.

Servon, L. J. 2002. *Bridging the Digital Divide.* Malden, MA: Blackwell.

U.S. Department of Commerce, National Telecommunications and Information Administration. 2002. *A Nation Online.* Washington, DC: U.S. Department of Commerce. Available at http://www.ntia.doc.gov/ntiahome/dn/anationonline2.pdf.

U.S. Department of Commerce, National Telecommunications and Information Administration. 2000. *Falling through the Net: Towards Digital Inclusion.* Washington, DC: U.S. Department of Commerce. Available at http://www.ntia.doc.gov/ntiahome/fttn00/contents00.html.

Westat. 1999. "Evaluation of the Telecommunications and Information Infrastructure Assistance Program for the 1994 and 1995 Grant Years." Washington, DC: U.S. Department of Commerce. Available at http://www.ntia.doc.gov/otiahome/top/research/EvaluationReport/evaluation_report.htm#1994_5.

Chapter 14

The Vertical (Layered) Net
Interrogating the Conditions of Network Connectivity

Greg Elmer

This chapter briefly discusses the implications of critical cyberculture's overreliance on horizontal or narrative-driven forms of analysis. In particular, I argue that central concepts and critical claims in cyberculture studies—specifically those that suggest an unqualified degree of individual user empowerment—stem from dated interpretations of technological infrastructure, software, and protocols. Given the limited scope of my contribution to this book, I will restrict many of my remarks to the Web. And although my arguments could be easily extended to video games and Digital Video Recorders (e.g., TiVo and Replay TV), there are valid reasons for focusing on the Web. The Web has offered myriad networks, environments, and software a standard platform and interface; for this reason it often serves as an archetype of "new media."

In what follows, I suggest that while the Web offers both decentered and distributed characteristics, it has become increasingly operationalized through hierarchical methods that subtly direct users toward preferred —and allied providers of—content, goods, and services. In this discussion I embrace the term "cyberculture" as defined by Robert Burnett and David P. Marshall (2003, p. 25): "Cyber comes from the Greek which means 'to steer.'" To many people, though, the argument might sound counterintuitive that cheaper, smaller, faster, mobile, and distributed forms of media technology might somehow restrain or otherwise control users. From a comparative media perspective (indeed, within the contemporary media environment), this argument might even sound patently absurd. My purpose though is not to make such a precipitous leap, for it would be foolhardy and downright wrong. Rather, my aim is to simply suggest that much work in cyberculture studies has taken us too far in the opposite direction, arguing that new media has effectively leveled the playing field or flattened hierarchies. Unfortunately, in so doing, the emancipatory claim also threatens to evacuate *power* as a long-standing hermeneutic tool of media and cultural criticism.

At the beginning of *Inventing the Internet,* Janet Abbate (2000, p. 44) offers one of the central claims of the emancipatory position in cyberculture studies, that "the culture of the Internet challenges the whole distinction between producers and consumers." A page later, though, Abbate qualifies her position, stating, "In the early days of the ARPANET, the distinction between users did not even exist" (pp. 4–5). Abbate's point, of course, is that ARPANET users were a relatively homogeneous bunch, sharing a common set of interests, scientific/academic goals, and technological competencies. Contemporary theorists of new media and cyberculture, however, have not been as quick—or have completely failed—to qualify their claims about contemporary emancipated users. Mark Poster (2001), for instance, a widely published theorist of new media, offers us a glimpse into the technological rationale for the emancipated, horizontal argument. In his book, provocatively or perhaps playfully titled *What's the Matter with the Internet?* Poster seemingly conflates the qualities of "hypertext" with the Net in general, a common fallacy found in many emancipatory arguments. After introducing his concept of "underdetermination" as a defining characteristic of the Internet in general, Poster explains that

> certain objects that I call virtual (hypertexts, for example) are overdetermined in such a way that their level of complexity or indeterminateness goes one step further. Not only are these objects formed by distinct practices, discourses, and institutional frames, each of which participates in and exemplifies the contradictions of capitalism and the nation-state, but they are also open to practice; they do not direct agents into clear paths; they solicit instead social construction and cultural creation. (2001, p. 17)

And although one can clearly find some truth to Poster's claims, his invocation of an underdetermined media form with no clear—or indeed *preferred*—paths leads to the conclusion that "the Internet is ruled by no one and is open to expansion or addition at anyone's whim as long as its communication protocols are followed" (p. 27). While clearly engaging in dubious technohyperbole, Poster does add an important caveat: the universality of protocols. Poster, though, has little to say about the manner in which protocols set operational limits and govern compatibility and new media corporate alliances. In short, protocols do not exist in a vacuum; they are deployed by particular actors to both include and exclude, open or close new media capabilities (Elmer 2002; Galloway 2004).

In large part, the emancipatory arguments within cyberculture studies are invoked by a narrow or romantic reading of hypertext history, with many proponents choosing to favor Ted Nelson's more radical, open, multiauthored, and nonlinear Xanadu program.[1] I argue that contemporary forms of hypertextuality (particularly on the Web) have much more in common with Vannevar Bush's "Memex" machine.[2] And while the virtual nature of Xanadu might provide a compelling and equivalent social diagram,[3] it also distances the decidedly personalized, closed, and proprietorial form of hypertext described in Bush's writing and, of course, the form of hypertext we now find on the Web (HTML).

The early examples of Memex and, later, Apple's Hypercard detail the emergence of a decidedly individualized and proprietorial form of hypertextual information management and computing. As is the case with the World Wide Web's version of hypertext (HTML), these earlier manifestations of hypertext promised a personalized (meaning single-authored) and intensely customized form of hypertext. Graphic representations of Memex, for example, often take the form of a personal desk, with no visible signs of multiauthorship or social forms of networking whatsoever. Moreover, in such proprietorial visions, the ability for many individual users to both read and write hypertextually linked documents was seriously curtailed.

Tim Berners-Lee's account of the birth of the Web and its first browser (Berners-Lee and Fiscetti 1999) likewise details the translation of hypertext from interactive, reading-writing, nonsequential labyrinth to a much more centralized, proprietorial media form (HTML). At the outset of the book, Berners-Lee offers some introductory philosophical remarks on his vision of the Web project, one that at first glance maintains antihierarchical and participatory elements: "New webs could be made to bind different computers together, and all new systems would be able to break out and reference others. Plus anyone browsing could instantly add a new node connected by a new link" (p. 1).

As the book's historical narrative develops, however, its author begins to document the emergence of a Web hypertext increasingly defined by the much more passive act of "browsing." At the very early stages of institutionalization Berners-Lee notes that "for the [Web-hypertext] proposal . . . I would have to sell this project as a documentation system—a perceived need at CERN—and not as a hypertext system, which just sounded too precious" (p. 19). In addition to the hierarchical and entrepreneurial limitations and biases of Berners-Lee's working environment, he later notes that in the development of the first Web browser "we decided not to take the time to develop the line-mode browser as an editor. Simply being able to read documents was good enough to bootstrap the process" (p. 33). He later goes on to lament that "it left people thinking of the Web as a medium in which a few people published and most browsed. My vision was a system in which sharing what you knew or thought should be as easy as learning what someone else knew" (p. 33).

The clash between Berners-Lee's own more radically open and hypertextually defined Web and the more proprietorily defined HTML are also highlighted in a series of early technical position papers written for Berners-Lee's World Wide Web Consortium at the Massachusetts Institute of Technology. Of all the Consortium's technical discussions of the Web, the question of links seems to best encapsulate the clear philosophical differences between previous forms of hypertext and hypertext markup language (HTML). Under the appropriate heading "Topology," for example, Berners-Lee and other members of the Consortium question the applicability of two or multiended links, a seemingly quite logical question, as the term "link" itself connotes two ends. The disadvantages of such a scheme, moreover, provide further evidence of an emerging, hierarchical hypertext system on the Web (HTML), one that lends a good deal more power to technical writers: "If [links] are bidirectional, a link always exists in the reverse direction. A disadvantage of this being enforced is that it might constrain the author of a hypertext—*we might want to constrain the reader*" (emphasis added).[4]

Some three years later, Berners-Lee characterizes the decision to enact a "mono-directional" hypertext link topology as a "fundamental compromise."[5] Thus, as discussion progresses on the contours of a proprietorial HTML, questions of protection and individual "domains" begin to take over the Web lexicon, to such an extent that discussions of the "collaborative possibilities of hypertext" on the Web are reduced to simple annotative possibilities of hypertext links. Accordingly, the accompanying technical discussion notes that "an annotation does not modify the text necessarily: one can separate protection against writing and annotation."[6]

Such restraints and conditions of computer networking, however, largely continue to be bypassed by many cyberculture scholars. For instance, Nina Wakeford's (2000) otherwise engaging discussion of research methods for Web scholars relies upon Mitra and Cohen's (1999) characterization of the "web text" as a space where "the reader becomes the author, in a sense, as he or she actively selects which links to follow" (Wakeford 2000, p. 33). And while the insertion of quotation marks indicates a slight qualification of what is meant by "authorship," such a radical statement on the very nature of cultural production surely requires some degree of critical analysis. Mitra and Cohen and Wakeford are, of course, not the exception. Discussing the lack of any one dominant corporate interest on the Net—a contention that could very well be refuted given the immense growth (vertically and horizontally) of the AOL/Time Warner, Microsoft, and most recently Google media empires—Gerald Goggin (2000, p. 111) unequivocally contends that "there is a very real sense in which internet users are choosing where they wish to go." And although one could perhaps substantiate this point—at least in relation to other media technologies such as television—the author's lack of substantial qualification and critical analysis of this statement unfortunately takes us no closer to understanding constraints or limits on users and the manner in which cybercapital enforces particular structures of knowledge on the Web.

Thus, in addition to narrative and horizontal analyses of the Web, I propose reviewing the critical possibilities of vertical analysis. Such an endeavor is of course not without precedent—or bias, for that matter. Just as horizontal and emancipatory arguments have come out of a literary tradition (death of the author, etc.), a vertical approach owes a great deal to questions of technological history and political economy. Again, it should be emphasized that I am not proposing a radical about-turn in cyberculture studies, one that would displace important work on virtual environments, CMC, blogging or other forms of "amateur," vernacular, and noncommercial interaction, communication, and publishing. Rather, I prefer to offer a balanced horizontal and vertical view that ultimately looks to radical successes and failures of new media as indicators of potential critical fissures opening and of possibilities for progressive social and political change.

One need not look far for vertical inspirations. The history of the Internet, at least from a technological perspective, is often written and rewritten as a history of layering—and connections between layers—of network infrastructure (hardware and software). That is to suggest that the innovation was seen, and articulated, in architectural terms, as a technology that was constructed vertically. For the purposes of setting standards and shared protocols, telecommunications networking in general was likewise often parsed into various levels of networking. The "Open System Interconnection" (OSI) reference model, for instance, is a system developed by the International Organization for Standardization (ISO), and a number of other international organizations conceptualized networks as a system where "each layer performs a related set of functions, utilizing and enriching the services provided by the immediately lower level" (Siris 2002, p. 2). The OSI model thus outlined seven distinct layers: physical, data link, network, transport, session, presentation, and application (Siris 2002, p. 3).

While the OSI model has faced much revision over the years, in an attempt to recognize converging functions among layers, there is increasing interest in theorizing connectivity between levels. Abbate (2000, p. 51), for instance argues, "A layered system is organized as a set of discrete functions that interact according to specific rules. The functions are called 'layers' because they are arranged in a conceptual hierarchy that proceeds from the most concrete and physical functions (such as handling electrical signals) to the most abstract functions (e.g., interpreting human-language commands from users)."

In addition to this technological or infrastructural perspective, economists have also increasingly conceptualized the Internet as a series of layers that demonstrate levels of economic production and employment. A recent report from the Center for Research in Electronic Commerce at the University of Texas at Austin (Barua et al. 1999), for example, argues that the Internet should be divided into four layers. Following a relatively similar topography as the OSI model, the report, entitled "Measuring the Internet Economy," begins with an Internet Infrastructure layer that includes back bone, fiber optic, switching, and server functions. Layer two, the "Applications" layer, would consequently "build upon the . . . IP network infrastructure." The report's third "intermediary" layer attempts to recognize the functions (and corporations, of course) that "increase the efficiency of electronic markets by facilitating the meeting and interaction of buyers and sellers over the Internet." Finally, the fourth layer, "Commerce," focuses almost exclusively on the terrain of e-commerce (pp. 4–5).

Ultimately, the relation between layers, or the distinctiveness of levels, remains debatable and open to change. Yet at the same time, there is a common hierarchical thread among vertical layered analyses, namely, that upper layers (and their companies and services) are dependent upon lower-level corporations and technologies that have explicit technological standards (protocols). Such "genetic" (and henceforth monopolistic) links between layers of the Net have been of prime concern for critics of some of the largest and most powerful new media corporations, particularly those engaged in sales and research on multiple layers (Microsoft, Intel, IBM, etc.). Not surprisingly, critics of Microsoft, especially legal historian and theorist Lawrence Lessig (2002), have similarly adopted vertical, layered concepts to critique the increasingly monopolistic, anticompetitive, and antidemocratic trends in networking innovation, standardization, governance, and commerce. In comparison to the OSI or the University of Texas models, Lessig's layers are broader and more abstract in their recognition of (1) infrastructure, (2) computer language or "code," and (3) simply "content."

Cyberculture studies have, however, perhaps suffered too much under the weight of abstraction or, at least, generalization. What is needed now, in addition to critiques of textuality and cultural expression, is a renewed conceptualization of the *conditions* of networking, along the lines offered above (i.e., from technologists, historians, economists, and lawyers). Underlying computer networking, the means by which we access networks, share resources, save or revise HTML pages, upload, download, etc., is the *moment of connectivity*—a meeting point, interface, language, exchange, intersection, or dialogue. While critical theories of media, communication, and culture have successfully questioned the discriminatory elements of such moments of connectivity, contact, and exchange, cyberculture studies is in danger of naturalizing and romanticizing this interface. A topography of contemporary computer networking, or an *archeology*, as Foucault would have it, would be a first step toward charting the *contemporary* terrain upon which normative networking (use) is encoded (e.g., AOL's user-friendly networking), economic monopolies are forged and strengthened, and radical political/proprietorial interventions are deployed across contemporary digital networks.

NOTES

1. See http://xanadu.com/.

2. Consider a future device for individual use, which is a sort of mechanized private file and library. It needs a name, and, to coin one at random, "memex" will

do. A memex is a device in which an individual stores all his books, records, and communications, and which is mechanized so that it may be consulted with exceeding speed and flexibility. It is an enlarged intimate supplement to his memory (Bush 1991, p. 82).

3. Gary Wolf (1995), for example, dubs Xanadu the archetypical virtual software or "vaporware" because it remains (since the early 1960s) a work in progress.

4. See http://www.w3.org/Designissues/Topology.html.

5. See http://www.w3.org/DesignIssues/Architecture.html.

6. See http://www.w3.org/DesignIssues/Multiuser.html.

REFERENCES

Abbate, Janet. (2000). *Inventing the Internet.* Cambridge, MA: MIT Press.

Barua, Anitesh, Jon Pinnell, Jay Shutter, and Andrew B. Whinston. (1999). "Measuring the Internet Economy: An Exploratory Study." Center for Research in Electronic Commerce, University of Texas at Austin.

Berners-Lee, Tim, and Mark Fiscetti. (1999). *Weaving the Web: The Original Design and Ultimate Destiny of the World Wide Web by Its Inventor.* San Francisco: HarperCollins.

Burnett, Robert, and David P. Marshall. (2003). *Web Theory.* London: Routledge.

Bush, Vannevar. (1991). "Memorandum Regarding Memex." In J. M. Nyce and P. Khan (eds.), *From Memex to Hypertext: Vannevar Bush and the Mind's Machine.* New York: Academic Press, pp. 81–84.

Elmer, Greg. (2002). "The Case of Web Browser Cookies: Enabling/Disabling Convenience and Relevance on the Web." In G. Elmer (ed.), *Critical Perspectives on the Internet.* Boulder, CO: Rowman and Littlefield.

Galloway, Alexander. (2004). *Protocol: How Control Exists after Decentralization.* Cambridge, MA: MIT Press.

Goggin, Gerald. (2000). "Pay Per Browse: The Web's Commercial Future." In D. Gauntlett (ed.), *Web Studies: Rewiring Media Studies for the Digital Age.* London: Arnold, pp. 103–112.

Lessig, Lawrence. (2002). *The Future of Ideas: The Fate of the Commons in a Connected World.* New York: Vintage.

Mitra, M., and E. Cohen. (1999). "Analyzing the Web: Directions and Challenges." In S. Jones (ed.), *Doing Internet Research.* Thousand Oaks, CA: Sage, pp. 197–202.

Poster, Mark. (2001). *What's the Matter with the Internet?* Minneapolis: University of Minnesota Press.

Siris, Vasilios. (2002). "The OSI Model and Switching." Institute of Computer Science—FORTH, Greece.

Wakeford, Nina. (2000). "New Media, New Methodologies: Studying the Web." In

D. Gauntlett (ed.), *Web Studies: Rewiring Media Studies for the Digital Age.* London: Arnold, pp. 31–41.

Wolf, Gary. (1995). "The Curse of Xanadu." *Wired,* June. Available at http:// www.wired.com/wired/archive/3.06/xanadu.html.

Chapter 15

The Construction of Cybersocial Reality

Stine Gotved

We do not know much about online life.[1] Despite a range of interesting studies, primarily ethnographic-based case studies of online groups and communities, we have only a few clues to the inner workings of the phenomena. The participants might get a sense of community and a feeling of belonging, and apparently the computer mediation of the interaction is no hindrance for developing significant relationships. Along the same lines, most of the studies have proven the participants to be competent individuals gathered around a common denominator—the interest in soap operas (Baym 1995, 1997, 2000), play-like hanging around (Kendall 2002), pre-movie Tolkien fandom (Gotved 2000), exchange of urban legends (Tepper 1997), and so forth. Some studies are focused on the methodology in studying online life, such as Hine (2000) and Markham (1998), or are reports from experience on how not to deal with the online groups (Sharf 1999). The richness of the different studies of online life during the past decade is shown in one anthology after another, yet still we are not familiar with the patterns of sociality. Very few (if any) studies deal directly with the basic social construction of online reality, time, and space, although some of the above-mentioned approaches touch upon the topics. Thus, this chapter is an attempt to combine our rather limited knowledge of online life with a basic sociological approach about the construction of social reality. The resources used in and re-created through the construction of cybersocial reality are thought of as limited to the online parts of our everyday life; however, this is an analytical construction without much empirical possibility. Nevertheless, in order to understand some of the subtle details in the construction of cybersocial reality, we have to demarcate it from the ever-present physical and embodied world, just for the sake of the analysis. The goal, therefore, is to develop a systematic methodology (and hence, the first step in a metatheory) to be employed in studies about cybersocial reality, online community, and computer-mediated communication.[2]

The Triangle Approach

The three basic sociological categories of culture, structure, and interaction—as outlined by Boudreau and Newman (1993)—inspired me to view the construction of cybersocial reality as a triangle. Boudreau and Newman, however, used the prefix "social" before both "structure" and "interaction," whereas I omit this word. This is not because cybersociality is not social (it certainly is) but because I see the prefix as an indirect opposition to the possible interplay with the environment and the technology. What is the opposite of "social," and why should the construction of social reality only take shape from areas already termed social? This is one of the blind spots in mainstream sociology, and of course, the point of broadening out the categories is even more important when talking about the construction of cybersocial reality, where we cannot ignore the central role of communication technology[3] and the Internet. As Jonathan Sterne reminds us, the Internet cannot be approached as just "new" because that is a normative judgment rather than an empirical description (1999, p. 259). We need to consider the role of the technology in everyday life, not as something with a deterministic relation (as in both the technophilic and technophobic variations) but as something deeply integrated in actions and interactions in the network society.[4] Especially when talking about online life and communication, the technology takes on an obvious role as basic condition and framing. The technology intervenes on the level of agency and in some ways becomes an independent agent on its own, and here again, the term *network* may be appropriate to describe the merging of agencies. Hence, the basic categories of culture, structure, and interaction must be extended beyond most sociological traditions[5] to include the technology, already integrated and thus nearly invisible in the ongoing cybersocial life.

Another detail in the basic triangle (see figure 15.1) is the way it is drawn, and here I follow the lead of Boudreau and Newman (1993). Instead of drawing the categories as dots to be connected with arrows (to represent the connections), it is the sides of the triangle that hold the meaning. The activity, the ongoing construction of cybersocial reality,

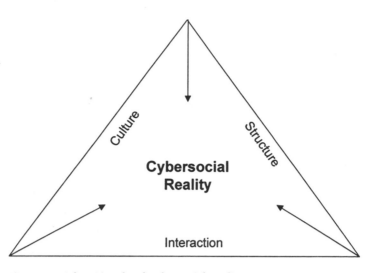

Figure 15.1. The Triangle of Cybersocial Reality

is found in the middle of the triangle, so to speak. This rather unusual model construction holds clear analytical advantages. First, there is no postulate about separability of the categories—the corners of the triangle are visual representations of the ever-existent overlaps of culture, structure, and interaction, areas where they cannot be distinguished. Second (and in the same vein), even with a specific focus on one of the categories, the connections to the other categories remain. Third, the sides of the triangle can be used as kinds of visual scales, where a specific event can be plotted as primarily in one category, with an asymmetrical association to the others. Finally, by collecting the activity in the middle, the triangle symbolizes the condition for the construction of social reality, the inescapable framing as well as the pool of resources. This is even more apparent when the matrix evolves and the basic triangle becomes embedded in time and space—eyes are drawn to the center of the triangle, where all the different factors and categories convene and where the cybersocial reality is constructed. Hence, the construction of the matrix is a conscious choice of representation in which the different categories and their interplay are united in the center instead of separated and drawn in the periphery.

The model also has great value with regard to the (rather false) dichotomy between online and offline. Although the design takes its departure from the need to know more about the online part in particular, all the categories could be used in a systematic approach to offline life as well. This is no surprise; after all, the three categories come from classical sociological thinking. Hence, the model has many recognizable elements, and this is a central point. Online life and sociality is not that different from offline; we use the same social competencies in slightly transformed ways, and when allowance is made for the mediation of the computer we have more similarities than differences. In sum, the matrix might be valuable to offline as well as online research into the construction of (cyber) social reality, and maybe even to an approach focused upon the life on the threshold between offline and online. However, the potential value of the matrix for research on offline life has yet to be explored, and in this chapter I will discuss the matrix solely in relation to the cybersocial parts of our constructions of reality.

The Basic Triangle

Cybersocial reality is constructed individually and collectively, and it is by no means static; it is the constantly interweaving patterns, actions, and interpretations of the ongoing life. The cultural side of the triangle represents the fluid processes of meaning and commonality; here we negotiate what is called common sense and the ever-shifting landscape of ideas and memory. This area is by no means value-free, and in analyses of online communication the cultural part is shown to raise frustrations as well as expectations and sometimes a perception of togetherness. The technology is inherent in the communication processes, where certain competencies (e.g., support or conflict management) are valued slightly differently than in the offline world. The construction of a common understanding, and especially the establishment of various norms (e.g., a local netiquette), represents an analytical move from the cultural flux to the more organized structure. On the triangle's structural side, the organization is in focus. Here, the possible role division and the hierarchy are to be placed, as is the underlying infrastructure—the communication's more or less given conditions (e.g., the protocols). Thus, the structure is the more stable part of the triangle, where the social structure and organization are intertwined tightly with the technology's interface and underlying design ideology. Lastly, interaction is the bottom line (without interaction, there is no social reality), and this element tends to be surprisingly hard for classic sociologists to comprehend. Interaction occurs not only between humans but also between humans and computers and between computers.

As previously stated, we cannot keep the different agencies separate, especially not when talking about the construction of cybersocial reality, and the triangle's interaction side includes all the variations.[6]

Even though the basic social complexity is the point of departure for the construction of the cybersocial reality (individually and/or collectively, visible and/or imagined), the technological variation is equally compelling. I have identified four levels of social complexity: the lone surfer in superficial communication with the waves of information; the dyadic couple focused upon each other; the interconnected network of relations; and the community basically concerned with defining insiders versus outsiders. Although there is a quantitative difference between the first two categories and the second two, the size is not important when talking about possible distinctions between network and community. The difference here is harder to define, but it relates to the levels of commitment and complexity in the involvement. In short, the four levels—the surfer, the dyad, the network, and the community—cover the social interactions in online communication, and this complexity is the context that underlies every construction of cybersocial reality. Merging the level of social complexity with the actual framing of the interaction, made by the technology in question, is one of the challenges on the level of interaction.

In sum, the three sides of the triangle are equally important in the cybersocial reality construction processes, although specific analyses might choose to put particular weight on one or two of the sides. The culture, structure, and interaction framework makes it possible to come to terms with the wide variety within online social life, whether we are talking about short-term communications between strangers or long-term establishment of cyber community. This point will be highlighted in the following sections, where the cybersocial reality is embedded in time and, later, space.

The Triangle of Time

The triangle of time (figure 15.2) is wrapped around the basic triangle as described above, and every side is thereby extended into a temporal dimension. The three time dimensions are based primarily on the sociology of Elias (1992) and also inspired from a wide range of scientific approaches to time. Time is one of the hardest topics to grasp, and to refer to the chronological order of things, the clock's mechanical or digital division of time, the body's biological aging, and so forth is just to touch upon

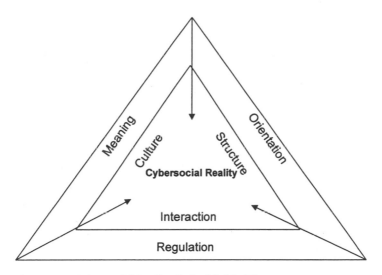

Figure 15.2. Cybersocial Reality Embedded in Time

an extreme complexity (see Adam 1995 for a brilliant analysis of time as a hidden focal point in social studies). The triangle of time extends the basic categories (culture, structure, interaction) into meaning, orientation, and regulation.

The cultural time dimension, *meaning*, relates to time understood as processes and memories of those processes. To establish certain patterns of meaning—central to the cultural part—time is necessary, and time is inscribed as a factor in every sort of communication. Time becomes history and takes on several layers of social meaning, as in discussions between newbies and oldies in any given online community, where the interpretations differ according to (among other things) time spent in the context. Again, the border between culture/meaning and structure/orientation may be a bit perforated and primarily defined through the stability and level of agreement about the organization. Thus, the *orientation* too is facilitated by clocks and calendars and, within online communication, also by recorded time like archives and FAQs. Furthermore, the basic protocol (whether the communication is synchronous or asynchronous) is important in many ways—the possible content, the speed, the interpretation patterns, and so on. The once balanced relation between space and time (long distances took a long time to travel) is totally out of balance with regard to the information technology, where the communication travels around the globe in nanoseconds. This speed is a challenge to the established time zones and the related GMT time, and at least two alternative ways of orientation, new ways of representing a global synchronicity, have been established.[7] In other words, the sheer speed of our communication makes it necessary to think of time differently, if coordination and orientation are to be achieved. The time dimension of interaction, the triangle's bottom line, is termed *regulation* to describe time's prime role in interaction. Time is used and interpreted as a significant parameter in interaction, mirrored in greetings during the day and across the year, and time plays important roles in interaction—from quality time to waiting time, from the endless minute to the experience of flow. The significance of even the smallest pauses in a communication, as well as the value attached to high-speed connections, is about time as regulating different aspects of interaction, which brings us full circle (or, rather, full triangle) back to the negotiation of meaning in the cultural dimension.

In sum, the triangle of time is a framework that allows us to talk about the often hidden roles of time in online communication. Inscribing the basic parameters of culture, structure, and interaction in a temporal dimension highlights the ways in which time holds importance in the construction of cybersocial reality. As Adam (1995) shows, the time aspects hold nearly indefinite potentials to rethink social analysis, and the triangle is at once a simplification of the matter and an opening toward a serious inclusion of time.

The Triangle of Space

Like the triangle of time, the triangle of space (figure 15.3) wraps around the basic triangle of cybersocial reality. The three basic categories are thus extended into spatial dimensions, with acknowledgment to the French sociologist Lefebvre (1974/1991). In general, sociology is relatively space-blind, with of course a few exceptions, such as Lefebvre (1974/1991) and Shields (1991, 1999). Other traditions, such as geography, architecture, and urban planning, are focused upon space (one way or another), and their inclusion of information technology, sociology, and other social sciences is often highly fertile (Dodge and Kitchin 2001). So, although the following categories are inspired by Lefebvre's take on space, they are primarily informed by more cross-disciplinary approaches. Named *re/construction, visibility,* and *practice,*[8] the three sides of the triangle of space are extensions of, respectively, the basic categories culture, structure, and interaction.

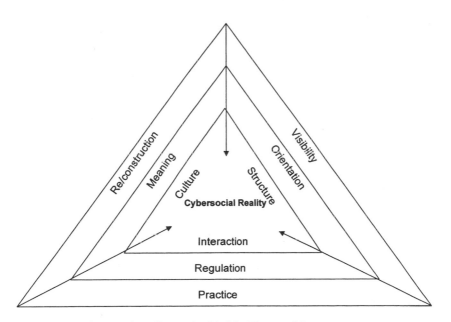

Figure 15.3. Cybersocial Reality Embedded in Time and Space

Re/construction is the spatial dimension of culture, and this is where the primary idea of (cyber) space is evoked. Through metaphors, analogies, objects, directions, expressions of sound, and so forth, the language (and, if implemented, the graphics) allows us to experience the conceived space behind the screen as an actual place. This is the re/construction of the physical world, as descriptive translations or negations, and language-wise very rich. Of course, there is an overlap to the next side of the triangle, *visibility*. This concerns the interface, where the spatial conditions are laid out—in the actual design, in the promise of navigational possibilities, and (as a common denominator) the screen's edges. The interface differences between blogs, chats, multiplayer gaming, and so on are huge and thus important to take into account—the visibility influences the construction of cybersocial reality. The last category in the space triangle is the interactional part, termed *practice*. This is the spatial perception derived from interactions and relations within the spatiality established by re/construction and visibility. The practice is loaded with imaginations about the possible extension of the spatiality and, especially, about the other participants. The social world is expressed in spatial terms—the hierarchy, the network, someone close to us—and our practice within this social world are accordingly related to imaginations about this spatial variation. The expressions of moving around in a MUD, for example, are simultaneously a way of experiencing the world and a way of establishing spatiality, and when this practice is combined with manipulating objects or using commands like "shout" or "push," there is an instant connection with the metaphorical level, the re/construction side of the triangle.

In sum, the re/construction, the visibility, and the practice together make up the spatiality experienced in online communication. Of course, the perception of space is an individual construction, but it is not made out of nothing—different factors are guiding us along. Basically, spatiality is central to our way of making sense of our surroundings, and this is true also in the case of cyberspace—the catchiness of the phrase stems at least partly from the reference to spatiality, which makes the concept easier to grasp.

Conclusion

By way of conclusion, I will rename figure 15.3 the Matrix of Cybersocial Reality.

Three basic sociological categories—culture, social structure, and social interaction—have been extended to include the ever-present technology and then embedded in time and space. Although such representations are always reductionistic, the triangle design leaves open the possibilities for overlap and fluid processes while at the same time defining the important factors to include. With this matrix, we are able to analyze and compare the variations within online communication, taking into account time, space, and complexity. The rich variation in cybersociality can be explained not only by the obvious different levels of social and technological complexity but also by their constructions and connections in the basic categories of culture, structure, and interaction, including their dimensions in time and space. In other words, the matrix establishes the frames of a metatheory in the area of cybersocial life, based on cultural sociology and the relatively few cross-disciplinary empirical studies of the phenomenon.

NOTES

1. I am grateful to the Ford Foundation and the Resource Center for Cyberculture Studies, which provided me the time to develop the latest part of this research area.

2. I do not discuss the possible differences between *cyber, online, virtual,* and *computer-mediated*. Historically, they are connected to different academic traditions and popular imaginations, and I will not provide more precise definitions.

3. Here, "technology" is shorthand for the complexity of hardware, software, protocols, browsers, and so on involved in online communication. To be sure, the technology holds a ballast of values, choices, designs, and so forth; the technology cannot be viewed as just an ideologically neutral communication tool.

4. Castells's (1996, 2000) term "network society" concerns the primary organizational form to be found, and I find this term more descriptive (and less ideological) than, for example, "high" or "late modernity," "postmodernity," the "information society." In my view, the network society incorporates the media as well as the communication technology and gives no prime position to physical meetings.

5. The exception is in the field of science of technology studies, where the merging of agencies results in the term "actants" to highlight that human-with-computer is an actor different from human-without-computer (or, for that matter, from computers-without-humans).

6. In broad terms, this discussion about the words "interaction" and "interactive" stems from the different views of the sorts of agency involved. Taking the triangle to another level of abstraction, we can see social science as focused on human-to-human interaction (the triangle's bottom line), the humanities as focused on the meaning arising from the interaction between a human and a text (the cultural part), and informatics as focused on the structural part, with the interface as framing the interaction between the human and the computer (and representing the intercomputer action as well).

7. Swatch Internet Time (http://www.swatch.com/internettime) divides the global day into one thousand beats. New Earth Time (http://newearthtime.net) uses the circle's 360 degrees. In both methods, the goal is to establish a "global now" to facilitate coordination and orientation when online.

8. In an earlier article (Gotved 2002), I termed the categories *metaphorical space, interface space,* and *social space*. The content, however, is the same.

REFERENCES

Adam, B. (1995) *Timewatch: The Social Analysis of Time.* Cambridge, UK: Polity.

Baym, N. (1995) The Emergence of Community in Computer-Mediated Communication. In S. Jones (ed.), *Cybersociety. Computer-Mediated Communication and Community,* pp. 138–163. Thousand Oaks, CA: Sage.

Baym, N. (1997) Interpreting Soap Operas and Creating Community: Inside a Electronic Fan Culture. In S. Kiesler (ed.), *Culture of the Internet,* pp. 103–120. Mahwah, NJ: Lawrence Erlbaum.

Baym, N. (2000) *Tune In, Log On: Soaps, Fandom, and Online Community.* Thousand Oaks, CA: Sage.

Boudreau, F. A., and W. M. Newman. (1993) *Understanding Social Life.* St. Paul, MN: West.

Castells, M. (1996) *The Rise of the Network Society.* Malden, MA: Blackwell.

Castells, M. (2000) Materials for an Exploratory Theory of the Network Society. *British Journal of Sociology* 51(1): 5–24.

Dodge, M., and R. Kitchin. (2001) *Mapping Cyberspace.* London: Routledge.

Elias, N. (1992) *Time: An Essay.* Oxford, UK: Blackwell.

Gotved, S. (2000) *Cybersociologi—det samme på en anden måde* [Cybersociology —Same Old Thing in a New Disguise]. Dissertation, in Danish, Department of Sociology, University of Copenhagen.

Gotved, S. (2002) Spatial Dimensions in Online Communities. *space and culture* 5(4): 405–414.

Hine, C. (2000) *Virtual Ethnography.* London: Sage.

Kendall, L. (2002) *Hanging Out in the Virtual Pub: Masculinities and Relationships Online.* Berkeley: University of California Press.

Lefebvre, H. (1974/1991) *The Production of Space.* Malden, MA: Blackwell.

Markham, A. N. (1998) *Life Online: Researching Real Experience in Virtual Space.* Walnut Creek, CA: AltaMira.

Sharf, B. F. (1999) Beyond Netiquette: The Ethics of Doing Naturalistic Discourse Research on the Internet. In S. G. Jones (ed.), *Doing Internet Research,* pp. 243–256. Thousand Oaks, CA: Sage.

Shields, R. (1991) *Places on the Margin: Alternative Geographies of Modernity.* London: Routledge.

Shields, R. (1999) *Lefebvre, Love and Struggle: Spatial Dialectics.* London: Routledge.

Sterne, J. (1999) Thinking the Internet: Cultural Studies versus the Millennium. In S. G. Jones (ed.), *Doing Internet Research,* pp. 257–287. Thousand Oaks, CA: Sage.

Tepper, M. (1997) Usenet Communities and the Cultural Politics of Information. In D. Porter (ed.), *Internet Culture,* pp. 39–54. London: Routledge.

Part III

Cultural Difference in/and Cyberculture

Chapter 16

E-scaping Boundaries
Bridging Cyberspace and Diaspora Studies through Nethnography

Emily Noelle Ignacio

Recent events demonstrate that the sociology of race and cultural studies should no longer be confined to national contexts, especially in the age of the Internet. Nations, "always already" entities, have been constructed and maintained largely through technological breakthroughs like print capitalism, easily reproduced prints and photographs, TV and satellite images, and even museums and maps (Anderson 1991). In all these cases, the images of a nation often go through a gate-keeping process, whereby some authoritative figures uphold and approve the images that reflect current political alignments. Often, these images are racialized and gendered, which historically has helped justify the creation and maintenance of existing inequalities. But what happens when images of a nation—or even race, culture, and gender—don't just cross national boundaries but are articulated through technological advances across national borders by anyone, regardless of authority?

We have seen how new technological advances can change the history of a nation. For example, in 2000, demonstrators in the Philippines who pushed for then-president Joseph Estrada's resignation from office congregated and organized largely through the use of "texting" through cell phones—with Filipinos within the Philippines as well as their friends and relatives around the world.[1] Similarly, the antiglobalization and antiwar protests from Seattle to Quebec to Genoa to Cancun in the late 1990s and early fall 2002 were also largely organized through alternative media sources on the Internet.[2] But, when studying diasporas, most scholars have not yet assessed the impact of these new technologies on members, particularly regarding members' ideas of national or ethnic identity or community. Because the Internet is a transnational space where people from all over the world can converge, I believe that through nethnography people interested in diasporic studies and/or computer-mediated communication can better examine how this kind of technology affects the construction of national, racial, ethnic, and gendered identities and can help create new coalitions apart from, rather than through the maintenance of, these socially constructed boundaries.

Building Diasporic Community

Scholars who emphasize the importance of deconstructionism and identity formation are often criticized for being stuck in the ivory tower, apolitical, and divorced from real-life social issues and demands for social justice. But, I argue, it is in the analysis of construction and reconstruction of these differences that we may be able to envision a new way to form communities and strive for social justice. As stated before, some social-justice-oriented communities have been able to use the Internet to learn more and articulate their concerns about various social issues, such as war and globalization. With respect to diasporas, it has been my experience that what starts out as a "cultural" newsgroup can swiftly turn into a place where social issues are discussed and debated, especially because sociopolitical policies, processes, and tactics affect various races, nations, social classes, and genders differently. And since members of diasporas, by definition, are located in different places, through these discussions the members of the newsgroup are able to see these processes at work. In my experience, they have also chosen to redefine themselves through a list of jokes that incorporates these sociopolitical issues as a common underlying history (Ignacio 2005).

National and Ethnic Identities in the Age of the Internet

The desire to find an authentic self by traveling to the homeland is not new. Although many studies concentrate on "external" factors such as the push and pull of immigration and the impact of the economy and governmental policies on assimilation, others have studied the relationship between the individual and society (see, for example, Boyarin 1994; Flores

1993; and Radhakrishnan 1996) and the importance of finding one's ethnic and/or racial identity (Espiritu 1996, 2003).

The importance of identity differs in various contexts. Studies on immigrants and racial and ethnic groups have revealed that because of increasing migration and transnational networks and the rise of nationalist and multicultural movements, establishing identity is desired not for assimilation but for differentiation (Espiritu 1994; Waters 1990). Many people wish to learn about their culture because they want to recapture the power to name themselves. That is, they need an identity, not only so they know their own roots but also so others can learn of their roots. And in the aftermath of September 11, 2001, as news spread of possible al-Qaeda members living within the United States, many people wished for easily identifiable ways to draw boundaries between "real" and "fake" Americans, as legal immigration papers and even naturalized citizenship no longer seemed to be sufficient.[3]

However, as stated before, cultures, nations, races, and identities are constantly being redefined in both real and virtual life, actively constructed and maintained through various media and the sciences (Anderson 1991). But in the age of the Internet, these categories have the potential to be redefined in different ways, as members of the diaspora have the opportunity to discover the global historical processes that underlie their local histories and personal experiences. I argue that the Internet makes possible the sharing of identities about culture and politics but that it also makes possible fierce debate over knowledge. In some circumstances, an Internet forum allows people to re-create a larger picture depending on the different information and/or experiences of the participants.

Furthermore, in their attempt to "go to the source," participants have the unique opportunity to discover that "the source" is itself defined and redefined. In the case of a former colonial subject, that redefinition is often still in relation to the colonial power. Therefore, it is important to study the impacts of globalization, colonization, racism, and other sociopolitical processes on each diasporic group separately so as to illuminate the specific ways inequalities are maintained. In doing so, we can put pieces of the puzzle together and better understand how and why inequalities are maintained and exactly who benefits.

While many scholars of computer-mediated communication have extensively studied how this technology changes gender identities, the link between postmodern subjectivities and the Net, and the prevalence of racial stereotypes on the Net (Jones 1995; Kolko, Nakamura, and Rodman

1999; Nakamura 2002; Poster 1995), we still have not yet systematically examined *continued* discussions online and their effects on an online community's ideas about national culture, race, gender, and/or ethnicity.

Merging Computer-Mediated Communication and Postcolonial Studies: Extending Ideas about Race, Class, Gender, and Nation

Both computer-mediated communication (CMC) and postcolonial scholars analyze the creation and re-creation of identity. Yet these discourses have not intersected with each other because their reasons for studying identity transformation are different.[4] Postcolonial theorists have been and still are focused on peeling away the "fixed shapes of historic ethnicity"; their studies often revolve around the fragmentation and (re-)creation of ethnic (as well as racial and gender) identities. Many seminal works on postcoloniality explore, through archival research on the colonial period, the development, maintenance, and possible decentering of national, cultural, racial, gender, and/or ethnic identities (McClintock 1997; Rafael 1993; Stoler 1997). By studying the images of male and female colonizers/colonized, we learn how both patriarchy and ethnocentrism (and their intersection) are used to justify imperialism and colonialism. Deconstructing "embedded" stereotypes and grand narratives are two major goals of postcolonial writers (Hall 1990). Studies of construction in the present show us how racialized/gendered images of the colonizer and colonized continue to be maintained (Gilroy 1993; Hall 1990; Radhakrishnan 1996). But they also show the importance of imagination and shared experience in possibly re-creating images in such a way that they are antiracist, antisexist, and empowering of the colonized.

Because global hierarchies were partially justified through the divisions between "civilized" and "uncivilized" and other dichotomies, images and/ or memories of one's "culture" must be included in the notion of "homelands," as well as in that of diasporic identity (Appadurai 1991; Boyarin 1994; Chow 1993; Radhakrishnan 1996). Identities are often not contingent upon a physical return (as many diasporic members cannot afford to go home) but on an imaginary return. Many second-generation immigrants define their ethnic identity against the memories of the homeland and against the images of the homeland and the stories of people who have traveled there (Abelmann and Lie 1995; Lie 1995). In addition, this return to the homeland is also desired by some people who *reside within* the homeland and who believe globalization has destroyed their motherland and culture (Ignacio 2005).

Since political struggles and personal experiences are intertwined, researchers argue that we must also examine the role of *experience* in the making of diasporic identity (Radhakrishnan 1996). Ethnicities are defined against lived and imagined experiences, as well as against perceived notions of "homelands" and "cultures" (Appadurai 1991). Images of the host countries and homelands travel across boundaries through transnational networks that blur boundaries between nations. These images also affect people's real lives. As an example, Arjun Appadurai describes the plight of the women involved in the sex tours in Asia. Here, women make money by catering to Western ideas of Asian women. These images of Asian women affect gender politics not only in these bars but also worldwide. Because images travel through these ethnoscapes so easily, he states that scholars must incorporate the links between imagination and social life into ethnographies.

A systematic analysis of experiences and these imaginary returns to either a home never seen or a home never experienced can provide insight into the workings of "global ethnoscapes" and the difficulties of forming communities based on an identification with static cultures.[5] In transnational cultural spaces such as Internet newsgroups, we can see how diasporic members identify membership in the culture. For example, I have found that in order to define "Filipinoness" the participants on soc.culture.filipino negotiated "culture" and, in doing so, uncovered the illusion of authenticity. As this negotiation occurred, they drew mostly upon images of the Philippines and the United States, common history, and lived and imagined experience to construct Filipino identity (Ignacio 2005).

Still, postcolonial writers study the maintenance of racial, national, cultural, and/or gendered imagery *outside* cyberspace. This is not to say that postcolonial scholars have not written about the present impact of new global media on diasporic members. Paul Gilroy (1993), Rajagopalan Radhakrishnan (1996), Stuart Hall (1990), and Arjun Appadurai (1991) are among many scholars who have traced cultural (re)productions across national boundaries. However, postcolonial studies remain in the realm of "real life" and usually within the colonial period largely because most postcolonial scholars have been concerned with exposing the *origin* of the constructed images. I argue that Internet research can add to our understanding of postcoloniality (and postmodernity) in that it allows us to see the process of redefinition among self-defined members of diasporas in a decentered space. Because of this, there is the potential for more voices to be heard simultaneously (Poster 1995, 1998).

Although CMC scholars have extensively studied gender identities, the link between postmodern subjectivities and the Net (Jones 1995; Poster 1995), and the continuation of racialized discourse in cyberspace (Kolko, Nakamura, and Rodman 1999; Nakamura 2002), none has systematically studied over a long period of time how people online radically alter their own ideas of national cultures, race, and/or ethnicity after continued discussion within one transnational community. The CMC study that has come closest to engaging postcolonial studies is Mark Poster's (1998) research on "Virtual Ethnicities." Poster's (1998, p. 209) analysis of a listserv, whose members were predominantly Jewish and which dealt with subjects pertaining to Jews, showed that because of the changing nature of Net content, "individuals in cyberspace cannot attach to objects in the fixed shapes of historic ethnicity." In other words, defining one authentic Jewish identity was extremely difficult because the listserv participants brought different experiences and information to the listserv and because the subjects they discussed changed so rapidly. However, given the conversations prevalent within Internet studies at the time, Poster focused mostly on proving that virtual communities are real communities, not on examining or describing the *process* by which the participants articulated ethnicity.

Furthermore, some scholars have added to a utopian vision of the Internet by documenting instances within newsgroups and Multi-User Dimensions (MUDs or Multi-User Dungeons, a class of multiplayer interactive game accessible via the Internet or a modem) where peaceful communication and collaboration take place (Baym 1995a, 1995b; Correll 1995; Rheingold 1993). They found that the cultures' characteristics and identities on these newsgroups and MUDs were negotiated by the participants. Since most newsgroups are currently used by participants who have no particular offline ties to one another to discuss hobbies and personal interests, the participants on these newsgroups actively try to form communities because they believe that more meaningful discussions can occur when a community is established (Baym 1995b). Thus, Internet communities are not dependent on formal membership or geographical space (Stacey 1969; Strauss 1978). Instead, like other "social worlds" (Shibutani 1955; Strauss 1978), they are groups with commitments to at least one main activity.

Sherry Turkle (1994) described the communities she studied as "parallel worlds"; that is, they were separate from the "real world," and new communities and community practices emerged in these locations. But many Internet communities are based on communities within the "real," nonvirtual world, for example, soc.culture Usenet groups. So even though the soc.culture newsgroups are located in a transnational space, they are still based on traditional, boundaried spaces (usually nations). Thus, I argue, these particular transnational locations are "perpendicular worlds," which computer-mediated-communication theorists have not yet systematically analyzed.

Unlike perpendicular lines, however, each world is constantly changing. That is, the Internet world changes as the participants debate issues and as the participants themselves change. Similarly, the lines connecting the Internet to the "real" world change. Each person brings different experiences and bodies of knowledge to Internet discussions. I argue that through nethnography scholars can better see how the participants in newsgroups or spaces dedicated to specific cultures rearticulate the "real world" categories as these discussions continue.

Doing Nethnography: Merging Participant Observation and Textual Analysis

People constantly rearticulate their identity in nonvirtual locations; I have witnessed this throughout my life. Although these events were sporadic, I saw my aunts' rearticulate their identity each time relatives from the Philippines or third-generation Filipino Americans visited our home. More-recent immigrants or visitors from the Philippines highlighted the "Americanness" of my first-generation family members, whereas third-generation Filipino Americans reinforced their "Filipinoness." However, my witnessing of these shifting identities occurred intermittently, usually during summer barbecues or at weddings and ending once people went home. In contrast, because soc.culture.filpino is centered upon the Filipino community and culture, I was able to watch this articulation and rearticulation take place between people physically located in different places on a daily basis (Ignacio 2005). By watching the debates unfold, I could see how members of the diaspora established what Filipino identity means with people back home and how people at home forged an identity with members of the diaspora, especially those in the old colonial country.

In the movie *Chan Is Missing* (Wang 1989), a cab driver (Jo) and his nephew (Rick) search for a man who has mysteriously disappeared (Chan

Hung). As the film progresses, we soon realize that Chan Hung symbolizes Chinese identity and that this identity is elusive. The director, Wayne Wang, illustrates this by showing the diversity of the Chinese American community; every Chinese immigrant and Chinese American Jo meets has different characteristics and describes Chan differently. At the end, Jo remarks that the more he looks for Chan/identity, the more confused he becomes. This exercise leads him to question and articulate his own definition of Chinese identity. He recounts the many conflicting descriptions of Chan he received from the people he met and concludes that the only way he can find identity is to "look into the puddle." In other words, he finds that definitions of Chinese identity are unique to each person and that there is no one unifying identity.

As a participant-observer of the newsgroup, my role was similar to Jo's in that I kept track of what people said about Filipino identity and how my own ideas changed. To do this, I chose to use the method of instances (Denzin 1998; Psthas 1995) to examine the features and structures of instances or occurrences on the threads in the newsgroup. Mikhail Bakhtin (1986) has argued that, when studying conversations, scholars should study utterances and responses rather than analyzing sentence structures. Each utterance has its own context and is in itself a rejoinder to another utterance. In addition, researchers should examine how others responded to the speaker's utterance. The method of instances is based on the same premise: each instance (in my case, each post) contains a context that members understand and respond to. I chose this method because I wanted to see what people debated, how the debates played out, and if and how they articulated Filipino identity during these debates.

Specifically, scholars use the method of instances to analyze (1) the mechanics of conversations (e.g., taking turns in conversation) and/or (2) participants' attribution of meaning to each utterance (e.g., did the participant think the last utterance was a question or an answer?). Because conversation analysis aims to describe the interactional phenomenon within the instance, it is not necessary to accumulate many instances before analysis. Additional instances only "provide another example of the method in action rather than securing the warrantability of the descriptions in the machinery itself" (Benson and Hughes 1991, quoted in Psthas 1995, p. 50). However, in my experience, analyzing collections of instances can reveal the complexity of the interactional phenomenon.

Researchers study these utterances to understand "culture in practice" and to learn about their reciprocal systemic relationship, not just the effects of structure on practice. By studying culture this way, researchers can understand how structures themselves change. And in using the method of instances and the cultural studies perspective, it is possible to analyze the *process* of identity formation. In my case, I was able to see how conversations on the Internet led to the rearticulation of nation, gender, race, and ethnic identity.

Conclusion

Lisa Nakamura (2002) has shown that U.S. racial classifications and negative stereotypes travel onto cyberspace and affect people's interactions. Through the utilization of the method of instances and nethnography, especially on newsgroups, researchers are able to study simultaneously the effects of local and global politics (e.g., global and local racial classifications) on participants' characterization of ethnic, racial, national, or even gender identity. And there is the possibility for them to study—and more important, to *show*—any efforts at new identity formations that are based on *underlying* histories that tie diasporic members' local and global politics. That is, the process of categorization—whether by race, ethnicity, culture, gender, or a combination of these concepts—is based on common sociopolitical issues.

In my research, I examine how technology affects the construction of national, racial, ethnic, and gendered identities. Specifically, through "nethnography" I was able to examine how national, racial, and ethnic identity was articulated, reified, and re-created within the soc.culture.filipino newsgroup on the Internet (Ignacio 2005). Through an extensive analysis of several debates, I witnessed community and identity formation of a diaspora in relation to various political and polemical arguments— mainly neocolonialism, Eurocentrism, Orientalism, and patriarchy. This was important not only because I was able to see the participants rearticulate their ideas of community building but also because I was able to see how participants anchored identity on experiences and cultural artifacts created by sociohistorical issues, rather than on an assumption of the authenticity of experience or culture. In doing so, I was able to see how computer-mediated communication can help members of a diaspora better understand their post- or neocolonial situation and can serve as a possible site for broader organizing and community formation. And as a result of seeing the impact of oppressive practices on members of the

Filipino diaspora, hopefully, people of all races and ethnicities will see the commonalities each community faces, instead of just focusing on the differences between them.

As more people depend on the Internet and other technologies that allow for swift, synchronous transnational communication to advance political agendas, studying the rearticulation of identities is increasingly important. As I write, the United States is in the middle of a war with Iraq and Afghanistan. Israel has just bombed Syria, and leaders of Arab nations around the world are outwardly putting aside national interests in the hope of creating a stronger coalition to defend citizens and noncitizens with whom they share a common history. In addition, people who have analyzed very carefully the creation, maintenance, and now realignment of the nation-states created through the Ottoman Empire are well aware that an anti-Western alliance has already been carefully formed. By citing historical and ideological commonalities, dangerous alliances have been formed across nation-states, alliances that threaten all of our lives, regardless of nation, culture, ethnicity, race, gender, or sexuality. Clearly national boundaries are porous, and an adherence to ideas of nations as boundaried could, analysts warn, lead to more international warfare and continued acts of terrorism. Yet while some members of our government insist upon forming national alliances and treating these wars as between nations, a close look at the opposition to these ongoing wars shows that similar transnational ties are being formed by people who wish to strive for peace. Like the Filipinos who mobilized against then-president Estrada in 2000, much of the initial organizing begins within diasporic communities across nations and on the Internet.[6] Because "real life" is increasingly influenced by computer-mediated communications, cyberspace and diaspora studies can only benefit from doing nethnography.

NOTES

1. In 2001, as President Estrada faced impeachment, an estimated seventy million Filipinos passed a message via texting to gather at a religious shrine and demand that Estrada step down from office. Four days later, after intense rallying at this shrine, Estrada stepped down (*Wired* 2001).

2. Internet 'zines such as commondreams.org and indymedia.org and online magazines such as thenation.com and znet.org have been instrumental in organizing antiglobalization and antiwar protests.

3. After September 11, people of many different ethnicities and races affirmed

their national pride by displaying the U.S. flag at their residences, on their cars, and on many other possessions. For racial minorities, particularly those who have physical characteristics that could be deemed "Arab looking," the prominent displays of the U.S. flag and other American symbols was particularly important, as the symbols "protected" them from their neighbors' wrath. Even though many of these people were well aware that they may be targeted by the government by virtue of their surnames, residential neighborhoods, national origins, and/or physical features, many felt they could deflect individuals' violence toward them by participating in visible acts of solidarity and patriotism.

4. Scholars who study CMC are generally concerned with how technology will affect traditional social units such as communities and the self (Baym 1995a; Danet 1998; Jones 1995). Thus, they often document either the transcendence and/or erasure of traditional identities, and they express a concern that cultural identities will be homogenized because of the current U.S.-centric nature of the World Wide Web. Both CMC and postcolonial scholars, however, show that the Internet can be an arena in which identity can be radically altered (because it is a constantly changing arena that transcends not only time zones but also traditional political boundaries).

5. The term "global ethnoscapes" captures the shifting of "social, territorial, and cultural reproduction of ethnic identity" (Appadurai 1991, p. 191). "Global ethnoscapes" captures the importance of the images of cultures as well as the migration of people. Because of migration, Appadurai argues, diasporas, and technological advances (including print capitalism and television), the definition of ethnicity is contingent upon both lived experience and imagined experience.

6. Editors at thenation.com, indymedia.com, and commondreams.org, possibly inspired by the success of e-mail and Web sites in organizing people at various antiglobalization protests and by the texting revolution in January 2001 that brought President Estrada down, have been actively recruiting supporters for their "No War in Iraq" letter-writing campaign.

REFERENCES

Abelmann, N., and Lie, J. 1995. *Blue Dreams: Korean Americans and the Los Angeles Riots.* Cambridge, MA: Harvard University Press.

Anderson, B. 1991. *Imagined Communities.* London: Verso.

Appadurai, A. 1991. "Global Ethnoscapes: Notes and Queries for a Transnational Anthropology." In *Recapturing Anthropology: Working in the Present,* ed. Richard G. Fox, pp. 191–210. Santa Fe, NM: School of American Research Press.

Bakhtin, M. 1986. *Speech Genres and Other Late Essays.* Austin: University of Texas Press.

Baym, Nancy. 1995a. "The Emergence of Community in Computer-Mediated

Communication." In *CyberSociety: Computer-Mediated Communication and Community*, ed. Steven G. Jones, pp. 138–163. Thousand Oaks, CA: Sage.

Baym, Nancy. 1995b. "From Practice to Culture on Usenet." In *The Cultures of Computing*, ed. Susan Leigh Star, pp. 29–52. Oxford, UK: Blackwell.

Benson, Douglas, and John Hughes. 1991. "Method: Evidence and Inference—Evidence and Inference for Ethnomethodology." In *Ethnomethodology and the Human Sciences*, ed. Graham Button, pp. 109–136. Cambridge: Cambridge University Press.

Boyarin, Jonathan. 1996. *Thinking in Jewish*. Chicago: University of Chicago Press.

———, ed. 1994. *Remapping Memory: The Politics of TimeSpace*. Minneapolis: University of Minnesota Press.

Chow, Rey. 1993. *Writing Diaspora*. Bloomington: Indiana University Press.

Correll, Shelley. 1995. "The Ethnography of an Electronic Bar." *Journal of Contemporary Ethnography* 24(3): 270–298.

Danet, Brenda. 1998. "Text as Mask: Gender, Play, and Performance on the Internet." In *Cybersociety 2.0*, ed. Steven G. Jones, pp. 129–158. Thousand Oaks, CA: Sage.

Denzin, Norman K. 1998. "In Search of the Inner Child: Co-dependency and Gender in a Cyberspace Community." In *Emotions in Social Life*, ed. Gillian Bendelow and Simon J. Williams, pp. 97–119. London: Routledge.

Espiritu, Yen Le. 2003. *Homebound*. Berkeley: University of California Press.

———. 1996. *Filipino American Lives*. Philadelphia: Temple University Press.

———. 1994. "The Intersection of Race, Ethnicity, and Class: The Multiple Identities of Second-Generation Filipinos." *Identities*, 1(2–3): 249–273.

Flores, Juan. 1993. *Divided Borders: Essays on Puerto Rican Identity*. Houston: Arte Público.

Gilroy, Paul. 1987. *There Ain't No Black in the Union Jack*. Chicago: University of Chicago Press.

———. 1993. *The Black Atlantic: Modernity and Double Consciousness*. Cambridge, MA: Harvard University Press.

Hall, Stuart. 1996. "Introduction: Who Needs 'Identity'?" In *Questions of Cultural Identity*, ed. Stuart Hall and Paul du Gay, pp. 1–17. London: Sage.

———. 1990. "Cultural Identity and Diaspora." In *Identity: Community, Culture, Difference*, ed. J. Rutherford, pp. 222–237. London: Lawrence and Wishart.

Ignacio, Emily Noelle. 2005. *Building Diaspora: Filipino Community Formation on the Internet*. New Brunswick, NJ: Rutgers University Press.

Jones, Steven G. 1995. "Understanding Community in the Information Age." In *CyberSociety: Computer-Mediated Communication and Community*, ed. Steven G. Jones, pp. 10–35. Thousand Oaks, CA: Sage.

Kolko, Beth E., Lisa Nakamura, and Gilbert B. Rodman, eds. 1999. *Race in Cyberspace*. New York: Routledge.

Lie, John. 1995. "From International Migration to Transnational Diaspora." *Contemporary Sociology* 24 (July 4): 303–306.

McClintock, Anne. 1997. " 'No Longer in a Future Heaven': Gender, Race, and Nationalism." In *Sites of Desire, Economics of Pleasure: Sexualities in Asia and the Pacific,* ed. Lenore Manderson and Margaret Jolly, pp. 89–112. Chicago: University of Chicago Press.

Nakamura, Lisa. 2002. *Cybertypes: Race, Ethnicity, and Identity on the Internet.* New York: Routledge.

Poster, Mark. 1998. "Virtual Ethnicity: Tribal Identity in an Age of Global Communications." In *Cybersociety 2.0,* ed. Steven G. Jones, pp. 184–211. Thousand Oaks, CA: Sage.

———. 1995. "Postmodern Virtualities." In *Cyberspace/Cyberbodies/Cyberpunk: Cultures of Technological Embodiment,* ed. Mike Featherstone and Roger Burrows, pp. 79–96. Thousand Oaks, CA: Sage.

Psthas, George. 1995. *Conversation Analysis.* Thousand Oaks, CA: Sage.

Radhakrishnan, Rajagopalan. 1996. *Diasporic Meditations: Between Home and Location.* Minneapolis: University of Minnesota Press.

Rafael, Vicente L. 2000. *White Love and Other Events in Filipino History.* Durham, NC: Duke University Press.

———. 1993. *Contracting Colonialism: Translation and Christian Conversion in Tagalog Society under Early Spanish Rule.* Durham, NC: Duke University Press.

Rheingold, Howard. 1993. *The Virtual Community.* New York: Harper Perennial.

Shibutani, Tomatsu. 1955. "Reference Groups as Perspectives." *American Journal of Sociology* 60: 562–569.

Stacey, Margaret. 1969. "The Myth of Community Studies." *British Journal of Sociology* 20(2): 134–147.

Stoler, A. 1997. "Educating Desire in Colonial Southeast Asia: Foucault, Freud, and Imperialist Sexualities." In *Sites of Desire, Economics of Pleasure: Sexualities in Asia and the Pacific,* ed. Lenore Manderson and Margaret Jolly, pp. 27–47. Chicago: University of Chicago Press.

Strauss, Anselm. 1978. "A Social World Perspective." *Studies in Symbolic Interaction* 1: 119–128.

Turkle, Sherry. 1994. "Constructions and Reconstructions of Self in Virtual Reality: Playing in the MUDs." *Mind, Culture, and Activity* 1(3): 158–167.

Wang, Wayne. 1989. *Chan Is Missing.* New York: New Yorker Video.

———. 1985. *Dim Sum.* Beverly Hills, CA: Pacific Arts Video.

Waters, Mary C. 1990. *Ethnic Options: Choosing Identities in America.* Berkeley: University of California Press.

Wired. 2001. "Estrada Got the Message." January 23. Available at http://www.wired.com/news/business/0,1367,41360,00.html.

Chapter 17

An Interdisciplinary Approach to the Study of Cybercultures

Madhavi Mallapragada

This chapter argues for an interdisciplinary approach to the study of cybercultures, an argument that has grown out of my frustration with the existing theoretical and analytical models dominant within the field of cyberculture studies. In my own work that looks at the cybercultures of Indian Americans, I found it productive and necessary to approach my project within an interdisciplinary framework that engages with the traditionally different disciplinary formations of diaspora studies, gender studies, postcolonial studies, and media and cultural studies. Although my larger argument is that cyberculture studies has a lot to gain by creatively engaging with the theoretical arguments and interventions made in these other overlapping yet distinct fields, in this chapter I will use the notion of "home" as discussed in diaspora and gender studies to illustrate my point.

Diaspora and gender studies offer valuable insights into the centrality of the notion of "home" in organizing, representing, and mobilizing our spatial worlds, social relations, and cultural imaginations. Gender studies' engagement with the politics of the "private" space of the home has illuminated the role of the physical space of the family unit in strategically articulating a gendered discourse of space and place to social relations. Diaspora studies extends the discussion of the "private" home and the "public" outside by addressing them within a transnational framework. For diaspora studies, the notion of the "homeland" has been central to addressing issues of identity and belonging in migrant contexts. Scholars of diasporic cultures have explored how the notion of the "homeland" facilitates the recasting of the "public" nation within the "private" homes of migrant subjects. Recasting the nation, the home of the national community as one's homeland is central to immigrants' negotiation of identity and belonging in their current locations. Home, in a transnational imaginary, is often also the homeland.

I focus on the notion of "home" to make my larger point that cyberculture studies has neglected to address key issues of gender, race, ethnicity, and the national and transnational within virtual cultures. However, the gap can be addressed by looking at the ways in which other disciplinary formations such as diaspora studies and gender studies have approached those very same questions. In particular, I contend that cyberculture studies needs to enter into a dialogue with diaspora studies that in turn would better illuminate some of the key issues at stake in the field of cyberculture studies, namely, the issues of border crossings, time-space compression, transnational connections, dislocation, and relocation. While the notion of "home" has been central to many of the theoretical debates on time, space, and place in diaspora studies, cyberculture studies' interest in "home" pages, ironically, has rarely extended to an engagement with the nuances of the "spaces of belonging" on the Web within specific sociohistorical contexts. Furthermore, cyberculture studies needs to creatively integrate gender studies' insightful analyses of the technologies of the "feminine" and the "masculine" within the household, family, nation, and community with its own traditional focus on virtual identities, digital realities, and virtual communities.

I

Where are you from?
From Holland.
No, where are you *really* from?

—quoted by Ien Ang (2001, p. 29)

Homes are "origin stories" . . . They are *made for coming from.*
—Dietmar Dath (Morse 1999, p. 68)

What are the political stakes in claiming (or sometimes being relegated to) a "home"? —James Clifford (1997, p. 247)

In recent years, diaspora studies has insightfully retheorized the idea of "home" to foreground the multiple histories, diverse contexts, and contradictory meanings of migration and the homeland. The scholarship of Paul Gilroy, James Clifford, Smadar Lavie, Stuart Hall, and Arjun Appadurai, among others, has complicated the conventional dualism between *home* (land) and *away* that has characterized traditional diaspora studies. By critiquing the imperializing discourse of the nation-state, the essentialized notions of cultural identity, and the universalizing history of the migrant condition, these scholars have emphasized the constructions and contestations of homes away from home—the homeland. In the process, they have dismantled static notions of home and homeland that had shaped traditional understandings of border crossings. In emphasizing the different imaginings of homeland, these scholars were writing against a dominant understanding of homeland that was embedded in conventional understandings of diaspora in academic and popular discourse.

William Safran's (1991) article "Diaspora in Modern Societies: Myths of Homeland and Return" is commonly acknowledged to be a classic example of a conventional understanding of diaspora. In this article, Safran offers a checklist of six characteristics to identify diaspora. Within his framework, to qualify as a diaspora, the members must have ancestors that are dispersed from one or two centers to many regions, must retain a collective memory of their original homeland, must believe they are not and perhaps cannot be fully accepted by the host society, must aspire to eventually return to their original homeland, must remain committed to the maintenance and restoration of the homeland, and finally must continue to relate to that homeland and to define their collective consciousness by that relationship.

After Safran's rigid formulation of diaspora emerged in the early 1990s, subsequent theorizations of the term have rigorously challenged his ideal model of diaspora including challenge to his overreliance on the official history of the Jewish diaspora as well as his conflation of migration with exile. Recent interventions, including those of Ella Shohat, James Clifford, Smadar Lavie, and Paul Gilroy have complicated the conventional dualism between *home* (land) and *away* that has characterized mainstream discussions of diaspora. By critiquing the "common territory and time" of the nation-state, the pure essence of cultural identity, and the universalizing history of migrant "roots/routes" (Clifford 1994, p. 302), these scholars have explored the construction of homes away from home. In doing so, they have introduced new vocabularies for imagining "home" across borders, through contact zones, and in hybrid cultures. Rey Chow (1993), articulating the notion of a "migrant sensibility," suggests that diaspora and hybridity need to be understood not just as experiences but also as epistemological categories in order to produce forms of knowledge that are dislocated and deterritorialized. The insights of these scholars continue to influence the rethinking of "homeland" and the nation-state in emergent migrant contexts.

Arjun Appadurai (1996), for instance, argues that given the contemporary patterns of border crossings, it is increasingly difficult to talk about homelands as the original territory that migrants leave behind. Appadurai's discussion of diaspora in *Modernity at Large: The Cultural Dimensions of Globalization* recalls Robin Cohen's (1997, p. 175) insightful remark that "globalization and diasporization are separate phenomena with no necessary causal connections, but they 'go together' extraordinarily well." In Appadurai's view, the contemporary global economy is marked by "fundamental disjunctures between economy, culture and politics" (p. 33). Included in the emerging dynamics of global interactions is the altered relationships between nations and states, communities and place, and time and memory. "The past," he says, "is now not a land to return to in a simple politics of memory" (p. 30). In the renegotiation of land, time, memory, and community, the meaning of homeland is reconstituted.

The revisionist accounts of diaspora such as those of Paul Gilroy and James Clifford reject simplistic and deterministic narratives of migrant histories and subjectivities. Paul Gilroy's (1993) study *The Black Atlantic* is a rethinking of the black diaspora, which is repositioned as a cosmopolitan Atlantic phenomenon. In his rethinking, Gilroy presents a transnational counterhistory to the questions of diasporic temporality, historicity, memory, and narrativity that have been "essential" to the discourse of diaspora. Gilroy reframes the terms of the debate about diaspora and homeland by "tracking," in Clifford's sense of the term, the dynamic "transnational migrant circuits" (Roger Rouse's famous phrase; Rouse 1991), constitutive of the black diaspora. In his excellent piece on diaspora, Clifford states that when histories of diaspora are written with a view to track rather than police the "roots/routes" of migrant peoples, the discourse of diaspora will of necessity have to shift to address the rearticulations of "travels, home, memories and transnational connections" (Clifford 1994, p. 311).

By tracking diverse migrant contexts and reading against the grain of traditional diaspora histories, contemporary diaspora studies has engendered a rethinking of the relationship between place, culture, home, community, and nation. This has in turn made the concept of migration more subtle in its scope to now include "migration that emphasizes contractual relationships, family visits, intermittent stays abroad, and sojourning as opposed to permanent settlement and the exclusive adoption of the citizenship of a destination country" (Cohen 1997, p. 157). As Clifford, among others, points out, the critical use of the term *diaspora* does not refer to any essential pattern of migration and settlement. It is a conceptual category that foregrounds movement, borders, dialogic processes, and constructs of *home* and *away* and of *self* and *other* as significant ways in which identity formation takes place (1994, p. 311).

II

Gender studies, especially from a postcolonial perspective, is particularly valuable for foregrounding the relations between home and nation, woman, culture, the public, and the private. In her work on Indian immigrants in the United States, Annanya Bhattacharjee (1998) illustrates the displacement of the community's dominant construction of Indianness in light of the question of domestic violence. Bhattacharjee's critique of the dominant construction of Indian national identity within the immigrant community reveals the centrality of notions of home—as household and homeland—in transnational settings. Furthermore, it reveals how a gendered discourse of social roles and power relations within the domestic household is critical to the maintenance of idealized constructions of the domestic space of the private home and the collective nationalist space of the immigrant community in the current location.

Bhattacharjee illustrates this by narrating an incident that occurred during a public celebration of the popular annual Hindu religious festival Diwali in New York City. She notes that although the organizers of the event did not have trouble with the idea that a Hindu religious festival was being recast as an "Indian" festival, they had strong objections to the participation of Sakhi, a South Asian women's organization, particularly because of Sakhi's idea of staging a play highlighting "select aspects of the family and women's roles in Indian society" (1998, p. 169). Bhattacharjee argues that recasting a Hindu festival as an "Indian" cultural event served the cultural agenda of the organizers, who participate in and benefit from a hegemonic discourse of India as a Hindu nation. On the other hand, the trouble with Sakhi was that its role as an organization addressing the needs of South Asian women facing domestic abuse disrupted the ideal narrative of the domestic home in diaspora as a microcosm of the ideal nation. Bhattacharjee notes that the very presence of Sakhi threatened to disrupt a "persistent theme of Indian nationalism," one in which the woman "becomes a metaphor for the purity, the sanctity and chastity of the Ancient Spirit that is India" (p. 170). By representing the violence against women within the domestic, the private, and the household, Sakhi offered a public image of the disjuncture between myth and reality in the lives of women in the household and the homeland.

Bhattacharjee's critique invokes postcolonial historian Partha Chatterjee's insights in *The Nation and Its Fragments* (1993), a study of nationalist thought in colonial India. In his study, Chatterjee argues that the hegemonic project of nation-building relied on the construct of the new Hindu woman as sign for nation in colonial India. Chatterjee's analysis of the nationalist response in colonial India reveals the centrality of the notion of home to the construction of a gendered discourse of the nation. Chatterjee argues that the discourse of nationalism divided the domain of culture into its material and spiritual spheres and constructed an analogous relationship between a material/spiritual divide and an outer/inner dichotomy. Furthermore, it applied the material/outer and spiritual/inner dichotomy to "the matter of concrete day to day living," thereby "separating social space into ghar and bahir, the home and the world" (p. 120). By marking the outer world as the domain of the material and the masculine and, correspondingly, the inner world as the domain of the spiritual and the feminine, the hegemonic nationalist project created an identification of social roles by gender to correspond with the separation of social space into inner and outer. This identification allowed the nationalists to make the case that as long as India held fast to its spiritual values, it could never be colonized in the true sense of the term. It followed that as long as the inner sphere (the domain of the spiritual) was preserved, colonialism was a failed project. Ultimately it was by casting the spiritual qualities of self-sacrifice, benevolence, devotion, and religiosity as the dominant characteristics of femininity and investing the middle-class Hindu woman with the task of cultural preservation in the private space of the home that the nationalist project succeeded in producing a discourse of the authentic uncolonized Indian nation as existing in the domestic/inner sphere.

In her study of the relationship between India's state-run television station Doordarshan and the construction of narratives about the "new Indian woman" in the late 1980s and 1990s, Purnima Mankekar (1999) echoes Partha Chatterjee when she argues that the construct of "Indian

womanhood" continues to frame the postcolonial nation's dominant construction of national culture and identity. In particular, Mankekar examines how the televising of the Hindu religious epic *Mahabharat* became
the site for the construction and contestation of narratives about the nation, woman, family, work, the domestic, and the public at a time of social
and cultural upheaval. Closely examining the construction of female identities in *Mahabharat* and the "meanings" female audiences made of it,
Mankekar insightfully points to the critical role of home technologies in
the construction and disruption of public, idealized narratives about the
nation and its women.

III

Cyberculture studies has for the most part neglected the relationship between home and cyberspace. Though it has enthusiastically embraced the
idea of the community and the homepage, it has rarely posed the question
What kinds of relations exist between virtual and "real" homes? In addressing issues of culture and identity, while some scholars, like Ziauddin
Sardar (1996), ponder the perils of cyberimperialism, others, like Alluc-
quère Rosanne Stone (2000, p. 504), wonder, "Will the real body please
stand up?" In dealing with issues of the cybernetic body, the virtual community, and the imperial/empowering Web, scholars have rarely paused
to interrogate the domains of social life such as the household, the neighborhood, and the nation, all of which shape and are in turn shaped by the
forms and practices of the Web.

   Early discussions of online communities clearly veered between utopian and dystopian visions of network-enabled relationships between
people stretched across time and space. Much of the deliberation revolved
around the disjuncture between the real versus the virtual identities of
communities. For some, including Howard Rheingold (1993) and Sherry
Turkle (1995), the communities enabled by online networks, overcoming
the barriers of space and time and, in turn, conferring anonymity and
interactive agency on the user, were nothing short of ideal. For others,
like Arturo Escobar (1996), Sardar (1996), and Shawn P. Wilbur (1997), it
is precisely the anonymity and displacement of "real" social relations in
cyberspace that is deeply unsettling. Furthermore, the so-called digital divide caused some of the early scholars to argue that the electronic frontier
was, not surprisingly, colonized by the First World elite. Others, such as

Mark Poster (1995), have introduced new modalities for framing community by articulating the ideas of democracy, citizenship, public interest, and public sphere to the online mobilization of constituencies of shared interests. While scholars like Poster intervene in the debate on community by inserting questions about the constitution of the "public" in any kind of community, they rarely ground their macro-theorizations of the public sphere on the Internet within the micro-processes of representations of the "private" home, the "public" homeland, and the "public and private" homepage, all of which are, as I argue, crucial to the enabling of community in online places. Ananda Mitra's (2000) essay "Virtual Commonality: Looking for India on the Internet," in which he discusses the Usenet group soc.culture.indian, offers an interesting though limited analysis of nation and homeland in the construction of community in cyberspace. Invoking Benedict Anderson's (1983) oft-quoted formulation of the nation as "imagined community," Mitra writes, "The national newsgroups become particularly important in this respect since the electronic community is produced in the *same way* that Anderson's imagined community becomes a nation" (2000, p. 687; emphasis mine). For Mitra, then, Usenet groups function in exactly the same ways as Anderson suggests the novel and the vernacular newspapers did in the context of Western nationalisms. In Anderson's argument about print capitalism, the conventions of the realist novel and the vernacular newspaper, including narrative temporality and simultaneity, enabled the collective identification of dispersed subjects around the idea of a shared time and space, which in turn were essential to the discourse of the nation. In Mitra's discussion, questions of narrative temporality and simultaneity are left uninterrogated. Although the movement of people across borders is acknowledged, the disruption and reconfiguration of the spatial and temporal imaginaries of the nation-state in cyber and diasporic places is ultimately left unaccounted for. Furthermore, the interesting and complex ways in which cyber technologies force a rethinking of notions of private and public, feminine and masculine, migrant and citizen, self and community, domestic and outside, nation and the transnational are left unexamined.

To conclude, current theorizations of home in cyberculture studies are woefully inadequate in addressing the diverse representations of home on the Web. Transnational social imaginaries and the reconfiguration of home in the new global order are issues that have not been adequately addressed in cyberculture studies. Take, for instance, the emergence of cyber Hindu Indian temples on the Web. Many of the cyber temples are virtual

replicas of existing temple structures in the "real" world. What is particularly fascinating about cyber temples is the attempt to re-create for the
virtual devotee the specific elements of a visit to the temple in the offline
world. Hence, in many instances, virtual visitors to cyber temples need
to "click" on the temple door to virtually enter its sacred space. Once
inside, they are invited to navigate their way through the different sections
of the temple by virtually clicking their way to the desired sections. This
act clearly attempts to reenact for the visitor the act of walking through
several doors to access different parts of a given temple in offline spaces.
Cyber Hindu temples strategically tap into diasporic desire and nostalgia
for the "original" temple and attempt to negotiate the realities of visiting
a temple in the current location. In the case of the United States, such a
visit involves driving long distances, an architectural style not very reminiscent of traditional Hindu temple structures, and perhaps most important, engaging with the temple as not merely a place of worship but as a
community space clearly organized with several goals in mind. These goals
include reinventing the temple space as a place for Sunday school, keeping
in touch with friends, and getting a date, among others. Cyber temples
emerge in this framework to negotiate multiple contexts. The computers
in the living rooms of diasporic subjects at once allow them to reconfigure
their relations to the immediate, the local, the national, and the transnational. Sitting in their private living rooms, the subjects connected by the
transnational technologies of the Web virtually enter the public space of
the nation's representative temples. Yet unlike the experience of visiting
an offline temple, the cyber visit is marked by an absence of other bodies
in the virtual space of the temple. Simultaneously part of the "public" and
"private" domains, yet interacting with/in them in new and imaginative
ways, immigrant users of cyber temples demonstrate some of the ways in
which Web technologies are refashioning home in virtual and diasporic
settings.

The role of the Web in reconfiguring the household, the homeland, the
family, and the community on the basis of a local, national, and transnational sense of belonging is a critical issue that has been neglected by
cyberculture studies. It is a gap that can be addressed by studying cybercultures within an interdisciplinary framework that engages with the traditionally different disciplinary formations of diaspora studies, gender
studies, postcolonial studies, and media and cultural studies. Although the
notion of the virtual community has offered useful insights into the poli-

tics of identity and belonging in virtual contexts, cyberculture studies has yet to imaginatively delve into the complexities of "home" pages and places on the Web.

REFERENCES

Anderson, B. (1983) *Imagined Communities: Reflections on the Origin and Spread of Nationalism.* London: Verso.

Ang, I. (2001) *On Not Speaking Chinese: Living between Asia and the West.* London: Routledge.

Appadurai, A. (1996) *Modernity at Large: The Cultural Dimensions of Globalization.* Minneapolis: University of Minnesota Press.

Bhattacharjee, A. (1998) "The Habit of Ex-Nomination: Nation, Woman and the Indian Immigrant Bourgeoisie." In S. D. Dasgupta (ed.), *A Patchwork Shawl: Chronicles of South Asian Women in America.* New Brunswick, NJ: Rutgers University Press, pp. 163–185.

Chatterjee, P. (1993) *The Nation and Its Fragments: Colonial and Post-Colonial Histories.* Princeton, NJ: Princeton University Press.

Chow, R. (1993) *Writing Diaspora: Tactics of Intervention in Contemporary Cultural Studies.* Bloomington: Indiana University Press.

Clifford, J. (1994) "Diasporas." *Cultural Anthropology* 9 (3): 302–338.

———. (1997) *Routes.* Cambridge, MA: Harvard University Press.

Cohen, R. (1997) *Global Diasporas: An Introduction.* Seattle: University of Washington Press.

Escobar, A. (1996) Welcome to Cyberia: Notes on the Anthropology of Cyberculture. In Z. Sardar and J. R. Ravetz (eds.), *Cyberfutures: Culture and Politics on the Information Superhighway.* New York: New York University Press, pp. 111–137.

Gilroy, P. (1993) *The Black Atlantic: Modernity and Double Consciousness.* London: Verso.

Mankekar, P. (1999) *Screening Culture, Viewing Politics: An Ethnography of Television, Womanhood and Nation in Postcolonial India.* Durham, NC: Duke University Press.

Mitra, A. (2000) Virtual Commonality: Looking for India on the Internet. In D. Bell and B. M. Kennedy (eds.), *The Cybercultures Reader.* New York: Routledge, pp. 676–697.

Morse, M. (1999) Home: Smell, Taste, Posture, Gleam. In H. Naficy (ed.), *Home, Exile, Homeland: Film, Media, and the Politics of Place.* New York: Routledge, pp. 68–73.

Poster, M. (1995) CyberDemocracy: Internet and the Public Sphere. Available at http://www.hnet.uci.edu/mposter/writings/democ.html.

Rheingold, H. (1993) *The Virtual Community: Homesteading on the Electronic Frontier.* Reading, MA: Addison-Wesley.

Rouse, R. (1991) "Mexican Migration and the Social Space of Postmodernism." *Diaspora* 1 (1): 8–23.

Safran, W. (1991) "Diaspora in Modern Societies: Myths of Homeland and Return." *Diaspora* 1 (1): 83–99.

Sardar, Z. (1996) Alt.civilizations.faq: Cyberspace as the Darker Side of the West. In Z. Sardar and J. R. Ravetz (eds.), *Cyberfutures: Culture and Politics on the Information Superhighway.* New York: New York University Press, pp. 14–41.

Stone, A. R. (2000) Will the Real Body Please Stand Up? In D. Bell and B. M. Kennedy (eds.), *The Cybercultures Reader.* London: Routledge, pp. 504–528.

Turkle, S. (1995) *Life on the Screen: Identity in the Age of the Internet.* New York: Touchstone.

Wilbur, S. P. (1997) "An Archaeology of Cyberspaces: Virtuality, Community, Identity." In D. Porter (ed.), *Internet Culture.* New York: Routledge, pp. 5–22.

Chapter 18

An Action Research (AR) Manifesto for Cyberculture Power to "Marginalized" Cultures of Difference

Bharat Mehra

This chapter explores action research (AR) in cyberculture studies in an effort to make cyberculture more inclusive toward disenfranchised users and achieve social equity for minority and "marginalized" populations. The object of AR is social practice and its transformations, along with the changes that occur in the social institutions and relationships that support it (Kemmis and McTaggart 1988). In the context of race, class, and gender issues in cyberculture, an AR shift seems desirable since it potentially allows traditionally defined "marginalized" users to change their disadvantaged life experiences and better "fit" cyberculture to their real-life needs and expectations. Such an agenda can lead to community-wide social empowerment of disenfranchised groups since it allows them to take action themselves toward scaling existing power and social imbalances based on a redefinition of relationships between various stakeholders in the community.

How can we incorporate action-oriented strategies in cyberculture toward support of democratic social change? How can cyberculture research contribute toward social equity for minority and "marginalized" cultures of difference? How can we as cyberculture researchers become more inclusive in the research process toward disenfranchised users? In order to answer these questions, this chapter presents some characteristics of AR through glimpses from a few projects involving different disadvantaged groups in East-Central Illinois. The presentation of example projects is not all encompassing in any manner; the focus in this chapter is only to identify AR characteristics in cyberculture studies that help to transfer cyberculture power into the hands of "marginalized" cultures of difference. Although the expression of identified AR characteristics varies in the different projects, the agenda is to present a range of different kinds of cyberculture research and demonstrate the potential of using AR toward social justice and social equity in the varied instances. The applicability of AR and the expression of its characteristics vary in the different cyberculture projects based on some of the following: vision, goals, and implementation plans of the project; degree of expectations for social justice; nature of cyber and offline interactions of participants; contextual realities of economics, social dynamics, and technical infrastructures; situational relationship between various project participants; and so on.

Cyberculture and Social Justice

The term *cyberspace* was coined by Gibson (1984, p. 51) as a "consensual hallucination experienced daily by billions of legitimate operators. . . . A graphic representation of data abstracted from the banks of every computer in the human system." Subsequent research traced cyberspace's development since the 1990s through three stages: popular culture, cyberculture studies, and critical cyberculture studies. This research has helped us define cyberculture more loosely by understanding "the relationships, intersections, and interdependencies between multiple areas," supporting "a series of negotiations" that "take place both online and off" (Silver 2000, p. 28). The focus of cyberculture research has been on documentation of human behavior, patterns of use, and development of theories and concepts to understand efforts of individuals and groups to express identity and achieve cohesion through the sharing of culture (values, language, rituals, icons) by means of the information infrastructure (Clarke 1997). What is missing in this research is its contribution to the processes of democratic social change. It also bypasses the issue of creating valid social knowledge, for it draws conclusions that are not inclusive of stakeholders during the entire research process. Consequently, findings identified in earlier research were interesting in their novelty and were described as "relevant" to research, but they did not have an impact upon bridging the sociocultural divides in our real-life geographic communities. Thus, it is now the opportune time to take cyberculture studies to the next stage of research conceptualization, the phase where it becomes a tool for social empowerment of the disadvantaged. AR provides one avenue for realization of this dream.

Several intertwining concepts and terms, such as the Internet, information superhighway, cyberspace, digital technologies, virtual reality, virtual/online communities, community/electronic networks, computer-mediated communication, networlds, and many others, have been used synonymously during different times and in different parts of the world to contribute toward our understanding of cyberculture studies in contemporary times. In this chapter, the term *cyberculture* is broadly and simply applied to the practices and use of computers by disadvantaged users.

Tenets of AR

AR is defined as a collaboration between a "professional action researcher and members of an organization or community seeking to improve their situation." All stakeholders involve themselves in the collaboration to "define the problems to be examined, cogenerate relevant knowledge about them, learn and execute social research techniques, take actions, and interpret the results of actions based on what they have learned" (Greenwood and Levin 1998, p. 4). Essential characteristics of AR are

- *Decentralization* of the inquiry into the local context as a means to solve real-life problems and bridge gaps between general laws and specific applications;
- *Deregulation* in movement away from "restrictive conventional rules of the research game, the overweening concern with validity, reliability, objectivity, and generalizability"; and
- *Cooperativeness in execution* where there are no functional distinctions between the researcher and the researched so that they all assume "equal footing in determining what questions will be asked, what information will be analyzed, and how conclusions and courses of action will be determined." (Stringer 1999, p. xii)

AR is closely tied to interpretative inquiry; hence, traditional criteria to evaluate rigor in experimental research—objectivity, reliability, validity, and generalizability—are inappropriate, and researchers pursuing AR may establish the trustworthiness of their study by reporting on credibility, transferability, dependability, and confirmability (Stringer 1999).

AR Manifesto in Cyberculture

Bringing together the philosophies of AR, cyberculture, and social equity, this section explores selected projects involving different disadvantaged groups in East-Central Illinois that are representative of a varied range of work that can come under the auspices of "cyberculture research." Detailed descriptions of the studies are not presented here; readers are directed elsewhere for that purpose. This chapter presents project highlights that were relevant to using AR strategies in cyberculture studies in order to show diversity in application of AR agendas and methods to achieve goals of social justice and social equity for different minority and "marginalized" populations.

Equal Participation of Disenfranchised Users in AR

Research, participation, and action are three pillars of AR, where use of participation in research and efforts to link research with action are intrinsically tied (McNiff 1995). In order to achieve social equity, AR practice in cyberculture needs to provide equal footing for all stakeholders "to come together to identify the problem to be investigated and then to collaborate throughout every phase of the research, dissemination, and utilization process" (Santelli et al. 1998, p. 211). In the Institute of Museum and Library Services (IMLS)–funded Afya project (http://www.prairienet.org/afya-project/index.html), participative alliances with SisterNet, a grassroots network of black women committed to addressing physical, emotional, intellectual, and spiritual health issues, have led to recruitment of local African American women as community action researchers to improve health information, services, and associated technological support (Bishop et al. 2000). Afya has an action-oriented agenda that has incorporated participants as equal beneficiaries throughout all stages of project development, from project conceptualization, needs assessment, data collection and analysis, decision-making in project implementation and assessment of Web-based resources, development of situated usability studies, and identifying relevant outcomes and future directions of growth (Bishop et al. 2001). For example, African American women in the community have been instrumental in creating culturally appropriate content for their Web site (http://www.sisternetonline.org/index.html). This has made progress toward equating imbalances in power dynamics between participants, health care information providers, and technological experts (Mehra et al. 2002). Black women have also been involved in the process of information system design and digital library evaluation in order to develop these as socially grounded activities that are situated in the social practice and used by "marginalized" members in society (Bishop et al. 2003).

Learning in Collaboration

AR recognizes the diverse skills, expertise, and perceptions of all stakeholders involved in the project (Whitney-Thomas 1997). For example, AR considers the expertise and knowledge of local participants as equally important to research and action as the contributions of professional researchers, for the former best know about the local contexts, conditions, and problems (Salisbury et al. 1997). This results in building collaborative teams and partnerships (Turnbull and Turnbull 1996) in which everybody contributes in ways that lead to mutual learning and sharing (Reason 1994).

Ongoing work in the online development of the Paseo Boricua Community Library (PBCL) (http://www.prairienet.org/pbclp) has involved building collaborative partnerships between faculty and students from the University of Illinois at Urbana-Champaign (UIUC) and teachers, students, and neighborhood volunteers at the Puerto Rican Community Center (PRCC) located in Chicago's Paseo Boricua neighborhood. These partnerships are blurring the categories of "researcher" and "participant" as traditionally defined. Various AR strategies in cyberculture are helping to build a "community of learners." Through summer 2003, the collaborative activities included the following:

- All participants worked collaboratively through online and offline interactions toward developing a vision and strategic plan for cultural development and preservation and community revitalization.
- In the process of creating the project Web site, though all participants provided input in different areas, academic researchers shared more in technological implementation and management issues, while community researchers provided a great deal of feedback in knowledge domains associated with local conditions, cultural values and philosophical ideologies, aesthetic sensibilities, and content characteristics.

- Decision-making and Web implementation of various information and communication tools took place via democratic consensus and knowledge sharing.
- Simple online tools helped in Web compilation of culturally appropriate research and local knowledge in order to build online content. These tools also allowed members to share and learn from one another based on their own level of individual expertise, knowledge, and time commitment. For example, "inquiry units" allowed team members to create relevant content (see, e.g., http://www.inquiry.uiuc .edu/bin/update_unit.cgi?command=select&xmlfile=u12265.xml).
- "Researchers" and "participants" interacted collaboratively to prepare and present a workshop for the 3D World Conference (http://www .twcfinternational.org/) that took place in Chicago in March 2003.
- In conceptualizing a Department of Commerce (DoC) Technology Opportunities Program grant that envisions connecting neighborhood teens, public health issues (diabetes, HIV/AIDS), creation of a "homework net" (community tech centers), and the PBCL project, local activists and community members were able to identify relevant areas of concern that were situated in local realities, while academic professionals were able to share their knowledge about expectations of funding agencies and grant stipulations.

Community Inquiry into Participants' Everyday Experiences

Action research is highly relevant to democracy because it allows all stakeholders to contribute collaboratively toward an inquiry into their own experiences (Dewey 1902) in order to focus on shared predicaments by learning from one another. This helps to develop a community of reflective practitioners (Schon 1983) who engage in processes of "reflective analysis" (Dewey 1988, p. 26) and apply a "rich blend of theory and practice" as they are tested against everyday experiences and real-world conditions (Hickman 2002). As part of the PBCL project, collective inquiry and action research strategies are being used to develop Community Inquiry Labs that include use of information and communication technologies to "support community learning and action that addresses critical local problems in a democratic manner" (Bishop 2003, p. 1). For example, curriculum units based on intersection of race, class, and technology-related issues are being incorporated into computer training classes for high school students at the Pedro Albizu Campos High School in Paseo Boricua. The process is helping to get feedback from participants about an online community information system and is contributing toward culturally relevant content for Paseo Boricua's online community library.

Online-Offline Convergences

Action research in cyberculture studies has to recognize the connections between people's virtual lives and their everyday real-life experiences (Wellman and Haythornthwaite 2002). For example, as part of the service-learning activities in the East St. Louis Action Research Project (http://www.eslarp.uiuc.edu), UIUC faculty, students, and staff are working with local neighborhood groups to build technical and social infrastructures in the city's most distressed communities, in ways that help build online support systems that are tied to people's offline lives. During spring 2002, Martin Wolske, instructor of the course Introduction to Network Information Systems, had students from his class establish six community technology centers (CTCs) across the city (http://www.eslarp.uiuc.edu/outreach/0203/). Action research strategies included site surveys and evaluation as well as developing trusting networks with community members in order to ensure that the CTCs were appropriately embedded within everyday social and spatial geographies of local residents.

Use of Mixed Methods

AR adopts a variety of social research techniques, and its implementation in cyberculture calls for the use of multiple and mixed methods (qualitative and quantitative) depending upon the "nature of the research question" (Meyer et al. 1998, p. 168). This helps to represent online-offline connections and provide a holistic understanding and recognition of diverse perceptions in the research initiative. For example, in a recent AR study with sexual minorities at UIUC, I used multiple methods to identify the role of an online mailing list in the participants' everyday lives. Content analysis of online postings and qualitative informal interviews with members provided complementary feedback that helped contextualize the use of the online mailing list in terms of online-offline crossovers and actions that the community perceived to promote its empowerment on multiple levels (Mehra, Merkel, and Bishop 2004).

Situated Nature of Applications and Concrete Outcomes

AR focuses on useful and concrete outcomes that help participants improve their situations through strategies that address goals in context (Carr and Kemmis 1986). In cyberculture research, this means developing situated and practical applications that are meaningful to the community. In a recent initiative sponsored by a Partnership Illinois Grant, under the auspices of the Prairienet Community Network (http://www.prairienet .org), I was involved in building a small digital library of Web resources for the purpose of developing small-business information resources for disadvantaged individuals from the business community and residents living in the north end of Urbana-Champaign. The project entailed building culturally relevant cyber content through participation and feedback from members of the Community Collaboration for Economic Development (CCED), a self-motivated group of individuals that has come together to develop entrepreneurial training programs for disenfranchised and minority people interested in starting a small business or expanding an existing business. The cyber resources incorporated concrete and practical content that low-income users employed for their small-business needs; constant feedback from the community to evaluate developed content was important for this task. AR involved developing strategies for training of low-income individuals, incorporating feedback from CCED members, especially for the evaluation of existing online and offline information resources, analyzing business information needs of potential users, developing Web resources to meet those needs, and understanding the political and social dynamics between CCED and disenfranchised members in the community (Mehra, forthcoming). Such efforts helped match the provision of the small-business information services to local needs and expectations of the disadvantaged community members.

Conclusion

The most important goal of AR in cyberculture studies is to build capacity for empowerment of "marginalized" cultures of difference. Empowerment can occur at various levels of overlapping and intersecting domains: individual, social, community-wide, or in whichever way the participants perceive. For example, black women in the Afya project gained personal and social empowerment by building their technological skills; the Puerto Ricans in Paseo Boricua hope to gain empowerment by community revitalization, preserving their cultural heritage against the forces of gentrification, and building an online community library (Flores-Gonzalez 2001); sexual minorities at UIUC conceived of their political, social, cultural, and educational empowerment by connecting their use of an online mailing list to their everyday "marginalized" experiences. As cyberculture researchers it is our task to ensure empowerment of all individuals by making the research process more inclusive of "marginalized" users and by building local capacity. AR provides an avenue toward this goal.

REFERENCES

Bishop, A. P. (2003). "Creating Community Inquiry Labs for Democratic Learning and Action Across Racial and Digital Divides." Unpublished project proposal.

Bishop, A. P., Mehra, B., Bazzell, I., and Smith, C. (2003). "Participatory Action Research and Digital Libraries: Reframing Evaluation." In A. P. Bishop, N. Van House, and B. Buttenfield (eds.), *Digital Library Use: Social Practice in Design and Evaluation.* Cambridge, MA: MIT Press.

Bishop, A. P., Mehra, B., Bazzell, I., and Smith, C. (2001). "Scenarios in the Design and Evaluation of Networked Information Services: An Example from Community Health." In C. R. McClure and J. C. Bertot (eds.), *Evaluating Networked Information Services: Techniques, Policy, and Issues.* Medford, NJ: Information Today.

Bishop, A. P., Mehra, B., Bazzell, I., and Smith, C. (2000). "Socially Grounded User Studies in Digital Library Development." *First Monday* 5(6) (June). Available at http://www.firstmonday.org/issues/issue5_6/bishop/index.html.

Carr, W., and Kemmis, S. (1986). *Becoming Critical: Education, Knowledge, and Action Research.* London: Falmer.

Clarke, R. (1997). "Encouraging CyberCulture." Address to CAUSE in Australia '97, Melbourne, April 13–16. Available at http://www.anu.edu.au/people/Roger.Clarke/II/EncoCyberCulture.html (accessed 26 September 2003).

Dewey, J. (1988). "Experience and Nature." In J. Boydston (ed.), *The Later Works of John Dewey, 1925–53, Volume 1: 1925.* Carbondale: Southern Illinois University Press.

Dewey, J. (1902). *The Child and the Curriculum.* Chicago: University of Chicago Press.

Flores-Gonzalez, N. (2001). "Paseo Boricua: Claiming a Puerto Rican Space in Chicago." *Centro Journal* 13(2) (Fall): 165–181.

Gibson, W. (1984). *Neuromancer.* New York: Ace.

Greenwood, D. J., and Levin, M. (1998). *Introduction to Action Research: Social Research for Social Change.* Thousand Oaks, CA: Sage.

Hall, B. (1996). "Participatory Research." In A. C. Tuijman (ed.), *International Encyclopedia of Adult Education and Training* (pp. 187–194). Oxford, UK: Pergamon.

Hickman, L. A. (2002). "Democracy and Global Citizenship: Creating Value by Educating for Social Reform." Presentation at the Boston Research Center, June 1. Available at http://www.brc21.org/hickman.html (accessed 26 September 2003).

Kemmis, S., and McTaggart, R. (1988). *The Action Research Planner,* 3rd ed. Victoria, Australia: Deakin University Press.

McNiff, J. (1995). *Action Research Principles and Practice.* New York: Routledge.

Mehra, B. M. (forthcoming). "Library and Information Science (LIS) and Community Development: Use of Information and Communication Technologies (ICTs) towards a Social Equity Agenda." *Community Development Society.*

Mehra, B., Bishop, A. P., Bazzell, I., and Smith, C. (2002). "Scenarios in the Afya Project as a Participatory Action Research (PAR) Tool for Studying Information Seeking and Use across the 'Digital Divide.'" *Journal of the American Society of Information Science and Technology* 53(14): 1259–1266.

Mehra, B., Merkel, C., and Bishop, A. P. (2004). "Internet for Empowerment of Minority and Marginalized Communities." *New Media and Society* 6(5): 781–802.

Meyer, L. H., Park, H., Grenot-Scheyer, M., Schwartz, I., and Harry, B. (1998). "Participatory Research: New Approaches to the Research to Practice Dilemma." *JASH* 23(3): 165–177.

Reason, P. (1994). "Three Approaches to Participative Inquiry." In N. K. Denzin and Y. S. Lincoln (eds.), *Handbook of Qualitative Research* (pp. 324–339). Thousand Oaks, CA: Sage.

Salisbury, C. L., Wilson, L. L., Swartz, T. J., Palombaro, M. M., and Wassel, J. (1997). "Using Action Research to Solve Instructional Challenges in Inclusive Elementary School Settings." *Education and Treatment of Children* 20(1): 21–38.

Santelli, B., Singer, G. H. S., DiVenere, N., Ginsberg, C., and Powers, L. E. (1998). "Participatory Action Research: Reflections on Critical Incidents in a PAR Project." *JASH* 23(3): 211–222.

Schon, D. A. (1983). *The Reflective Practitioner: How Professionals Think in Action.* New York: Basic.

Silver, D. (2000). "Looking Backwards, Looking Forward: Cyberculture Studies 1990–2000." In David Gauntlett (ed.), *Web Studies: Rewiring Media Studies for the Digital Age* (pp. 19–30). Oxford: Oxford University Press.

Stringer, E. T. (1999). *Action Research.* Thousand Oaks, CA: Sage.

Turnbull, A. P., and Turnbull, H. R. (1996). "Participatory Action Research." In National Council on Disability (ed.), *Improving the Implementation of the Indi-*

viduals with Disability Act: Making Schools Work for All of American Children (pp. 685–710). Washington, DC: National Council on Disability.

Whitney-Thomas, J. (1997). "Participatory Action Research as an Approach to Enhancing Quality of Life for Individuals with Disabilities." In R. Schalock (ed.), *Quality of Life: Applications to Persons with Disabilities,* vol. 2 (pp. 181–198). Washington, DC: American Association on Mental Retardation.

Wellman, B., and Haythornthwaite, C. (2002). *The Internet in Everyday Life.* Malden, MA: Blackwell.

Chapter 19

Cyberstudies and the Politics of Visibility

David J. Phillips

This rumination began with a note from David Silver, the organizer of the Critical Cyberculture Studies Symposium, saying that he was especially interested in having me devote some of my paper to issues of sexuality. I was a little taken aback by this. I don't consider my work to be essentially, or even especially, about sexuality. And of course I wanted to discuss my current project, on the implementation of location capabilities in wireless phone networks, which seems about as unsexy as you can get. I called David and asked why he wanted me to address sexuality. He said, in brief, "I've read your work." So I find myself, yet again, flummoxed by having been read.

On reflection, I can't disagree that my sexual identity pervades my work. As a teacher and scholar, and to the extremely minor degree that I am a public intellectual and a political activist, I try to make it clear to my audience that they are responding to the work of just another regular old lefty liberationist homo. The "just another" part has always been rhetorically crucial. It has always seemed politically important to take for granted that old lefty liberationist homos are central to society, central to technology research, are not in need of translation to the mainstream. I position my work with respect to class, sexuality, and gender, and I make explicit the aspects of those social positions that make them particularly useful entry points into the research. But on the whole I leave it to readers to triangulate my perspective with their own, and to tease out useful consonances and contradictions.

This chapter explores further these themes of personal voice, marginality, and useful research in two threads. The first is an autobiography of a particular research project—in process and perhaps to be abandoned soon. The intent of this first part is to foreground the ways in which my awareness of my identity, my history, and my social position informs the development of my research questions, as well as the theory and method brought to bear on those questions. The second part of the chapter is a reflection on whether this example has lessons for the constitution of the field of "cyberstudies" itself in relation to other, more fully institutional-ized fields.

The Development of a Research Project

Surveillance is one of the continuing focuses of my research. For years, I've been exploring the relations among Foucauldian discipline, the political economy of information, and technologies structuring access to infor-mation, especially cryptographic technologies. I've been interested also in ideological discourses of technology, especially the technolibertarian ideology of cypherpunks.[1] I was thrilled and fascinated when, during the dot-com boom, a group of entrepreneurs, venture capitalists, and cypher-punks started Zero-Knowledge Systems, a company whose flagship product was a pseudonymity service named Freedom. The Freedom service allowed users to establish several pseudonyms and choose among them during online interactions. The pseudonyms were unlinkable and untraceable, but persistent, so each pseudonym could accrue visibility and repu-tation.

Though I never shared the cypherpunks' faith in market capitalism, I personally welcomed Freedom as a much needed intervention into evolv-ing structures of Internet surveillance. More formally, I also thought that studying Freedom would allow me to begin to update Goffman's theories of self-presentation and identity management from the world of restau-rant dining rooms and kitchens to online contexts (Goffman 1959), and to incorporate issues of the political economy of personal information. I started my project by subscribing to the Freedom service and simply try-ing to use it during my regular online sessions. As I went about my busi-ness with my new multiple identities, I became confused, troubled, and frustrated about the practicality and the politics of my behavior. I found that a lot of this confusion spoke directly to my history and self-identity as a middle-aged, professional, gay man who had been "out" all of his adult life.

I began questioning the decisions I was making. Why was I, in each in-stance, choosing to be "djp" or "DrPhillips" or "Corky"?[2] Why was I choos-ing a particular persona in a particular context? What was I revealing, and to whom, if I confessed as "djp" that I also went as "DrPhillips"? What benefits and risks were involved in that revelation?

This reminded me a lot of negotiating the closet and led to a paper entitled, oddly enough, "Negotiating the Digital Closet: Online Pseudonyms and the Politics of Sexual Identity" (Phillips 2002). In that paper, I suggested that simple pseudonymity was far too blunt a tool for the sort of face management that people do by second nature every day. I tried to suggest the kinds of tools that would be needed for more successful face management. More important, though, I suggested that framing the issues surrounding personal information systems in terms of privacy flew in the face of the political work of coming out—the creation of identity, community, and social/economic/political power—that is the hallmark of the modern gay rights movement.

The Freedom project caused me to reframe my scholarly investigations as being more about visibility and identity than privacy and surveillance. My research questions turned to the development, deployment, integration, and use of tools for managing, not privacy, but trust, intimacy, community, representation, and context. How do we share different facets of ourselves, based not on the innate "sensitivity" or "stigma" of that facet but on our relation with the person with whom we are sharing or the social context of that interaction? How do we even know "where we are" in online contexts, and how do we know who is sharing that "space" with us? How do we know how, and to what end, we are known? Most important, how and with what information tools do we make online locales and settings? Most intriguing, how do we each live, simultaneously and copresently, but in different locales (that is, seeing different things, interpreting through different codes, each guided by different maps overlaid upon the same space)? What forces impose locales upon us? What is at stake as we do this?

Understanding these questions of the mediation of activities that sustain identity, subcultural knowledge, and regenerative places becomes even more important as physical space—our offices, our homes, our shopping districts—become more and more shot through with "pervasive" or "ubiquitous" or "context-aware" computing and information systems. I had been working with geographers in another project on location-aware information systems (Phillips, Curry, and Regan 2002), and the link between information environments and physical spaces became more and more fascinating to me. I kept returning, in my mind, to a quote from the developer of GeePS, a location-based marketing service:

Think of GeePS as a local market, a one-mile circle of energy around a potential customer, which moves with him or her, providing local information that fits individual needs. This information is dynamic and controlled by the merchants, communities and establishments in that radius. (Mack 2000, p. 38)

Who is it that decides what "local market" to present to the individual? Who determines the individual's "needs"? Upon what social ontology are those determinations made, and with what social goal? Who constructs the place that the individual inhabits? How can we understand, both empirically and theoretically, the conditions necessary to live interstitially or counterculturally in the face of pervasive computing?

It is important to note that it was not any theoretical bent but my embodied history as a gay man that led to these questions. Or rather, the theory that informs this project was not learned in graduate school but is an expression of an ontology derived from myriad personal influences. The investigation into these questions cannot and should not be separated from their political and historical genesis, yet they nevertheless have importance beyond their origin. They are "mainstream" issues.

It seems to me that a research project designed to answer these questions would have three prongs. The first prong would be to understand, historically and empirically, how individuals and subcultures in fact have managed context, place, and identity. The second would explore various technologies of visibility and identification, and how these could possibly mediate historical social practices. Finally, the research would limn the social processes and historical forces through which such techniques become part of the infrastructure of daily life, suggesting points of intervention in these processes so that future developments in media might be more likely to support liberatory activities. There are certainly other ways to approach these questions, but this approach concurs with my training in critical media studies and the social shaping of technology. Again, my autobiography runs through the project design. So do my political goals: the project assumes that relatively marginal identities are appropriate points of entry into a broad sociological project; it affirms the centrality of that marginality. The project is holistic, embracing the confluence of all kinds of power. It is interventionist.

In addressing the first prong of the research, I have been looking to queer theory, gay and lesbian history, and postmodern and feminist geography. For me, the most provocative and instructive of these have been the gay and lesbian history works. What has come out of this, for me, is the problematic between two modes and goals of place-making—the subcultural and the overtly political. Chauncey (1994, pp. 187–89) provides an example of the first, describing how, in early-twentieth-century New York City, gay people developed private, local knowledge, "developing tactics that allowed them to identify and communicate with each other without alerting hostile outsiders to what they were doing. Such tactics kept them hidden from the dominant culture, but not from one another." In part, this involved "constructing a gay map of the city," which "had to consider the maps devised by other, sometimes hostile, groups."

The second mode of place-making is the generation of explicit, public places and milieus that support specific public identities and relationships—gay bars, gay neighborhoods, gay shopping districts, gay political districts, gay vacation spots. This is the "coming out," the identity politics, that has informed the gay rights movement since the early 1970s (Armstrong 2002; D'Emilio 1983).

These two tactics of social positioning—subcultural signaling and overt identity and place claiming—are entwined. They interact in various ways. Each is essential to the claiming of social power. First, "coming out" as a tactic of political claim-staking always occurs in a context of power. It involves risks that are historically specific and that vary with the circumstances of the actor. Popular chanteuses face a very different cost-benefit analysis in coming out than do tenured professors or truck stop waitresses. In certain moments it may be politically and personally expedient to proclaim one's sexuality at a public rally but not at work. In other moments, the opposite might be true—anonymous declaration in a crowd would be meaningless, whereas coming out in the workplace would catalyze powerful economic and political forces. Being "out" or closeted is not a binary condition; it is a negotiated and fluid identity status. It is the management of revelation in specific social contexts. The ability to construct, limit, understand, and segregate these contexts is a measure of social power.

A second area also highlights the strategic interplay between subcultural and overt identity making. This involves the social cost of stable, globally recognized identity categories. Identities classify and typify. They turn humans into knowable objects. This stabilization is necessary if the political goal is to bring an excluded group within the mechanisms of bureaucratic power and to begin to exercise that power on behalf of that group. These stable identity categories become both the tools for, and the outcome of, stable, enduring social relations and interactions. So the decision to be "out" comes with the decision to be out *as what?* What does the proclaimed identity *do?*

One thing identities do a lot of lately is to facilitate the regulation of consumer demand. The reification of identity categories, and their enmeshment into regulatory regimes, is running full-throttle in capitalist rationality. An example of this is Claritas's PRIZM system, which defines sixty-two distinct "lifestyle types" and describes each U.S. neighborhood in terms of these types. For example, in West Hollywood, Greenwich Village, and Dupont Circle one is likely to find the "Bohemian Mix"—professional singles and couples aged between twenty-five and forty-four with household incomes of about $38,500 who use call answering, shop at The Gap, have a rollover IRA, and watch *Face the Nation* (Claritas Corp. n.d.-a, n.d.-b). The social issue here is not so much that these descriptions are untrue or inaccurate but that they are useful, and they are used. They guide the decisions of marketers and so reify the types they describe. As Eliza Doolittle noted, "The difference between a lady and a flower girl is not how she behaves, but how she is treated" (Shaw 1951, p. 99). Differential treatment of social types, especially in the marketplace for essential goods, reentrenches pernicious discrimination and stereotyping (Gandy 1995) and destroys a sense of national citizen identity (Turow 1997). In reconfiguring social groups as markets, issues of social justice are subordinated to issues of appropriate consumption, and economically undesirable groups (that is, the poor) are excluded, again, from public discourse (Chasin 2000; Sender 2001).

Because every category excludes as it includes, because imputed membership in identity categories determines or influences each individual's life chances, identity is the site and object of economic and political struggle. Since every category is partial, fluid, and contingent, there is a continual, vital redefinition and realignment of identities and relations. Donna Haraway and Judith Butler both insist on the political necessity of seriously playing with the boundaries and meanings of constructed identities. Haraway (1991) calls for a radical integration of, a radical networking of, a radical dispersion of, social locations and identities via *strategic affinities* between social identities, and the blurring and ad hoc reconfiguration of identity boundaries. Likewise, Butler (1998, p. 1518) asks how to "use [an identity] in such a way that its futural significations are not *foreclosed?* How to use the sign and avow its temporal contingency at once?" She answers that this may be possible through drag, through *ironic performance,* by signaling identities self-consciously. Both authors refer to these activities as play, but both insist that the play is, while pleasurable, deadly serious.

Together, this sociohistorical research attempts to understand the stakes, strategies, and tactics of social visibility—of identity—and place-making for, through, and within power. Identity categories are constructed and fluid, yet they can be stabilized to form parts of enduring political, cultural, and economic relations. There is not one set of categories and one set of relations common to all; some are bureaucratized and rationalized within dominant forms of government and business, while others are closely guarded as trade secrets or as subcultural knowledge. These social relations have a spatial component. Not only are they used to organize physical and virtual space, but spatial metaphors organize the relations themselves. The next phase of the research project is to theorize how, exactly, identity is constructed, claimed, or imputed. What is the role of information technology in this process?

One way of looking at the role of information technologies in the construction of social identity is through the Foucauldian paradigm of panopticism. In its idealized form, panoptic surveillance individualizes each member of the population and permits the observation and recording of each individual's activities then collates these individual observations across the population. From these conglomerated observations, statistical norms are produced. These norms are then applied back to the subjected individuals, who are categorized and perhaps acted upon, either with gratification or punishment, according to their relation to the produced norm. Thus, surveillance produces both discipline (that is, conformity to the norm) and the disciplines (regulated fields of knowledge and expertise). Importantly, the observer, the operator and coordinator of the panoptic system, is invisible to the observed. This invisibility helps to ensure the silent, efficient operation of the whole (Foucault 1979).

This metaphor is in fact useful for understanding the personal information systems that operate every day, usually silently and without notice, in computer-mediated communication systems. A paradigmatic example is the Wall Street Journal Online. The system uses "cookies"[3] to uniquely *identify* individual users, then to *monitor* and *track* their traversal of the site. The information thus gathered is *statistically analyzed* to place each user in one of eight *categories* (car buffs, consumer techies, engaged investors, health enthusiasts, leisure-minded, mutual-fund aficionados, opinion leaders, or travel seekers). This categorical identification then becomes the *knowledge guiding the treatment of each individual,* as different advertisements are served to members of different classes (Ives 2003).

Yet information technology need not be organized in a top-down, panoptic structure of visibility and classification. Haraway (1991) and Stone (1995) celebrate the way that new information technologies can permit the queer crossing and blurring of boundaries, mediating cyborg transgressions and deep coalitions. And technical research continues into communication protocols that facilitate subcultural knowledge, resistant play, camp, irony, and transgressive performance. For example, consider protocols for subcultural knowledge. danah boyd's SecureId is an identity management tool that allows users to segregate their personal information into "facets" of identity. Before a visitor can have access to a particular facet, the visitor must answer a question that proves in-group membership. In this way, SecureId mimics, in part, the social signaling work of fashion and speech codes (boyd 2002). John Canny (2002) addresses the issue of the discriminatory "pushing" of information based on demographic models and develops collaborative filtering techniques that allow participants to choose the ways in which their activities recursively construct and rely upon those demographic models.

At the level of performance and identity play, we have protocols such as the Freedom pseudonymity suite discussed earlier, which permits the user to segregate performances according to context. Likewise, Ellison (1997) has described identification systems that permit of local but interlinked naming structures. In a sense, these protocols allow one to give one's friends or associates the power to vouch for one's identity, but only under certain circumstances. Again, the user, the performer of identity, has some capacity to link personae to context. But performances are self-reflexive— dancers rehearse before a mirror, actors rely on the director to let them know what "plays." Translating this to an information context, Nguyen and Mynatt (2002) propose *Privacy Mirrors*—interfaces that enable users to self-monitor the data-impression they are exhibiting to others.

So techniques for queer identity management exist, or are possible. But why is it that queer techniques are mere possibilities, while more panoptic techniques such as unique IDs, cross-site tracking, and centralized consumer profiling are integrated into the communication infrastructure, into the architecture that, as Benjamin (1968, p. 240) says, we encounter "habitually, and in a state of distraction"?

This question initiates the third phase of the research process—an investigation into the political economy and the social construction of infrastructures of visibility. Such an investigation combines structuration and actor-network theories. Structuration theory, as applied to the study of technology, suggests that the determining influences among technical systems and social structures are mutually recursive—that technological systems are both medium and outcome of social practices (Giddens 1984; Orlikowski 1992). Actor-network theory understands the social topology as a constantly reforming constellation of actants, each attempting to enlist and translate the positions and capacities of other actants to gain some end (Law 1990). Both theories are concerned with how action in the here and now is translated into institutional structures enduring through time and space. They suggest that the way to study technological change is to focus on the genesis of particular systems in specific historical contexts, to bring to light the social positions and resources of actors as they attempt to refashion existing institutional, cultural, and technical linkages.

Bowker and Star refer to this integration of artifact, practice, and institution as *infrastructuring*. Their *Sorting Things Out* (1999) offers wonderful lessons for studying how particular processes and, especially, particular categories are institutionalized and woven into the fabric of everyday life. Sites of infrastructuring include entrepreneurial organizations, standards-setting bodies, regulatory agencies, courts, the workplace, and the home. Infrastructuring is astonishingly complex, and it is unique for each instance. Therefore, case studies are the preferred investigatory method.

The study of the infrastructuring of visibility, attempting to understand the conditions of institutionalization of particular mediated practices of identity and visibility, would require a set of cases of the attempted deployment of systems of identification, tracking, and profiling. These would include successful and unsuccessful attempts, at different scales, in different political regions, and in different institutional contexts. Together, their comparison might give us an idea of the forces (economic, political, ideological, legal, cultural, global, local) that shape and constrain our ability to engage in identity construction and place construction.

The aim of such a study is twofold. First, it would reflect a constellation of pressures shaping everyday visibility practice and suggest points of intervention where oppressive practices might be effectively challenged and liberatory, or queer, practices nourished. Second, though, it denaturalizes the very notions of identity, identification, and classification. It foregrounds the constructed nature of those entities and makes the boundaries of their use apparent. In so doing, it makes apparent the "social and political work" that infrastructure is doing (Star and Bowker 2002, p. 160). It makes infrastructure itself available as a camp or ironic object, to be recognized and used as a prop in the performance of social truth.

So there is my ideal research project. It links the autobiographical with the universal, the here-and-now with the spacious and the enduring, culture and ideology with technology and economics, high theory with empirical investigation. It is critical, reflexive, and active. But is it cyberstudies?

Well, why not? Of course, it's also telecommunications policy, sociology of technology, media studies, computer science, gender studies, and American studies, at least. It fits amply within my own home department, Radio-Television-Film, though it directly addresses neither radio, television, nor film. But that is because my department has always considered itself essentially concerned with cultural representation, economic structures, and social justice and has consistently expanded beyond its name to include foci on media of all ilk. That, as far as I am concerned, is the most important political fact—not that cyberstudies, as a field, needs to be integrated into institutional practice but that critical study, as a practice, needs to be integrated into institutionalized fields. This means, perhaps, recognizing that we are never at home; we are always marginal. Perhaps we will always, of necessity, work in contingent alignments and coalitions of "computer scientists," "sociologists," "geographers," "political economists," and "literary theorists." The political work is to make such contingency commonplace, to recognize the marginal as pervasive, to understand that the proper place for yet another lefty liberationist homo is wherever he happens to be.

NOTES

1. Too briefly and broadly, this ideology holds that anonymity and untraceability, especially in payment systems, would reduce or eliminate governmental power in cyberspace. Freed from state regulation of markets, cyberspace would bloom as a capitalist utopia.

2. Not my real pseudonym.

3. Cookies are a mechanism by which Web site operators can place a unique identifier on each user's machine, so that the site can compile a history of each user's activities on that site across browser sessions. For a more complete description of cookies, see Cookie Central n.d.

REFERENCES

Armstrong, E. (2002) *Forging Gay Identities: Organizing Sexuality in San Francisco, 1950–1994.* Chicago: University of Chicago Press.

Benjamin, W. (1968) "The work of art in an age of mechanical reproduction." In H. Arendt (ed.), *Illuminations.* New York: Schocken.

Bowker G., and Star, S. L. (1999) *Sorting Things Out: Classification and Its Consequences.* Cambridge, MA: MIT Press.

boyd, d. (2002) "Faceted Id/entity: Managing representation in a digital world." Unpublished master's thesis, Massachusetts Institute of Technology.

Butler, J. (1998) "Imitation and gender insubordination." In D. H. Richter (ed.), *The Critical Tradition: Classic Texts and Contemporary Trends,* 2nd ed. New York: Bedford/St. Martin's.

Canny, J. (2002) "Collaborative filtering with privacy via factor analysis." Paper presented at SIGIR '01, Tampere, Finland.

Chasin, A. (2000) *Selling Out: The Gay and Lesbian Movement Goes to Market.* New York: Palgrave.

Chauncey, G. (1994) *Gay New York: Gender, Urban Culture, and the Making of the Gay Male World, 1890–1940.* New York: Basic.

Claritas Corp. (n.d.-a) "You are where you live:j1." Available at http://cluster2 .claritas.com/YAWYL/Default.wjsp?SystemWL (accessed 23 June 2003).

Claritas Corp. (n.d.-b) "You are where you live:j1." Available at http://cluster2 .claritas.com/YAWYL/clusterlookup.wjsp?cluster10&zipcode10011 (accessed 23 June 2003).

Cookie Central. (n.d.) "The cookie concept." Available at http://www.cookiecentral .com/content.phtml?area=2&id=1 (accessed 21 September 2003).

D'Emilio, J. (1983) *Sexual Politics, Sexual Communities: The Making of a Homosexual Minority in the United States, 1940–1970.* Chicago: University of Chicago Press.

Ellison, C. (1997) "What do you need to know about the person with whom you are doing business?" Written testimony before House Science and Technology Subcommittee Hearing of 28 October: Signatures in a Digital Age. Available at http://world.std.com/~cme/html/congress1.html (accessed 21 September 2003).

Foucault, M. (1979) *Discipline and Punish.* New York: Vintage.

Gandy, O. (1995) "It's discrimination, stupid!" In J. Brook and I. A. Boal (eds.), *Resisting the Virtual Life.* San Francisco: City Lights.

Giddens, A. (1984) *The Constitution of Society: Outline of the Theory of Structuration.* Berkeley: University of California Press.

Goffman, E. (1959) *The Presentation of Self in Everyday Life.* New York: Doubleday.

Haraway, D. J. (1991) *Simians, Cyborgs, and Women.* New York: Routledge.

Ives, N. (2003) "Online profiling, separating the car buff from the travel seeker, is a new tool to lure advertisers." *New York Times,* June 16, sec. C, p. 10.

Law, J. (1990) "Technology and heterogeneous engineering: The case of Portuguese expansion." In W. E. Bijker, T. P. Hughes, and T. J. Pinch (eds.), *The Social Construction of Technological Systems: New Directions in the Sociology and History of Technology.* Cambridge, MA: MIT Press.

Mack, A. M. (2000) "Going local." *Adweek,* July 10, pp. 38–39.

Nguyen, D. H., and Mynatt, E. D. (2002) "Privacy Mirrors: Understanding and shaping socio-technical ubiquitous computing systems." Georgia Institute of Technology Technical Report GIT-GVU-02-16. Available at http://www.erstwhile.org/writings/PrivacyMirrors.pdf (accessed 21 September 2003).

Orlikowski, W. (1992) "The duality of technology: Rethinking the concept of technology in organizations." *Organization Science,* 3: 398–427.

Phillips, D. J. (2002) "Negotiating the digital closet: Online pseudonyms and the politics of sexual identity." *Information, Communication, and Society,* 5: 406–24.

Phillips, D. J., Curry, M., and Regan, P. (2002) "Implications of the deployment of wireless emergency response systems." Paper presented at the Sixth ETHICOMP International Conference on the Social and Ethical Impacts of Information and Communication Technologies, Lisbon, Portugal.

Sender, K. (2001) "Gay readers, consumers, and a dominant gay habitus: 25 years of the *Advocate* magazine." *Journal of Communication,* 51: 73–99.

Shaw, B. (1951) *Pygmalion.* Baltimore: Penguin.

Star, S. L., and Bowker, G. (2002) "How to infrastructure." In Leah A. Lievrouw and Sonia Livingstone (eds.), *The Handbook of New Media.* Thousand Oaks, CA: Sage.

Stone, A. R. (1995) *The War of Desire and Technology at the Close of the Mechanical Age.* Cambridge, MA: MIT Press.

Turow, J. (1997) *Breaking Up America: Advertisers and the New Media World.* Chicago: University of Chicago Press.

Chapter 20

Disaggregation, Technology, and Masculinity
Elements of Internet Research

Frank Schaap

Keeping with the eclectic spirit of *Critical Cyberculture Studies,* I will discuss three topics in the, admittedly brief, space of this chapter. The first topic will outline why it is important to think about "the Internet" as a collection of different online environments rather than as one monolithic entity to which a variety of qualities and effects can be attributed. The second topic will extend this line of argument to the need to be aware of the premises on which the technologies that enable "the Internet" were (and are being) built, and the need to investigate that technology's constraints and affordances for social interaction. The third topic will focus on the articulations of gender in the first two topics, and I will discuss why it is important in the context of online social interaction to pay particular attention to masculinity.

The social scientific study of various online environments as social, cultural, political, and economic places has come a long way since the first half of the 1990s, when almost every study laboriously described the minutiae of computer-mediated communication in a MUD, chatroom, or on IRC. It is not that the practical aspects of online interaction are less important than they were but that a body of work has accumulated and, in general, people are better acquainted with the Internet now and know, even if not through hands-on experience, about chatting and role-playing. More-recent studies consequently introduce the setting of their study briefly and proceed to discuss social and theoretical aspects of importance to that particular setting. However, between meticulously explaining what happens on the screen and the acceptance of the "thereness" of the underlying technology lies a middle ground where the interplay and mutual construction of the social/cultural and the technological aspects of online interaction can and must be explored. The Internet is a fundamentally technological medium, and virtually every study deals, implicitly or explicitly, with what "the Internet" adds to the mix that makes online communication different from offline, "unmediated" communication. In this chapter, then, I aim to articulate two rather pragmatic issues and one more political issue of importance for doing "Internet research."

I started thinking about the importance of these issues after meeting "in the flesh" some of the players of the role-playing MOO I had previously researched (Schaap 2002). During my time on the MOO, I had learned that some of the other players lived near one another and met up offline more or less regularly. Some of the players had met online and then discovered that they lived close to one another; other players were already friends when they started playing on the same MOO. Most of the meetings of these players were not formally organized but simply a group of friends getting together for a beer, dinner, or console gaming. What I, as one of the isolated players, didn't quite realize was the extent to which the online world of the role-playing games was discussed in the offline meetings. The MOO that they all played on and what went on "in there" was one of the main returning topics for conversation. One of the players actually used the term "oral history" to describe how they talked about the virtual world in their offline meetings. Not only were practical matters such as easy ways of making money or possible vulnerabilities of the program code discussed, but the everyday social interactions and in-game politics were discussed as well. Feats of social or technological accomplishment were recounted—how a gang war was won or how a powerful character was tricked. In the course of recounting them, these stories eventually took on the form of landmarks in the social history of their shared real *and* virtual lives.

"The Internet": The One and the Many

Although the Internet entered the popular consciousness some ten to fifteen years ago, the term is still capitalized and comes only preceded by the article "the," reinforcing the idea that there is only one such thing as "the Internet." Other terms, such as "Electronic Highway" or "cyberspace," are also predominantly used in the singular. The capitalization also shows the (still) relative newness of the Internet, because we no longer capitalize other media such as television, radio, and telephone. There are several aspects that feed into the idea of a singular Internet.

The first aspect is that the everyday experience of using the Internet is structured by sitting in front of one screen and one machine. That machine presents us with a windowed graphical user interface, where different windows provide access to different (online) applications, but in the end, they appear on one and the same screen. Whereas television, radio, and telephone provide access to their media through physically separate objects (despite all the hype about convergence), the various Internet applications are united by their appearance on the same screen, in similarly styled windows. A second unifying aspect is that the various online applications, such as e-mail, the Web, chatrooms, IRC, and so on, rely on a common set of technologies. A computer must connect to the Internet and set up a TCP/IP connection on top of which other protocols allow the various applications to do their thing. One can argue that the "Transfer Control Protocol/Internet Protocol" in combination with the physical layer of computers and cables really *is* the Internet and that hence it really is *one* thing, but that argument misses the point that the everyday experiences of the Internet are with and through the various applications. The third aspect, manifest mostly in the academic study of the Internet, is the twin forces of extrapolation and macro analysis. Manuel Castells's *The Internet Galaxy: Reflections on the Internet, Business, and Society* (2001) is an example of a macro-scale analysis that attempts to map a wide variety of social, cultural, political, and economic developments to "the Internet." Mostly, the Internet is rendered as a source or amplifier of these developments. Castells, for example, draws extensively on the case of the Amsterdam Digital City to discuss the rise of the "netizen," who is a politically engaged "local/global citizen," taking part in the inherently democratic public sphere created by the Internet.

It is, however, problematic to conflate any single online application— or a collection of different applications—under the umbrella of a "Digital City," with the Internet as a whole and discuss "the Internet's" potential as a public sphere or, as with MUDs, chatrooms, and IRC, take the identity play in those environments as exemplary for the Internet as a whole. TCP/IP may be a common "carrier wave" for these applications, but we are not conflating or comparing television, radio, and mobile phones just because they use a piece of the electromagnetic spectrum to transmit their signal. There are of course similar practices across different applications and legitimate comparisons to be made, but those must be made after establishing the basis on which they are to be compared. There are many things for the social scientist to learn from studying MMORPGs,[1] but there are substantial differences between EverQuest, Ultima Online, and Lineage that influence the articulations of identity, gender, community, and so forth that you will find in these games. In order to make the similarities and comparisons meaningful, you have to first indicate the differences, and hence you have to name the game.

Taking a step back and first looking at a particular online environment in and of itself is of course a first step toward making those isolated cases meaningful in a larger framework again. That larger framework, however, may not necessarily look the same as what the term "Internet" calls up.

> For both researchers and participants, a central aspect of understanding the dynamics of mediation is to "disaggregate" the Internet: not to look at a monolithic medium called "the Internet," but rather at a range of practices, software and hardware technologies, modes of representation and interaction that may or may not be interrelated by participants, machines or programs (indeed they may not all take place at a computer). What we were observing was not so much people's use of "the Internet" but rather how they assembled various technical possibilities that added up to *their* Internet (Miller and Slater 2000, p. 14).

One of things that my encounter with the role-players and Miller and Slater's study of Internet use on Trinidad makes clear is that in the everyday experience of users, "the Internet" is not one thing, nor is its practice confined to computer-mediated spaces only. As Miller and Slater describe in their study, for many Trinidadians the central application of *their* Internet may be an ICQ channel called De Trini Lime, whereas for the role-players in Minneapolis it may be their virtual world, while for an Internet researcher it might be the Association of Internet Researchers' mailing list. These central applications gain meaning and use in the context of various other online and offline practices of work and leisure, in public and private spheres. Not only, then, is it important to disaggregate the Internet on the level of the technology and social practices; it is also important to locate the different uses and meanings of the technologies and social practices in *both* online and offline contexts.

The Shape of Technology

In a recent article in a game magazine, several game-industry luminaries were asked the question, "What would be your ultimate online gaming experience—your dream game?" Warren Spector, studio director at Ion Storm, answered,

> I'd like to be able to play with friends scattered all around the country and all around the world. I'd like sufficient tools to interact with them in ways that didn't feel forced or—a chat line with pretty pictures just doesn't cut it. I'd like all of this in the context of a narrative that's richer and more varied that the typical fantasy or sci-fi scenario. I mean, killing monsters and going on random questions is all well and good but how about something more? Not too much to ask, is it? We're pretty close to providing that experience already. (Quoted in "Player 1 Ready! Player 2 Press Start" 2002, p. 74)

Yuji Naka, president and CEO of Sega's Sonic Team, answered,

> My ultimate online gaming experience would be a game that allows you to experience virtual senses through the network, not with television as a medium. You would not only be able to hear, see and feel but also even taste and smell. (Quoted in "Player 1 Ready! Player 2 Press Start" 2002, p. 74)

Sylvian Constatin, project manager at Ubisoft Entertainment, answered,

> I think that some kind of global virtual world, recreating a better clone of our world, and in which anything possible in real life (and more . . .) would be possible, would be absolutely fantastic. (Quoted in "Player 1 Ready! Player 2 Press Start" 2002, p. 74)

The visions of these developers progress from a rich and varied game that is conducive to rich and varied social interaction, via a sensorially fully immersive game world to an even-better-than-the-real-world virtual world. In many ways, these visions echo William Gibson's original and originary descriptions of cyberspace in *Neuromancer* (1984) and Neal Stephenson's vision of the "metaverse" in *Snow Crash* (1992).

Cyberspace as Gibson described it was a physically inhabitable, electronically generated alternate reality. It was entered by means of direct links to the brain; that is, it was inhabited by refigured human "persons" separated from their physical bodies, which were parked in "normal" space. In cyberspace, the physical laws of "normal" space did not need to apply, although some experiential rules carried over from the normal space; for example, the geometry of cyberspace as Gibson described it was Cartesian (Stone 1995, p. 34).

Cyberspace, the concept of an inhabitable, electronically generated alternate reality, has become the dominant metaphor for thinking about the nonspace of electronically represented and mediated symbolic interaction. Indeed, the metaphor of cyberspace has gone beyond the conceptual, and not only are game worlds now modeled along the lines of an electronically inhabitable, navigable virtual space, but future visions of the Internet and access to it are also cast in these terms and have been for some time. This vision is being implemented as we speak: numerous online multiplayer game spaces are under development; real-time speech interaction, including voice distortion technology, is available; faster graphics cards are released on a merciless six-month product cycle; and at least one blind person already has a miniature camera wired directly into his brain via a custom signal processor, allowing him, when all parts of the plan come together, to "see" the image the camera provides (Kotler 2002).

The technical reality of cyberspace as envisioned by Gibson and Stephenson is approaching fast. But what is the social reality of these cyberspaces going to be? What social conventions, norms, and rules about the "physical" properties of objects and modes of social interaction, about identity, race, ethnicity, gender, physical appearances, and (dis)abilities are the programmers encoding into the very fabric of those virtual worlds? An enormous amount of work goes into developing fantastical virtual environments, life-like animated avatars, and artificial intelligence routines for computer-controlled characters, but the mechanics animating these worlds and shaping the tools and conventions for social interaction in them are, mostly implicitly, based on our everyday commonsense understandings of how the world works. These understandings are formalized, reified, and encoded as the natural way of doing business in virtual environments, while the social implications of this process remain largely invisible to developers and users alike. This shouldn't be much of a surprise, because much of our day-to-day cosmology is shrouded by the fact that it simply is "the way things are." With more and more of our everyday communication, business, and life taking place in computer-mediated environments, it becomes more and more important to make visible the sociocultural machinations and presuppositions that are (being) encoded in it. Stone (1995, p. 27) puts it emphatically when she writes that

> [w]ithin a short time, the number of hours that a broad segment of children will spend playing computer-based games will exceed the number of hours that they spend watching television. It is entirely possible that computer-based games will turn out to be the major unacknowledged source of socialization *and* education in industrialized societies before the 1990s have run their course.

Although the last years of the twentieth century have proven Stone's expectation a bit too bold, I believe that it would not be wise to underestimate the importance of the matter.

In the technologized and mediated Western societies, technology is often viewed as a transparent and neutral tool. Technology, however, is developed by people who are embedded in a particular social, cultural, political, and economic situation. The programmers of the text-only virtual environment re-created by the MUD, for example, proceeded from a commonsense understanding of what it means to speak with one another in a physical environment and applied that understanding to the MUD. One player can have his or her character, for example, "whisper" to another character. Both the sending and receiving players see the intended message on their screen, but the players of other characters who happen to be in the same room will only see a message to the effect that Character A whispered something to Character B. Had the player of Character A chosen to "say" something to Character B, then everyone in the same room would have been able to "hear" what Character A said to Character B. And if the player had made Character A "shout" at Character B, even players in adjoining rooms would have heard what the conversation was about.

The implementation of different commands for "spoken" interaction in a MUD is a relatively straightforward illustration of how commonsense social and cultural understandings shape online environments, which in turn shape our online interactions. In his article "Living inside the (Operating) System: Community in Virtual Reality," John Unsworth details how Unix (the operating system that runs most Internet servers) and MOO program code reflect/encode the cultural and institutional beliefs of the people and the institutions that spawned them.

MOOs in general take shape under twin forces not unlike fate and free will, where free will is what we always have understood it to be, but where the role of fate is played by the operating system in which the MOO is embedded. The aporia in this analogy, and it is an important one for my argument, is that unlike transcendental fate, computer operating systems are historically and culturally determined. (Unsworth 1996)

Unix is that operating system in which MOOs are embedded. It was developed by AT&T's Bell Labs during the 1960s and 1970s to offer multiple users simultaneous access to then very expensive mainframe computers.

The Unix file system is hierarchical in its organization, and the particular kind of hierarchy is, in essence, dendritic: file systems have a treelike structure, with a "root" directory containing files and other directories, or branches, of the file system, which in turn can contain other files and directories. In Unix, every file (and, indeed, every process) has an individual owner, and the hierarchy of owners explicitly mirrors the hierarchy of the file system itself, with the superuser of all users and user groups called "root" (Unsworth 1996).

Unsworth mentions several factors that were of crucial importance for the development of Unix. Bell Labs received a relatively large amount of money for research from AT&T, the former telecom monopolist, which gave researchers quite some leeway on their projects, although, working for a commercial company, a certain amount of research was still expected to "pay off." AT&T, mindful of the then recently settled antitrust lawsuits, decided to distribute Unix at or near cost to universities while setting a prohibitively high price for other companies. That meant that AT&T offered next to no support, which in turn lead to the formation of an informal, cooperative support system in which the users helped one another. These factors, combined with the fact that Unix was designed with communication and the sharing of precious mainframe resources in mind, led to an operating system that incorporated both the institutional, hierarchical qualities "ordained" by the company where it was developed and the individual but cooperative and communicative qualities of the programmers who made it.

On the one hand, as a mental representation of the universe of information, Unix is deeply indebted to culturally determined notions such as private property, class membership, and hierarchies of power and effectivity. On the other hand, this tool, shaped though it was by the notions of ownership and exclusivity, spawned a culture of cooperation, of home-made code, of user-contributed modifications and improvements—in short, of "fellowship" (Unsworth 1996).

MOO-code was developed at Xerox Parc, also in a well-funded research facility where researchers could "get away" with doing some research that didn't have any immediate commercial applications. MOO-code runs, first and foremost, on Unix machines, and Unsworth details how the MOO-code and Unix share quite a few characteristics. A MOO is also a hierarchical system, where the users (wizards, programmers, players) have tightly controlled access to the MOO's objects, depending on the permissions detailed by their hierarchical status. The objects, the building blocks that form the very fabric of the MOO, are themselves ordered in a hierarchical fashion; different orders of objects relate to one another in a parent-child (directory and file) system, and the first object (#0) from which the MOO universe proceeds can be likened to the Unix "root directory."

Mainstreaming Masculinity

A number of important articles about gender and the Internet appeared in the first half of the 1990s, roughly bookended by the publication of Michael Benedikt's *Cyberspace: First Steps* (1991) and Sherry Turkle's *Life on the Screen* (1995). In 1990, the Internet as a whole was still mostly an, admittedly overgrown, academic research project, but important social technologies such as Usenet, IRC, and MUDs were already in place. For social scientists, the rapid expansion and adoption of the Internet in the first half of the 1990s came on the heels of poststructural and postmodern theory. Important elements of everyday life such as nationality, race, sexuality, and gender had become redefined as discursive constructions, held in place in society by power relationships. In gender studies, these theoretical movements reinforced and completed the transition from thinking about gender as a natural or biological given to gender as a social construction. And race, for example, had become but a very tenuous explanation for past and present hierarchies of power, as even the biological sciences posited African Eve, who presumably lived about fifty thousand years ago, as the common ancestor of every woman and man alive today.[2] Theoretically at least, identity appeared to have come under the individual's control, a matter of personal choice up to a point. Up to the point, really, of everyday reality, where the established webs of power and knowledge constrain and ascertain the outer limits of idiosyncrasy and where change happens much slower than wishful thinking and the giddy bubble economy of the 1990s would have.

However, the mostly textual and disembodied communication on the Internet connected strongly with the postmodern view of the world as inherently mediated and constructed, and IRC and MUDs in particular offer the possibility of (co)constructing the self, the other, their genders, and their surroundings in direct textual interaction. Most studies of gender focused on the implications of being able to deconstruct gender in online environments, because even though theory allowed deconstruction of gender in the everyday world, only the Internet appeared to offer spaces where this theory could be "lived." Deconstructing gender, or showing the arbitrariness of the qualities attributed to masculinity and femininity as "natural facts" and showing the very real political, economic, and everyday effects of those "natural facts," was and is particularly important from a feminist point of view. When the "natural facts" of life really are our own social constructions, then we can "rewrite" the rules and create a world better suited to ideals of equality and democracy.

The early studies (Reid 1991, 1994; Bruckman 1992; Cherny 1994, 1995; Turkle 1995) broke the ground by introducing IRC, MUDs, and computer-mediated communication in general as a field of social-scientific study and by developing a vocabulary for it. These studies focused on three aspects of gender in text-only online interaction: first, that, indeed, the gender of your online representation is a choice and that you can choose the opposite gender of your real-life gender (gender swapping); second, that you can choose a nonconventional, neither male nor female, gender (gender bending);[3] third, how these possibilities tied in with gender studies and what their effects were or could be. The possibilities for "playing" with gender were accessible to a growing number of people, and the general perception of the researchers seemed to be that this could lead to a shift in the popular understanding of gender, similar to the shift that had occurred in the social sciences.

An interesting side effect of studying gender on IRC and in MUDs and their possible effects on everyday life was that the researchers had to somehow define or show the "importance" or "reality value" of what happened online, vis-à-vis more pessimistic notions of the Internet (and MUDs in particular) as inconsequential at best or outright dangerous at worst. Bruckman's and Turkle's psychologically oriented work provided a compelling theory in that respect. They argue that playing a character in a

MUD allows the players deal with everyday, real-life problems by playing their characters and interacting with other players. Playing with gender in the relative safety and anonymity of IRC or a MUD allows the players to explore different aspects of their identity, and when returning to their everyday life from their life on the screen the therapeutic effects of the MUD allows them to better deal with their real-life problems and problematic social conventions. This argument carried and still carries a lot of weight and returns in one form or another in many later articles. Although I do not deny the reflexive nature of playing a character in a MUD and the possible personal advantages that it may yield, my main critique of this argument is that, in essence, it doesn't take the online experience seriously. It seems that what makes the online "play" worthwhile is not the experience itself but the expression of that experience in a substantial gain for the "MUDder" in his or her everyday real life. The virtual reality is acknowledged as a social space of importance for the players, but it is made unreal and Other with respect to the real reality, which is thereby restored as the one true and final reality and kept safe from the possibly disruptive forces of an Other reality. But I am getting ahead of the argument here.

The possibly disruptive forces of gender and identity being uprooted in virtual reality, however, have largely failed to materialize. This probably will not have surprised Susan Herring (1994), who early on claimed that communicative processes on mailing lists largely reflected everyday gender biases and showed a remarkably clear male-versus-female dichotomy. Only recently (Kendall 2002; Schaap 2002) it seems a similar notion has made its way into the analyses of MUDs. Here the focus is not so much on discerning male from female "speech" but, rather, on the stereotypical ways in which players choose to enact masculinity and femininity through their characters. Lori Kendall (2002, p. 107) explains that while the "electronic medium that makes gender masquerade possible and conceivable for a wider range of people [it] also enables both the masqueraders and their audiences to interpret these performances in ways that distance them from a critique of 'real' gender." The parodical and subversive gender reenactments that gender theorist Judith Butler wrote about in her influential book *Gender Trouble: Feminism and the Subversion of Identity* (1990a) are thwarted by "the understanding that the limitations of the medium *require* performance allows online participants to interpret online gender masquerade selectively as *only* performance" (Kendall 2002, p. 107). This is exactly the concern that Butler voices in another article (1990b, p. 278), when she likens gender enactments to stage plays and notes that the subversive qualities of political plays can be demoted by reading/reframing them as "just an act."

The potentially subversive effects of online games and social interaction prove to be quite limited, but the traditional gender conventions that were supposed to be questioned online appear to be doing quite well. Although gender bending occurs regularly in MUDs, Roberts and Parks (1999) conclude that the vast majority of participants choose to swap genders, sticking to more traditional notions of gender and gender relations, rather than choose a potentially more subversive nonconventional gender. In my own study (Schaap 2002), I found that role-players largely rely on conventional and socially legible expressions of masculinity and femininity to enact their characters, while developing finely tuned mechanisms for reading one another's performances for cues about the players' real-life gender. And Kendall (2002) and Herring (1994) find that online spaces in many instances are masculine spaces, where expectations of behavior and identity are shaped by traditional notions of heterosexuality and standards of hegemonic masculinity.

Most gender studies regard the naturalized, heterosexual, masculine normativity of many everyday locations and interactions as problematic from a feminist or queer point of view, and rightly so. However, this masculine normativity is only rarely problematized for (heterosexual) men themselves, which is my main concern here. Even though conventional constructions of gender appear to cast white heterosexual masculinity in a more favorable hierarchical position, what is often overlooked is that these constructions are in many ways just as constrictive and restrictive as the other gendered identities "recognized" in society. When particular traits commonly associated with masculinity, such as aggressiveness and self-reliance, are problematized, it is through pathologization, as in the case of aggression in video games or noncommunicativeness and technological "obsession" of nerds and geeks. Meanwhile, normative images of heterosexual masculinity are not only (re-)created by MUDders, who have a relatively large say in how they wish to shape and portray their character, but also in mass-market video games and commercial graphical multiuser online role-playing games (MMORPGs). Recently I bought a video game called Splinter Cell. This is not an online game, but I find it an intriguing example of how masculinity is more often than not constructed in game environments. In the game, the player plays a character called Sam Fisher, who looks a lot like movie star George Clooney and whose description reads as follows:

> Fisher has been on the front lines of espionage in several defining conflicts throughout the past decades. He's a survivor and excels in covert operations through hard work, insatiable curiosity, and brutal honesty. He has little time for diplomatic niceties and even less for lies. Though fully aware of and confident in his abilities, Fisher understands that his survival has often been a matter of luck. He knows he is human and fallible and does not want to die. He has a strange and slightly dark sense of humor. He is quiet, instinctive, and observant: somebody who watches from the outside. Combat, espionage, and combat training have defined his adult life; his tactical experience has become part of his instinct. Now, even outside of work he is most comfortable on the fringes of society, keenly observant but still removed. Fisher has acquired an admirable collection of scars and secured his place in Valhalla; he has little left to prove to the world. Now older and wiser, he has no interest in glory. If he fights, it is because he believes the cause is necessary and he is capable. ("Who Is Sam Fisher?" 2002, p. 8)

Interestingly enough, halfway through the game the player learns that Sam has a daughter (and presumably a wife, but I haven't finished the game yet), who then provides yet another motive for Sam to fight his righteous fight, while at the same time introducing/reinforcing the heterosexuality of the lead character. I am a white, fair-haired, blue-eyed, heterosexual, thirty-something, middle-class male with a university degree. Presumably, I fit the game's target demographic. Do I as a player identify with this character? Well, for gaming purposes I do. The character locates my "point of being" (Wilhelmsson 2001) in the game world, and I enjoy Tom Clancy's international-spy-thriller storyline through him. However, do I as a player identify with the image of masculinity expressed by Sam and articulated through his role and actions in the game's narrative? Well, if you have to be a guy anyway, why wouldn't you want to be a good-looking, broad-shouldered, smart, and capable man with an intriguing dark sense of humor and a dangerous but rewarding job, working for a top-secret American government outfit protecting humanity's freedom. However, Sam's character feels strained, stereotypically male, even for someone like me, who might be every control group's favorite subject, and I find it hard to take seriously and thus to identify with this character. It is my firm belief, and something I'm working toward in my current research, that we need to look more closely at how masculinity is shaped in online and game spaces, without forgetting or, rather, building on the work already done on femininity and traditional power relationships in these spaces. Too long has masculinity been feminism's and queer studies' Other, and it is time to break down the monolithic image of white heterosexual masculinity.

NOTES

1. MMORPG: Massively Multiplayer Online Role-Playing Game.

2. Interestingly, we never get to hear much about African Eve's significant other.

3. "Gender swapping" or "gender switching" are the terms usually used to indicate women taking on male personae or vice versa, while "gender bending" is usually used to indicate a broader range of "gender play," including nonconventional genders, but usually also including gender swapping.

REFERENCES

Benedikt, M. (ed.). (1991) *Cyberspace: First Steps.* Cambridge, MA: MIT Press.

Bruckman, A. (1992) "Identity Workshop: Emergent Social and Psychological Phenomena in Text-Based Virtual Reality." Available at http://www.cc.gatech.edu/~asb/old/papers-index-dec01.html#IW.

Butler, J. (1990a) *Gender Trouble: Feminism and the Subversion of Identity.* New York: Routledge.

Butler, J. (1990b) "Performative Acts and Gender Constitution." In Sue-Ellen Case (ed.), *Performing Feminisms.* Baltimore: Johns Hopkins University Press.

Butler, J. (1993) *Bodies That Matter: On the Discursive Limits of "Sex."* New York: Routledge.

Castells, M. (2001) *The Internet Galaxy: Reflections on the Internet, Business, and Society.* Oxford: Oxford University Press.

Cherny, L. (1994) "Gender Differences in Text-Based Virtual Reality." Available at http://www.usyd.edu.au/su/social/papers/cherny2.html.

Cherny, L. (1995) "'Objectifying' the Body in the Discourse of an Object-Oriented MUD." Available at http://fragment.nl/mirror/Cherny/Objectifying_the_body.txt.

Gibson, W. (1984) *Neuromancer.* New York: Ace.

Herring, S. (1994) "Gender Differences in Computer-Mediated Communication: Bringing Familiar Baggage to the New Frontier." Available at http://www.cpsr.org/cpsr/gender/herring.txt.

Kendall, L. (2002) *Hanging Out in the Virtual Pub: Masculinities and Relationships Online*. Berkeley: University of California Press.

Kotler, S. (2002) "Vision Quest." *Wired* 10.09, August. Available at http://www.wired.com/wired/archive/10.09/vision.html.

Miller, D., and Slater, D. (2000). *The Internet: An Ethnographic Approach*. Oxford, UK: Berg.

"Player 1 Ready! Player 2 Press Start" (2002) *XBox Nation* 3, pp. 68–77.

Reid, E. M. (1991) "Electropolis: Communication and Community on Internet Relay Chat." Available at http://www.aluluei.com/electropolis.htm.

Reid, E. M. (1994) "Cultural Formations in Text-Based Virtual Realities." Available at http://www.aluluei.com/cult-form.htm.

Roberts, L. D., and Parks, M. (1999) "The Social Geography of Gender-Switching in Virtual Environments on the Internet." *Information, Communication and Society* 2, no. 4, pp. 521–540.

Schaap, F. (2002) *The Words That Took Us There: Ethnography in a Virtual Reality*. Amsterdam: Aksant Academic.

Stephenson, N. (1992) *Snow Crash*. New York: Bantam Spectra.

Stone, A. R. (1995) *The War of Desire and Technology at the Close of the Mechanical Age*. Cambridge, MA: MIT Press.

Turkle, S. (1995) *Life on the Screen: Identity in the Age of the Internet*. London: Phoenix.

Unsworth, J. (1996) "Living inside the (Operating) System: Community in Virtual Reality." Available at http://www3.iath.virginia.edu/pmc/Virtual.Community.html.

"Who Is Sam Fisher?" (2002) Tom Clancy's Splinter Cell, Dutch Xbox game booklet, Ubisoft Entertainment. Translated by the author.

Wilhelmsson, U. (2001) "Enacting the Point of Being: Computer Games, Interaction and Film Theory." Ph.D. diss., University of Skövde, Sweden.

Chapter 21

Gender, Technology, and Visual Cyberculture
Virtually Women

Kate O'Riordan

This chapter examines simulations of femininity through commercial digital media products, drawing on Ananova, a simulated newsreader, and other figures that have formal similarities, such as Lara Croft. This discussion also links representation on the Web with mobile communications and wireless networking.

Ananova is, after Kyoko Date (and with the exception of the game avatars), the most celebrated virtual persona to date. Ananova was launched as an Internet newscaster for a news portal of the same name and heavily publicized in January 2000 as the "cyberbabe" to read the news. The figure is an animated character, designed by the Digital Animations Group, that reads news clips on the Internet news agency site (www.ananova.com) through the deployment of RealSpeak text-to-speech programming. With the refinement of Wireless Application Protocol (WAP), mobile telephony as an Internet portal, and the purchase of Ananova by the Orange mobile network, the character has become part of the convergence of mobile telephones and the Internet. Orange uses aspects of the Ananova portal, including Ananova's video reports, to deliver a news service through mobile telephony.

Producers posit digital media products such as Ananova as a bridge between the technology and human users. These products are represented as a development in the human-computer interface where the interface is so friendly that communication technologies are "humanized." As noted in previous work—and discussed extensively by Lev Manovich (2001)—the desire to represent photographic realism is a main development path in digital media production. Among what Manovich calls the "icons of mimesis" is the flesh, the human body, and within that, at the apex of these design goals, are the movements of the face and the sound of speech. Linked to this "naturalization" of simulated images is the "naturalization" of the human body, and as the marked body, the female body represents the most naturalized body image. So in an order of naturalized simulacra we have first the flesh/human bodies/figures (e.g., crowd scenes in films); second, the individual person (e.g., game characters, personalities, mimetic avatars); third, the female body, the sexed and gendered form (e.g., Ananova, Lara Croft, Kyoto Date). These last elements represent both an apex of programming and design achievement and the strongest signifier of the concept of the natural—feminized forms—in the semiotic patterns of masculine, feminine, artifact, natural.

> Although . . . technology makes possible the destabilisation of sexual identity as a category, there has also been a curious but fairly insistent history of representations of technology that work to fortify—sometimes desperately —conventional understandings of the feminine. (Doane 1990, p. 20)

Redrawing on Mary Ann Doane's assertion, which mirrors Raymond Williams's (1975) claim along the same lines (that technological change works to fortify conventional social values), I highlight some issues and questions I have about simulations of femininity. There are three themes here:

- The gendering of the interface through a paradigm of friendship (corporate address);
- Aesthetics and heteronormative binary sex/gender conflations;
- The implications of the shift from representation to simulation and the virtuality/visibility/body relation implicit in this shift (Kember 1998).

Simulations as the Interface with "New" Technologies

Digital art, animation, and Human Computer Interaction/Interface (HCI) development trajectories have long pursued the notion of "user friendly." The obvious goal of such trends is to develop an interface (interface having the property of being between faces) that could be conceived of in the same paradigm as a friend.[1] In addition to this, cultural figures such as the cyborg and the posthumanistic, as well as actor-network theories, contribute to the development of this logic. A simulated person is the contemporary realization of this HCI research and aesthetic realism.

In line with the favored characters in offline media, these personae are young, attractive, female celebrities. The friendly female face is thus the future present of the convergence of cybercultural forms such as mobile telephony, computer games, hand-held devices, and the Internet. Ananova is a primary example, a product developed at the same time as Mya, a virtual persona who was developed to "link the real world with the virtual" (Barboza 2000).

In 2000, this corporate move to "personalize the impersonal" (technology) revolved around these two virtual personae, both of which are represented as female, single, and stereotypically attractive. Ananova, for example, is reported to be a combination of popular iconic figures Posh Spice, Kylie Minogue, and Carol Vorderman and is attributed with having "a full range of human characteristics" (ITN 2000) and with enabling a personalization of the "impersonal" information networks. Ananova also marks a shift from visual design for the Web to design objectives for mobile screens.

Simulations as "Female" and "Friendly"

The technology is represented as female—now not only extratextually, such as the science-fiction examples analyzed by Doane (1990). But now the female is inserted into the technology, and vice versa, to more fully conflate female with technology. There are a variety of implications of the technology-as-female dynamic within psychoanalytic theories of visual culture. Analyses such as those by Mary Anne Doane (1990), Sarah Kember (1998), and Christian Metz (1982) have produced much discussion of the gendering of technology and the dynamics of technology/gender/sexuality. An example of this is Doane's (1990, p. 31) observation when discussing Freud, Metz, and Bailble: "In both cases the theory understands the obsession with technology as a tension of movement toward and away from the mother . . . the conjunction of technology and the feminine is the object of fascination and desire but also of anxiety." When "the mother" continues to be understood as female, these narratives of gendering reposition gender in a heterosexualized optical binary of maternal/paternal, female/male, which still repositions female as lack.

These analyses often separate out the simulation (or digital image) from the photograph or analogue film. Kember's (1998, p. 10) focus on photography, medical imaging, and video surveillance, for example, although explicitly offering "a critique of the technologically determined split between photography and new imaging technologies," also serves to maintain a partial distinction between the referential and nonreferential image, a distinction that has ceased to be sustainable in the context of digital production. As Manovich (2001) points out in relation to the history of art, this distinction has always been tenuous.

The emphasis on the referential image in work such as Kember's (1998) leads me to deal with a different aspect here, that of simulations or nonreferential images. These are often dismissed as cartoon or animation and therefore irrelevant except in relation to children or an "underground" history of film. However, simulated characters are significant sites of identification and commodification within the circuit of culture (to paraphrase Hall [1997]) and particularly within the circuit of cyberculture. They are also constructed through a near obsession with a reality aesthetic (Manovich 2001). Therefore, as catalysts for thinking about both the extremely real and the extremely gendered, they perhaps enable us to draw out further implications for sex/gender dynamics and the virtual/visible/body relation.

The combination of the reality aesthetic and the insistence on simulations as friendly results in a concentrated effect. In much traditional media reception the consumer can be said to *view* the media content. In the computer game scenario the user *operates* the content (Lara Croft). With the simulated newscaster (Ananova) the consumer can instigate a relationship with the content, as the concept of interpellation is reenacted through digital media. This relationship can thus be compared to the relationships formed with other "others," i.e., interpersonal ones. The relationship is mediated by our understanding of a difference between persons and digital images—although there has been a cultural shift from humanism to an understanding of persons as integrated with machines, the cognitive division remains strong. However, a relationship with Ananova is in some ways intended to be comparable to an interpersonal relationship.

I am not suggesting that the simulation fools the consumer but that we have reached a cultural moment in which the concept of interpersonal extends beyond humanism to encompass phenomena other than organic humans (the concept of posthumanism is relevant here). Our concepts of realism as an aesthetic also allow us to look at illusion in terms of the effect it has on us rather than its "reality."

Consumers form emotional, psychological, and physical relationships with media celebrities. The subject engages with a variety of actors material, symbolic, and both. The "reality" status of these actors and images is relatively unimportant; there have, for example, long been fan groups for the characters played by actors. In terms of these animations, Lara Croft has a thriving fan base, and when Kyoko Date was publicized through magazine features, some consumers thought that the images referred to an organic human person. A difference between these simulated characters and the acted characters is the ontology of the object.

There is a person who looks and sounds like the character played by an actor. The character may be fictional, but it has a body. The simulation's body is informational. This simulation reverses the avatar-user relationship where the avatar is the vehicle for the body to navigate cyberspace: the virtual personae is the avatar of cyberspace for "it" to navigate the actual.

Many of the virtual personae that have emerged on the market to date are simulations of young, attractive females. These personae are clearly being constructed through a heteronormative paradigm. This gendering of the interface as young (white) females invokes a familial relationship of fathering.[2]

This structures the technology through a "preferred reading" (which we might, after Price [2002], reterm "corporate address") as malleable, semi-innocent, vulnerable, attractive, and naturalized. Through the construction of a familial relationship, the personae are simultaneously desexualized and eroticized (e.g., the price paid for Ananova was reported as "the dowry"). There has been speculation that the prevalence of female fantasy figures is related to the dominance of men in software engineering and programming. This is, I think, an oversimplification of the way discourses of gender and sexuality are deployed, and it also reduces an understanding of contemporary digital media production, which is as much about graphic design, art, and animation as programming. I argue that these figures relate to a much wider cultural ideology mobilized through the two intersecting discourses of masculine/feminine and machinic/natural.

A game hero catalogue, *1000 Game Heroes* (Choquet 2002), provides a classification, "sexy heroes," that conveys an image of the feminine body that is hypersexualized in that its femininity is predicated on the gender/ sex conflation. The bodies connote "female" through the morphology of having no penis (lack) and through having breasts (excess). They have a Victorian aesthetic of tiny waists and large breasts, but without the excessive fabric. In another recent publication, *Digital Beauties,* Wiedemann (2001) claims to detail the range of products now available. The launch advertising for the book reads as follows:

> Here you'll discover a host of digital beauties from all around the world and a dizzying array of styles and techniques—moody black-and-white nudes, surreal portraits, Lara Croft–style adventure chicks, sleek ultra-futuristic babes, etc. Both 2D and 3D design are covered, with an emphasis on the latter; some images are so stunningly lifelike it's hard to believe they're 100% computer generated. (Taschen 2001)

"Digital beauties" are all simulations of the female body, "babes," "chicks," and "nudes," artifacts positioned as the current apex in digital aesthetics. These figures are all very traditional, however, and these "futuristic" beauties are already aesthetically "dated," having close links to anime, cartoon, and styles of gothic and cyberpunk subcultures rather than being anything new. They do, however, point to another development in the relationship between the body and representations of the body in cyberculture; they represent another element of the "reality" genre: the idea of a simulation has come to represent something that is virtually real.

Research in the 1980s pointed to a popular conceptualization of computers as impersonal and frightening (Turkle 1995). Computing-related activities are still seen as both impersonal and destructive to human relationships—concepts of Internet addiction are a case in point.[3] Cultural myths about artificial intelligences, read through computers and robots, antagonistically dominating the human race are prevalent in the media (see films such as *War Games,* 1983; *Terminator,* 1984; and *The Matrix,* 1999). In the 1990s, Turkle (1995) pointed to a shift in conceptualizations that occurred as the personal computer became more widely available in the 1980s and in the 1990s became viewed as "personal."

Another point in this shift occurs when computers are being both marketed and increasingly conceptualized as integrated with the human (notions of the cyborg, wearable computing, counseling software programs, Stelarc). The gendering of the interface mentioned earlier points to a conceptualization of digital hardware as actively friendly, nonthreatening, desirable, and malleable. One of the cultural fears about cybercultural forms is that they may be too "intelligent" and hyperrational. This gendered figuration demotes these levels of perceived intelligence and rationality. As feminized figures, the level of intelligence can be understood as that culturally attributed to women. Thus, computers can even be conceptualized as more emotional and less rational than their (hu)man users.

Reality Aesthetics and Heteronormativity

Having set up these feminized/technologized imaginary friends, I want to think about them by returning to Kember (1998) and, before that, to Benjamin (1969). With tools from these theorists, further implications for sex/gender dynamics and the virtual/visible/body relation can be drawn out. First, the aesthetics of the heteronormative binary sex/gender conflation are worth dwelling on because at issue is the question of how these simulations are so clearly female (in addition to their discursive construction as such by Wiedemann [2001], for example). The femininity is symbolic, coded and read as expression, language, hair, actions, costumes, and colors. They are after all not bodies—they are representations. They cannot be sexed through chromosomes, genital arrangement, mammary glands, hormones. However, it is of course partly the obverse, they are gendered through morphology. They are sexed, and then gendered in conflation, precisely through the shape of the pelvis, the lack of the penis, and the excess of breasts. Figure-hugging costumes, endemic in new media animations (and naturalized as a "demand" of programming constraints), serve to recast the body as unambiguous and to "show" that there is indeed lack (of the penis) and excess (of the breasts): the classic psychoanalytic figuration of the naturalized feminine.

Implications

The reason that I think it is significant to highlight the femaleness of these figures is partly only to say, Look—new technologies, for all their apparent newer, faster, liberating auras, are of course marketed through one of the most traditional and stereotyped sites of commodification—the sexed female body.

However, more important for me is the visibility/body relation, and to return to Kember's (1998) notion of the trace of the real (Benjamin's "aura") in relation to the photograph, I want to ask what happens if we relate this to the nonreferential image, like the simulation. I do this to suggest that simulations produce a new experience of *having been* (having material traces). They provide a way of looking at how the symbolic and psychic produce material realities and residue. These icons have an existence in a similar way that memory exists, and they reproduce the simulated female as a "real" agent with which the viewer/user has a relationship. In this way they are both a successful rendering of the technology as "friend" (as in user-friendly) and a successful manifestation of new normative bodies because of their visible signification as bodies. So the reality aesthetic in the simulation can force us to accept new (cyber) bodies in the social. But my concern is that these bodies reproduce deeply problematic versions of identity and bodies, renewing old templates, against which normality beauty and legitimacy can (again) be judged. (These same issues have been raised in relation to medical imaging by Kember [1998], Thacker [1998], and Doyle and O'Riordan [2002].) Theorists of cyberculture have long considered the implications of the body's entering cyberspace through some version of immersion or jacking in. This expectation has been preempted by the bringing of the virtual out to the body and the embodiment of the virtual. Virtual bodies, it turns out, are not the human translated into data but the data embodied as a fantasy of the female.

These virtual personae are simulations, then, that in some ways converge with traditional representational practices but also signify differently. Unlike the cartoon or phantasmagoria characters, these virtual personae are attempts not to realize the fantastic but to idealize the real. The concept of the perfect copy of which there is no original is familiar from the work of Walter Benjamin (1969)and Jean Baudrillard (1994 [1981]). These ideal women, for which there is no referent, are like Frankenstein's creature and like the projected goals of artificial intelligence (AI) and artificial life (AL) development: imagined ideal forms materialized. They have a virtual materiality, imagined, planned, and contained in software and hardware, realized through cyberspaces and through the aesthetic moment of reception. This does not make them, psychologically and materially, less real. There is an obvious problem in drawing a distinction between the virtual and actual because the virtual cannot accurately be described as less "real." Real and nonreal is a cognitive division like nature and culture —an attempt to separate realms of existence into different zones by constructing an opposition. This division does not have an ontological guarantee, and the slippage of these zones into each other cannot be described solely in terms of eccentricity or irrelevancy. If the real is never in the mediation but in the experience of the subject, then images have always been virtual (Kember 1998; Manovich 2001).

Conclusion

Simulations such as Ananova work, as Doane (1990, p. 20) has said, "to fortify—sometimes desperately—conventional understandings of the (hyper) feminine" as "female." At the point of production these figures thus close off understandings of what it means to signify as female, reinforcing visual encodings of hyperfemininity as the definition of "female." They do this by operating through a visual morphology of the sexed body (i.e., to be female is to appear as hyperfeminine). This reinforces the elision of sex into gender by remapping it onto a male/female binary. Although this chapter deals only with form and production (rather than accounting for consumption and interpretation), this closure, and the conflation of sex and gender into a static template, is not useful. It reproduces sexed hierarchies of difference and reintroduces one-dimensional understandings of gender, in a world where we have the need, and opportunity, to understand that gender and sex are constituted through multiple manifestations, variables, and processes.

As Kember (1998, p. 22) notes of the techniques that enable image simulation, "here the object world is regarded as not simply mutable but as totally malleable. It no longer exists as something exterior but marks the realization of the subject's desire and imagination."

The attempt to produce perfectly friendly and contained women, and perfectly friendly and contained technology, through these simulations marks the desire to realize technology and the female as in control (again) of the gaze that was disturbed by the emergence of the digital image and that produced the "virtual anxiety" that Kember highlights.

To bring these things together, these simulations simultaneously fortify conventional understanding and mark the realization of the subject's desire. The drive for the photographically real in visual cyberculture creates an object world that for the subject is populated by stereotypes, conventions, and normative subject/objects (Hillis 1999). The virtual is integrated with the actual, rendering the actual with the wallpaper of the screen, and this object world of images has a centrality to the mediated landscape. My point here is that the design of visual cyberculture is the design of the object world of the subject, and my question is, What does this mean for relations of power if we include simulations in accounts of the mediation of power? My argument has been that these figures cannot be relegated to a notion of the insignificant through a discourse of animation but must be examined in the very real context of the power that digital imaging has for the investment of the subject in the image.

Two final points: First, if these figures are a significant cultural interface, the power of corporate address in the visual rhetoric of these images to position the subject into a world of corporate design limits notions of developing new or resistant cultural forms linked to visual digital culture. Second, if the other of the digital object world is always malleable and homogenized, do not cultural understandings of difference always become turned forever and always toward a compulsion to colonize and control? The question that emerges from this is, If we understand the digital image as malleable, how does the cultural status of the image relate to power relations of social difference, and what is the implication for the other if the subject is always called into a vision of the self as author of the world?

NOTES

1. Human-computer interaction is a discipline concerned with the design, evaluation, and implementation of interactive computing systems for human use and with the study of major phenomena surrounding them.

2. The ethnicities that are being simulated—and how they are being simulated —require further analysis and are beyond the scope of this project. However, the fact that these simulations replicate and exaggerate not only heterosexual and patriarchal relations but also those of whiteness needs to be stated here.

3. See also Kraut et al. 1998 for a description of this "disorder" and Reed 2000 for an analysis of the discursive formations of health and computer use regulation.

REFERENCES

Abbate, Janet. 1999. *Inventing the Internet.* Cambridge, MA: MIT Press.

Barboza, David. 2000. "Motorola Hopes a Computer-Generated Character Will Link the Real World with the Virtual One." *New York Times,* April 25, p. C8.

Bassett, Caroline. 1997. "Virtually Gendered." In K. Gelder and S. Thornton (eds.), *The Subcultures Reader.* London: Routledge.

Baudrillard, Jean. 1994 [1981]. *Simulacra and Simulation.* Trans. S. F. Glaser. Ann Arbor: University of Michigan Press.

Benjamin, Walter. 1969. "The Work of Art in the Age of Mechanical Reproduction." In Hannah Arendt (ed.), *Illuminations.* New York: Schocken.

Braidotti, Rosi. 1996. *Between Monsters, Goddesses and Cyborgs: Feminist Confrontations with Science, Medicine and Cyberspace.* London: Zed.

Carter, Cynthia, Gill Branston, and Stuart Allan. 1998. *News, Gender and Power.* London: Routledge.

Castells, Manuel. 1996. *The Information Age: Economy, Society and Culture.* Cambridge, MA: Blackwell.

Cherny, Lynn, and Elizabeth Reba Weise (eds.). 1996. *Wired Women: Gender and New Realities in Cyberspace.* Emeryville, CA: Seal.

Choquet, David. 2002. *1000 Game Heroes.* Köln: Taschen.

Doane, Mary Anne. 1990. "Technophilia: Technology Representation and the Feminine." In M. Jacobus, Evelyn Fox Keller, and Sally Shuttleworth (eds.), *Body/Politics.* New York: Routledge.

Doyle, Julie, and Kate O'Riordan. 2002. "Virtually Visible: Female Cyberbodies and the Medical Imagination." In A. Booth and M. Flanagan (eds.), *Reload: Rethinking Women and Cyberculture.* Cambridge, MA: MIT Press.

Gibson, William. 1996. *Idoru.* London: Penguin.

Hall, Stuart (ed.). 1997. *Representations: Cultural Representations and Signifying Practices.* London: Sage, in association with the Open University.

Haraway, Donna. 1991. *Simians, Cyborgs and Women: The Reinvention of Nature.* London: Free Association.

Harcourt, Wendy. 1999. *Women@Internet: Creating New Cultures in Cyberspace.* London: Zed.

Herring, Susan. 1996. *Computer-Mediated Communication: Linguistic, Social and Cross-Cultural Perspectives.* Amsterdam: John Benjamins.

Hillis, Ken. 1999. *Digital Sensations: Space, Identity, and Embodiment in Virtual Reality.* Minneapolis: University of Minnesota Press.

ITN Online. 2000. "Ananova Turns a New Shade of Orange." Available at http://www.itn.co.uk:80/Business/bus20000705/070505.htm (accessed June 7, 2000).

Kember, Sarah. 1998. *Virtual Anxiety: Photography, New Technologies and Subjectivity.* Manchester: Manchester University Press.

Kraut, Robert, Sara Kiesler, Vicki Lundmark, Tridas Mukopadhyay, Michael Patterson, and William Scherlis. 1998. "Internet Paradox: A Social Technology That Reduces Social Involvement and Psychological Well-Being?" *American Psychologist* 53, no. 9 (July): 1017–1032.

Manovich, Lev. 2001. *The Language of New Media.* Cambridge, MA: MIT Press.

The Matrix. 1999. Dir. Andy and Larry Wachowski. Warner Bros.

Metz, Christian. 1982. *Psychoanalysis and the Cinema.* London: Macmillan.

Price, Stuart. 2002. "Masculinity and Corporate Address." Paper presented at University of Reading: Fourth Annual Conference of the Media, Cultural and Communication Studies Association (MeCCSA), December 19–21.

Reed, Lori. 2000. "Regulating Computer Use(rs): Corporate Engagements, Behavioural Science, and the Sponsorship of Health and Illness." Paper presented at the University of Birmingham: Third International Crossroads in Cultural Studies, June 21–25.

Taschen. 2001. "Almost Real: Building Women Out of Bits and Bytes." Taschen Web site. Available at http://www.taschen.com/ (accessed April 1, 2005).

The Terminator. 1984. Dir. James Cameron. Orion Pictures.

Terranova, Tiziana. 2000. "Affective Images: Videogames and the Cybernetic Rewiring of Vision." Paper presented at the University of Birmingham: Third International Crossroads in Cultural Studies, June 21–25.

Thacker, Eugene. 1998. ". . . /visible_human.html/digital anatomy and the hypertexted body." CTHEORY, Article A060. Available at http://www.ctheory.net/text_file.asp?pick=103 (accessed April 1, 2005).

Turkle, Sherry. 1995. *Life on the Screen: Identity in the Age of the Internet*. New York: Simon and Schuster.

War Games. 1983. Dir. John Badham. Metro-Goldwyn Mayer.

Weird Science. 1985. Dir. John Hughes. Universal Studios.

Wiedemann, Julius (ed). 2001. *Digital Beauties*. Köln: Taschen.

Williams, Raymond. 1975. *Television: Technology and Cultural Form*. New York: Schocken.

Part IV

Critical Histories of the Recent Past

Chapter 22

How Digital Technology Found Utopian Ideology

Lessons from the First Hackers' Conference

Fred Turner

In the mid-1990s, as the Internet and the World Wide Web went public, a utopian near-consensus about their likely social impact seemed to bubble up out of nowhere. The Net would level social hierarchies, distribute and personalize work, and dematerialize communication, exclaimed pundits and CEOs alike. The protocols of the Net were said to embody new, egalitarian forms of political organization. They offered the technological underpinnings for peer-to-peer commerce, and with them, claimed many, an end to corporate power. And well above the human plains of financial and political haggling, suggested some, those same protocols might finally link the now-disembodied species in a single, harmonious electrosphere.

Individually, these predictions popped up across American culture—and ultimately, around the world—throughout the following decade. But where did they come from? And how did they suddenly seem to be everywhere at once?

I raise these questions not so much to try to answer them (oh, the pages that would take!) as to turn our collective attention backward. Over the past ten years, cyberculture scholars have examined myriad forms of social life emerging in and around the wires. Many have also turned a critical eye on the discourses of cyberspace and their ideological effects. Yet almost all have left these two tasks unconnected.

To see what I mean, consider the two dominant approaches to explaining the rise of digital libertarianism in America. In the first, scholars have pointed out that new technologies as diverse as telephones and airplanes have always generated utopian hopes (Agre 1998, 2000; Healy 1997; King

2000; Miller 1995; Sardar 1996; Sobchack 1996). "The basic conceit is always the same," writes Langdon Winner (1997, p. 1001), "new technology will bring universal wealth, enhanced freedom, revitalized politics, satisfying community, and personal fulfillment." In the second approach, critics have read techno-utopianism as the self-serving ideology of an emerging "virtual class" (Barbrook and Cameron 1998; Borsook 2000; Kroker and Weinstein 1994; Terranova 1996; Turner 1999). Some, like Barbrook and Cameron (1998), have focused on the ways in which versions of techno-utopian discourse have helped manage the structural and cultural contradictions of working in high-tech. Others, such as Kroker and Weinstein (1994), have asserted that a new, transnational class has emerged alongside networked computing machinery and that its members have developed a techno-utopian ideology to support their class position.

Each of these perspectives has substantial analytical value. The first reminds us that the Internet and the Web were not the first "revolutionary" technologies, and it invites us to compare our digital present to a steam-powered or newly electrified past. The second points to the ways that emergent social groups have turned networked computers into ideologically charged symbols and asks us to keep our eye on the ways that new media can be recruited into ongoing power struggles. Yet, despite their usefulness, neither of these perspectives explains just *how* digital technologies and utopian ideology came together. Instead, each reifies an analytical category—technology in the first case, class in the second—and then declares it a source of ideology. In the process, each walls off from discussion all the social work that sociologists (Becker 1982; Berger and Luckmann 1966) and, particularly, sociologists of science and technology (Bijker, Hughes, and Pinch 1987; Bijker and Law 1992; Fleck 1979; Latour 1991, 1993; MacKenzie and Wajcman 1999) have shown goes into the construction of both ideology and technology.

To the extent that cyberculture scholars accept these walls, they tend to become readers of ideological texts. They might study the pages of *Wired* magazine and rail against its technophilic, macho prose, for instance, or search contemporary computer advertising for signs of virtual class self-promotion. This is useful work, but it leaves us critical amnesiacs: with it, we can articulate precisely where we are, culturally speaking, yet we can't say how we got here. For that, we need a historical version of what Stuart Hall has called a theory of "articulation" (Hall and Grossberg 1986, p. 45; see also Slack 1996). As Jonathan Sterne has pointed out, cultural studies scholars have long argued that "there are no necessary correspondences" between ideologies, practices, and social groups (Sterne 1999, p. 263). Rather, those correspondences are established by relevant social groups in particular times and places. It is these highly local, time-bound processes we need to explore. In the case of cyberlibertarianism, for example, we need to go back into the past and identify the social work that has gone into aligning emerging digital technologies with libertarian political ideals. By uncovering this work, we can relocate contemporary cyberculture in its historical context.[1] We can trace its emergence not simply to the rise of the Net or the Web but to negotiations surrounding the integration of those technologies into ongoing social and cultural transformations. At the same time, we can help integrate the study of technological culture into the study of culture more broadly.

The Case of the Hackers' Conference

To give a sense of what this kind of work might look like, I want to explore a single important moment in the development of utopian information ideology: the 1984 Hackers' Conference. In the early 1980s, hackers were widely depicted in the popular press as antisocial and potentially criminal (Levy 1984; Thomas 2002). By the mid-1990s, however, they had come to embody the liberated information worker. Their long hair and late-night prowlings were no longer depicted as evidence of deviance but as marks of genius. In popular accounts at least, hackers had become entrepreneurial hippies who wielded computers like LSD and were transforming America into a turned-on, high-tech New Economy. How did this happen?

Part of the answer is that a few hackers actually *were* hippies. Many individual computer developers in the 1960s and 1970s had countercultural sympathies, and countercultural ideals played an important role in the development of the personal computer (Freiberger and Swaine 1984; Markoff 2005). Yet this historical fact is only a piece of the puzzle. As a close look at the Hackers' Conference suggests, transformations in the symbolic character of hackers required face-to-face ideological work, carried out within a forum built for the purpose.[2]

This work began with the 1984 publication of San Francisco Bay Area journalist Steven Levy's book *Hackers: Heroes of the Computer Revolution*. In it, Levy identified three generations of computer hackers. The first emerged at MIT in 1959. They were undergraduates who clustered around a giant TX-o computer that had been built for defense research and then donated to the Institute. Within several years, these undergraduates were joined by a variety of Cambridge-area teenagers and MIT graduate students and were working with a series of computers donated by the Digital Equipment Corporation (DEC). By 1966, most gathered on the ninth floor of Technology Square, in Marvin Minsky's Artificial Intelligence ("AI") Laboratory.

Within the AI Lab, writes Levy, there were two kinds of workers: planners and hackers. The planners were theoreticians, usually of the mind, who thought of computers as tools that could be used to generate or model information. The hackers focused on the computer systems themselves and on seeing what they could do. Within the lab, a culture clash emerged. Theory-oriented graduate students, equipped with well-funded and well-organized careers but not necessarily with computer programming expertise, resented the hackers' claims for computer time, as well as their free-wheeling style. David Silver, for instance, was then a fourteen-year-old hanger-on at the lab who solved a seemingly impossible problem in designing a robot insect. He recalls that his work

> drove [the AI theoreticians] crazy . . . because this kid would just sort of screw around for a few weeks and the computer would start doing the thing they were working on that was really hard. . . . They're theorizing all these things and I'm rolling up my sleeves and doing it. . . . you find a lot of that in hacking in general. I wasn't approaching it from either a theoretical point of view or an engineering point of view, but from sort of a fun-ness point of view. (Quoted in Levy 1984, p. 104)

According to Levy, this point of view characterized the work of two subsequent generations of innovators. The first of these were the "hardware hackers" of the 1970s. Clustered in and around the San Francisco Bay area, they included the young founders of Apple Computer, Steve Jobs and Steve Wozniak, as well as early proselytizers for personal computing such as Lee Felsenstein, Bob Albrecht, and Ted Nelson. For this generation, Levy argued, computing could be seen as a form of political rebellion. Computers may have always been large and centralized, they may have always been guarded by institutionalized experts, they may have been used to organize the war in Vietnam, but programmers like Felsenstein and Nelson wanted to transform them into tools of personal liberation. The second generation to follow the AI hackers of MIT knew little of this countercultural legacy. They were the "young game hackers" of the early 1980s who had grown up working with the microcomputers that the previous generation had struggled to invent (Levy 1984, p. vi). They included Ken Williams, founder of game-maker On-Line Systems, and his wife, Roberta (designer of the game Mystery House), online-security expert Mark Ducheneau, and others. This generation worked in the shadow of Atari, the maker of Pac Man, but unlike Atari, which was infamous among computer designers for its organizational hierarchy, they also aimed to maintain an open management structure within their organizations. Though they worked in a corporate setting, their designers would be "hackers"—semi-independent, creative individuals—not drones.

Above all, Levy (1984, pp. 27–33) argued, though they had never met, members of all three generations shared a single set of six values, a "hacker ethic":

1. Access to computers—and anything which might teach you something about the way the world works—should be unlimited and total.
2. All information should be free.
3. Mistrust Authority   Promote Decentralization.
4. Hackers should be judged by their hacking, not bogus criteria such as degrees, age, race, or position.
5. You can create art and beauty on a computer.
6. Computers can change your life for the better.

In part because of the countercultural overtones of this list, Levy's work drew the attention of Kevin Kelly, future editor of *Wired* magazine, and Stewart Brand, former Merry Prankster and founder of one of the most influential publications to come out of the counterculture, the *Whole Earth Catalog*. Since the mid-1970s, Brand had edited a magazine devoted to cybernetics, ecology, and right living, called the *CoEvolution Quarterly*, as well as occasional reissues of the *Whole Earth Catalog*. He had recently hired Kelly, a former backpacker and Christian mystic, to edit the *Quarterly*. In 1983, Brand had been given a $1.3 million advance to create a *Whole Earth Software Catalog*, in the hope that he could do for the booming PC market what he had done for the back-to-the-land movement fifteen years earlier. After reading Levy's book, Brand and Kelly decided to hold a conference at which they would bring the three generations of hackers together.

As Kelly later recalled, he and Brand wanted to see whether hacking was "a precursor to a larger culture," and they wanted to "witness or have the group articulate what the hacker ethic was" (Kelly 2001).

Something like 150 hackers actually arrived to spend a weekend at Fort Cronkhite, in the Marin Headlands just north of the Golden Gate Bridge. They included Steve Wozniak of Apple, Richard Stallman, Ted Nelson, and Theodore Draper—known as Captain Crunch for his discovery that a toy whistle he found in a box of the cereal gave just the right tone to grant him free access to the phone system. Some worked alone, part-time at home; others represented such institutions as MIT, Stanford, Lotus Development, and various software makers. Most had come to meet others like themselves. Their hosts offered them food, computers, audio-visual supplies, and places to sleep—and a regular round of facilitated conversations.

By all accounts, two themes dominated those conversations: the definition of a "hacker ethic" and the description of emerging business forms in the computer industry (Brand 1985; Elmer-DeWitt 1984; Markoff, Robinson, and Shapiro 1985; Schrage 1984). The two themes were of course entwined. The "hacker ethic" that Levy described—the single thread ostensibly running through all of the participants' careers—had emerged at a moment in the commercial development of computing at which sharing products and processes improved profits for all. By the mid-1980s, however, the finances of computer and software development had changed radically. As Stewart Brand pointed out, in what would soon become a famous formulation, information-based products embodied an economic paradox. "On the one hand," he said, "information wants to be expensive, because it's so valuable. The right information in the right place just changes your life. On the other hand, information wants to be free, because the cost of getting it out is getting lower and lower all the time. So you have these two fighting against each other" (Brand 1985, p. 49).

Throughout the conference, hackers discussed different ways they had managed this dilemma. Some, like Richard Greenblatt, an early MIT hacker, argued that source code must always be made freely available, in keeping with the ethos of what has since become the Free Software movement. Others, like Robert Woodhead, suggested that they would happily give away the electronic tools they had used to make products such as computer games but that they would not give away the games themselves. "[T]hat's my soul in that product," explained Woodhead. "I don't want anyone fooling with that" (quoted in Brand 1985, p. 48). Bob Wallace discussed how he had marketed his text editor PC-WRITE as Shareware (in which users get the software for free but pay if they want documentation and support), while Andrew Fluegelman discussed how he had marketed his telecommunications program PC-TALK as Freeware (in which users voluntarily pay a small fee to use the software). Still others, like Macintosh designer Bill Atkinson, defended corporate prerogatives, arguing that no one should be forced to give away the code at the heart of his or her software.

The debate took on particular intensity because according to the "hacker ethic," certain business practices—like giving away your code—allowed you to claim the identity of a "hacker." In part for this reason, participants in a morning-long forum titled "The Future of the Hacker Ethic," led by Levy, began to focus on other elements of the hacker's *personality* and to modify their stance on the free distribution of information goods. For instance, participants agreed that hackers were driven to compute and that they would regard people who impeded their computing as bureaucrats rather than legitimate authorities. By and large, they agreed that the free dissemination of information was a worthy ideal, but in some cases, it was clearly only an ideal (Brand 1985). If they could not agree on proper hacker business practice, they could agree that being a hacker—in this case, being the sort of person who was invited to the Hackers' Conference—was valuable in its own right. As Lee Felsenstein (2001) pointed out, "that little bit of cultural identity [was] extremely important." In the popular press, hackers had been characterized as machine-obsessed loners. Gathered together in the stucco halls of Fort Cronkhite, hackers could recognize themselves as something else. Lee Felsenstein recalls feeling empowered: "Don't avoid the word 'hackers.' Don't let somebody else define you. No apologies: we're hackers. We define what a hacker is . . . nobody else" (ibid.).

In the end, the group did not come to any consensus on the right approach to take toward the emerging challenges of the software industry. But regarding the shift in public understandings of hacking, what was most important was simply that the hackers had brought the definition of hacking into alignment with emerging economic conditions. At the Hackers' Conference, Brand and company provided computer workers with a venue in which to develop and temporarily live a group identity around the idea of hacking and to make sense of emerging economic forms in terms of that identity. This work had the effect of rehabilitating hackers in the public eye, but it also had the effect of explicitly and securely linking countercultural people and a countercultural ethos to the world of computing. Virtually all the journalistic reports to emerge from the conference echoed John Markoff's comments in *Byte*: "Anyone attending would instantly have realized that the stereotype of computer hackers as isolated individuals is nowhere near accurate" (Markoff, Robinson, and Shapiro 1985). Yet, a few of those same reports picked up on another theme as well. Several either quoted or paraphrased Ted Nelson when he exclaimed, "This is the Woodstock of the computer elite!" (Markoff, Robinson, and Shapiro 1985; Schrage 1984). One report listed Stewart Brand among the "luminaries of the personal computer 'revolution'" (Markoff, Robinson, and Shapiro 1985); another described Brand as a "long-time supporter of hackers" (Florin 1985). Neither was quite true: until tapped to start the *Whole Earth Software Catalog,* Brand had had only fleeting contacts with the burgeoning computer industry. Quietly, almost without noticing it, the invited reporters had begun to intertwine the countercultural play of Woodstock, and countercultural players such as Brand, with an industry and a work style that had emerged within and at the edges of such culturally central institutions as MIT, Stanford, and Hewlett-Packard. Hackers were not simply highly individualistic and innovative engineers. They were cultural rebels—and their computers were the new tools of utopian cultural change.

Conclusion

The Hackers' Conference of 1984 was only one moment in the wedding of the libertarian idealism of the counterculture to the inventions and inventors of computing technology, but it was an important one. Over the next fifteen years, its attendees would play major roles in shaping both the computer industry and the press's coverage of that industry. New organizers in California turned the conference into an annual event, and programmers went on to stage similar gatherings in Israel, Malaysia, and Belgium.

For the field of cyberculture studies and particularly for that wing of it that deals with questions of technology and ideology, the Hackers' Conference offers several useful conceptual tools. Perhaps the most important is simply the evidence it presents that the ways we think about machines and technical workers have historical origins and that with a little digging, these origins can be identified. Finding these moments opens up the formerly closed analytical categories of technology and class and allows us to see them as categories that have in fact co-evolved. At the same time, it allows us to acknowledge the roles nontechnicians have played in shaping our perceptions of life with digital technologies. In the Hackers' Conference, we see that it is not hackers alone who bring together countercultural ideals and computer-based work; rather, it is hackers acting in concert with cultural entrepreneurs such as Stewart Brand and journalists such as John Markoff. In this sense, we can see that the hip, entrepreneurial hacker who would become so visible in the 1990s was not so much a hippie in his own right as the representative of a cultural category cobbled together by counterculturalists and technologists working in collaboration.

Moreover, we can see that this collaboration took place in a forum. This fact has two implications for cyberculture studies. The first is that if we hope to understand the rise of cyberlibertarianism and the development of future technoideologies, we would do well to try to identify the sorts of forums in which technologists and cultural entrepreneurs come together. A survey of work along these lines to date suggests that forums might be found within one of three concentric professional rings, arrayed in decreasing proximity to computing technologies. The first ring consists of those "close to the machine": inventor and designer communities and user communities (communities that often overlap in the digital environment). As research into the social history of earlier technologies has shown, such communities often play a key role in shaping both the mechanics and ideological impact of new technologies (Bijker 1995; Marvin 1988). We could imagine a second ring of midsized organizations that have as a primary or nearly primary function the turning of new technologies into symbolic goods. These organizations might range from think tanks to corporate marketing departments to e-business start-ups, and recently several have begun to attract attention from scholars (Brooks and Bowker 2002; Hassan 2003; Werry 2001). We can think of journalists, pundits, and commercial advertising agencies as a third ring. Though members of this ring will be connected to members of the other two (and may also even be members of the other two), they often serve as hosts for the sorts of collaborative gatherings represented by the Hackers' Conference.

The second implication of the Hackers' Conference is broader and, in relation to cyberculture studies' potential contribution to social theory, more serious. The Hackers' Conference happened to be an offline forum, an embodied weekend at a rundown former army base. But there is no reason that online forums could not also serve as sites at which to bring together representatives of multiple communities and develop ideological resources that could in turn be exported to the public at large. On the contrary, there is already substantial evidence that emerging online collaborative forums ranging from virtual communities to massive, multiplayer online games have been doing this work for some time (Kollock 1999; Li 2003; Rheingold 1993; Turner 2002). As we study new forms of technologically enabled sociability, we have an opportunity to explore not only online cultures but also the ways in which online collaborations help generate the symbolic and ideological resources out of which all cultures are made.

In short, we have an opportunity to make the study of cyberculture as central to the study of society as networked computers have become to the experience of social life.

NOTES

1. We do have precedents for this sort of work. Paul Edwards's study of Cold War computing, *The Closed World* (1996), offers a rich depiction of the multiple roles computers played in shaping geopolitics, psychology, and aesthetics during and after the 1950s. N. Katherine Hayles's book *How We Became Posthuman* (1999) explores the development of cybernetic subjectivity and, with it, a deep transformation in American cultural politics. Yet, Edwards and Hayles have written primarily about events that occurred some fifty years ago. What remains to be written are the histories of how we got from there to here. For a particularly insightful review of the literature in this area, see Rosenzweig 1998.

2. Developed by sociologist Bennett Berger, the concept of "ideological work" denotes the work a community must do when its shared beliefs encounter material conditions that render those beliefs inaccurate and ineffective as bases for action (Berger 1981, pp. 18–21). Faced with a conflict, Berger writes, groups can change or give up their beliefs, try to change their circumstances to make the beliefs more true, or, "[s]omewhere between these two, a group may accommodate its beliefs to the circumstances it cannot alter, while manipulating those it can to achieve the best bargain it can get" (p. 21). All three strategies require ideological work.

REFERENCES

Agre, Philip E. 2000. *Cyberspace as American culture.* Available at http://polaris .gseis.ucla.edu/pagre/sac.html (accessed October 10, 2001).

Agre, Philip E. 1998. "Yesterday's tomorrow." *Times Literary Supplement,* July 3, pp. 3–4.

Barbrook, Richard, and Andy Cameron. 1998. "The Californian ideology (main mix)." September 18. Available at http://cci.wmin.ac.uk/theory-californianideology-main.html (accessed October 10, 2001).

Becker, Howard Saul. 1982. *Art worlds*. Berkeley: University of California Press.

Berger, Bennett M. 1981. *The survival of a counterculture: Ideological work and everyday life among rural communards*. Berkeley: University of California Press.

Berger, Peter L., and Thomas Luckmann. 1966. *The social construction of reality: A treatise in the sociology of knowledge*. Garden City, NY: Doubleday.

Bijker, Wiebe E. 1995. *Of bicycles, bakelites, and bulbs: Toward a theory of sociotechnical change*. Cambridge, MA: MIT Press.

Bijker, Wiebe E., Thomas Parke Hughes, and T. J. Pinch. 1987. *The social construction of technological systems: New directions in the sociology and history of technology*. Cambridge, MA: MIT Press.

Bijker, Wiebe E., and John Law. 1992. *Shaping technology building society: Studies in sociotechnical change*. Cambridge, MA: MIT Press.

Borsook, Paulina. 2000. *Cyberselfish: A critical romp through the terribly libertarian culture of high tech*. New York: PublicAffairs.

Brand, Stewart. 1985. " 'Keep designing': How the information economy is being created and shaped by the hacker ethic." *Whole Earth Review* (May): 44–55.

Brooks, Lonny J., and Geoffrey Bowker. 2002. "Playing at work: Understanding the future of work practices at the Institute for the Future." *Information, Communication and Society* 5.1: 109–136.

Edwards, Paul N. 1996. *The closed world: Computers and the politics of discourse in Cold War America*. Cambridge, MA: MIT Press.

Elmer-DeWitt, Phillip. 1984. "Let us now praise famous hackers." *Time*, December 3, p. 76.

Felsenstein, Lee. 2001. Interview with the author, July 18.

Fleck, Ludwik. 1979. *Genesis and development of a scientific fact*. Chicago: University of Chicago Press.

Florin, Fabrice, prod. and dir. 1985. *Hackers: Wizards of the electronic age*. Documentary short film. Eugene, Oregon. Distributed by New Dimension Films.

Freiberger, Paul, and Michael Swaine. 1984. *Fire in the valley: The making of the personal computer*. Berkeley, CA: Osborne/McGraw-Hill.

Hall, Stuart, and Lawrence Grossberg. 1986. "On postmodernism and articulation: An interview with Stuart Hall." *Journal of Communication Inquiry* 10, no. 2: 45–60.

Hassan, Robert. 2003. "The MIT Media Lab: Techno dream factory or alienation as a way of life?" *Media, Culture & Society* 25: 87–106.

Hayles, N. Katherine. 1999. *How we became posthuman: Virtual bodies in cybernetics, literature, and informatics*. Chicago: University of Chicago Press.

Healy, Dave. 1997. "Cyberspace and place: the Internet as middle landscape on the electronic frontier." In *Internet culture*, ed. David Porter. New York: Routledge.

Kelly, Kevin. 2001. Interview with the author, July 27.

King, James. 2000. "The cultural construction of cyberspace." Ph.D. dissertation, King Alfred's College, University of Southampton, England.

Kollock, Peter. 1999. "The economies of online cooperation: Gifts and public goods in cyberspace." In *Communities in cyberspace*, ed. Peter Kollock and Marc A. Smith. London: Routledge, 220–237.

Kroker, Arthur, and Michael A. Weinstein. 1994. *Data trash: The theory of the virtual class*. New York: St. Martin's.

Latour, Bruno. 1993. *We have never been modern*. Cambridge, MA: Harvard University Press.

Latour, Bruno. 1991. "Technology is society made durable." In *A sociology of monsters: Essays on power, technology and domination*, ed. John Law. Sociological Review monograph 38. London: Routledge, 103–131.

Levy, Steven. 1984. *Hackers: Heroes of the computer revolution*. Garden City, NY: Anchor Press/Doubleday.

Li, Zhan. 2003. "The potential of *America's Army*: The video game as civilian-military public sphere." Master's thesis, Comparative Media Studies Program, Massachusetts Institute of Technology.

MacKenzie, Donald A., and Judy Wajcman. 1999. *The social shaping of technology*, 2nd ed. Buckingham, UK: Open University Press.

Markoff, John. 2005. *What the dormouse said: How the 60s counterculture shaped the personal computer industry*. New York: Viking Penguin.

Markoff, John, Phillip Robinson, and Ezra Shapiro. 1985. "Up to date." *Byte* (March): 355.

Marvin, Carolyn. 1988. *When old technologies were new: Thinking about electric communication in the late nineteenth century*. New York: Oxford University Press.

Miller, Laura. 1995. "Women and children first: Gender and the settling of the electronic frontier." In *Resisting the virtual life: The culture and politics of information*, ed. James Brook and Iain A. Boal. San Francisco: City Lights Books, 49–58.

Rheingold, Howard. 1993. *The virtual community: Homesteading on the electronic frontier*. Reading, MA: Addison-Wesley.

Rosenzweig, Roy. 1998. "Wizards, bureaucrats, warriors, and hackers: Writing the history of the Internet." *American Historical Review* 103.5 (December): 1530–1552.

Sardar, Ziauddin. 1996. "alt.civilization.faq: Cyberspace as the darker side of the West." In *Cyberfutures: Culture and politics on the information superhighway*, ed. Ziauddin Sardar and Jerome R. Ravetz. New York: New York University Press.

Schrage, Michael. 1984. "Hacking away at the future." *Washington Post*, November 18, p. F1.

Slack, Jennifer Daryl. 1996. "The theory and method of articulation in cultural studies." In *Stuart Hall: Critical dialogues in cultural studies*, ed. David Morely and Kuan-Hsing Chen. London: Routledge, 112–130.

Sobchack, Vivian. 1996. "Democratic franchise and the electronic frontier." In *Cyberfutures: Culture and politics on the information superhighway,* ed. Ziauddin Sardar and Jerome R. Ravetz. New York: New York University Press.

Sterne, Jonathan. 1999. "Thinking the Internet: Cultural studies versus the millennium." In *Doing Internet research: Critical issues and methods for examining the Net,* ed. Steve Jones. Thousand Oaks, CA: Sage, 257–287.

Terranova, Tiziana. 1996. "Digital Darwin: Nature, evolution, and control in the rhetoric of electronic communication." *New Formations* 29 (Autumn): 69–83.

Thomas, Douglas. 2002. *Hacker culture.* Minneapolis: University of Minnesota Press.

Turner, Fred. 1999. "Cyberspace as the new frontier? Mapping the shifting boundaries of the network society." Internet news service, Red Rock Eater News Service, June 6. Available at http://www.infowar.com/survey/99/survey_060799b _j.shtml.

Turner, Frederick C., Jr. 2002. "From counterculture to cyberculture: How Stewart Brand and the *Whole Earth Catalog* brought us *Wired* magazine." Ph.D. Dissertation, Department of Communication, University of California, San Diego.

Werry, Chris. 2001. "Imagined electronic community: Representations of virtual community in contemporary business discourse." *firstmonday* 4.9. Available at http://www.firstmonday.org/issues/issue4_9/werry/index.html.

Winner, Langdon. 1997. "Technology today: Utopia or dystopia?" *Social Research* 64.3: 989–1017.

Chapter 23

Government.com
ICTs and Reforming
Governance in Asia

Shanthi Kalathil

In China, job seekers in far-flung provinces can now consult Beijing's municipal portal for helpful relocation information and one-on-one advice. Those in search of business licenses in Vietnam can obtain them through one-stop shopping at a government Web site. Meanwhile, Singapore offers its citizens the opportunity to pay parking fines, register a change of address, or complain about corruption, all over the Internet.

By bringing governments and citizens into closer contact, Internet use in Asian developing countries is creating significant ripple effects throughout the region's political systems. International attention tends to focus on grassroots movements that use information and communication technology to organize and agitate for social and political causes. Yet, at the same time, unnoticed elites within many Asian governments are quietly pushing to streamline government and encourage transparency through use of the Internet.

Such measures, particularly those that use the Internet to increase popular oversight of government, may encounter internal hurdles in the years ahead. Policymakers should consider supporting e-government initiatives, especially those that promote transparency and accountability, when assessing how to utilize the Internet to promote good governance in Asian countries. Scholars should also take up the challenge of initiating thorough studies of the Internet and governance, with an eye toward ensuring that policy is based on solid, well-researched evidence.

E-government in Asia: Developing but Understudied

In recent years, the issue of transparency has risen to a place of prominence in public debate. Corporate scandals have highlighted the need for timely and responsible disclosure of information. The growth of the Internet has helped ordinary citizens gain easy access to information that might previously have been concealed by governments or placed in hard-to-find databases. The Internet has also helped to integrate data from many sources to present a more comprehensive picture than might otherwise have been available (Graham 2002).

Some Asian countries, having learned the political and economic lessons of faulty disclosure, have internalized the need for formalized transparency measures. With the introduction of advanced information and communications technology (ICT) such as the Internet, transparency in both the political and business spheres has become more than simply an ideal. Debate about transparency—how to define it, how to measure it, and how to achieve it—now informs grassroots discourse in many of Asia's consolidating democracies as well as in its more authoritarian regimes.

Against this backdrop, some government reformers in Asian countries —and particularly in new or consolidating democracies—are using the Internet to increase the transparency, accessibility, and accountability of government. These e-government reforms tend to take place under the general scope of national ICT plans, which envision the incorporation of ICTs into government, economy, and society. Particularly in Asian developing countries, ICTs are seen as crucial to the development of sustainable growth.

Several Asian countries have embarked on large-scale, ambitious national ICT plans that provide fertile ground for e-government reforms. China, for instance, has essentially mapped out how it wishes to develop information technology through a series of five-year plans. It has coined a new term, "informatization," to refer to the way in which ICTs factor into economic, political, and social developments. Government officials envision a not-too-far-off future in which the Internet, in particular, is incorporated into and helps modernize sectors ranging from education and health to agriculture and industry. In fact, the drive to enter the information age characterizes much of the country's current approach to development (Kalathil and Boas 2003, p. 23).

Yet, because these ICT initiatives take place not on center stage but in the background of political reform, many political scientists have not considered the long-term ramifications of the process. Certainly, with respect to China, only a few scholars pay lip service to the changes currently under way in the government's bureaucracy. Yang (2003) is one of the few to examine new e-government measures in the context of state capacity, arguing that improvements in bureaucratic transparency within China are part of a larger series of attempts to remake the state.

In fact, the broader literature on transitioning countries and consolidating democracies sets the tone for considerations of Internet use and state-initiated political reform. For the most part, it appears that the mainstream political-science community considers the Internet too new —or too "fringe"—a phenomenon to be addressed seriously. Moreover, the standards of the transitions literature were penned long before the Internet became a factor in politics, and discussion of even the traditional media's role in democratic transition and consolidation tended to be relegated to the background (Huntington 1991; Linz and Stepan 1996).

In the academic community, the topic is typically left to communications scholars. There is now a respectable body of literature on online political discourse, civil society, and media transformation in Asia within the communications discipline (Lee 1990; Zhao 1998). Yet communications scholars tend to skip topics like e-government in favor of analyzing the online public sphere and the myriad changes in the Asian media sector. Although these topics are naturally germane to the issue of ICTs and political change in Asia, they also deemphasize the role of the state and state elites in driving political change.

Finally, nongovernmental advocacy groups and the policymakers they target typically publicize grassroots use of the Internet, especially use by grassroots development groups and dissidents. Anecdotes about cell phone text messaging forcing the removal of Philippine president Joseph Estrada, or online Korean news sites enlisting ordinary citizens as journalists, tend to reinforce the perception that the bulk of politically significant Internet use within Asia takes place among civil society groups and the public.

Beginnings of Better Governance

In fact, reform-minded elites—often at the local level—are also instituting changes that may facilitate improved governance in many Asian countries. Many officials want the Internet to strengthen state capacity through administrative streamlining and automation. They may also look to e-government to shore up regime support by providing government services online.

A recent World Bank–funded study (infoDev 2002) has identified three phases of e-government. The first is the publishing phase, in which governments use ICTs to improve access to official information. ICTs such as the Internet can bring some of the large volume of government-generated information closer to the public, enabling citizens—particularly in developing countries—to bypass standing in long lines or paying bribes. The second phase is the interaction phase, in which ICTs facilitate broader civic participation in government. This is usually some form of two-way communication enabled by the Internet, and it can include anything from e-mail contact with government officials to online feedback on proposed legislation. The third phase is the transaction phase, in which actual government services are made available online. This may include anything from online tax filing to government e-procurement.

In Asia, despite many countries' enthusiasm for the Internet, most governments have not moved significantly beyond the second phase, interaction online. A United Nations study (2002) characterized the Asia/Oceania region as having only "minimal" e-government capacity, with a majority of the countries being classified as deficient. According to the United Nations, the enabling e-government environment is weak in many of the countries surveyed, meaning that problems with infrastructure and human capacity need to be addressed before e-government can properly function.

Despite this somewhat dim overall assessment, individual countries are making strides in improving their e-government capacities. China, despite its ambivalence about political use of the Internet, has embarked on a comprehensive e-government program. In 1999, several Chinese state organs launched the "Government Online" project, meant to bring all central government departments online within the next several years. Beyond simply posting government functions online, the project also seeks to implement online administration through use of electronic databases and online document transfer. Some of China's bigger cities are also establishing complex municipal Web sites that may pave the way for further innovation, particularly the creation of government-citizen feedback loops. Beijing's municipal Web site features information about government services, updates on laws and regulations, and a local news center (Kalathil and Boas 2003, pp. 31–32).

Other countries have thought innovatively about the very concept of e-government. Singapore is a standout model of e-government that other countries in both the developing and developed world aspire to emulate. Its "eCitizen" project provides several integrated services through a single Web site; citizens can visit the site, click on topics such as "family" or "care for the elderly," and immediately have access to a range of government services, all of which can be easily transacted online (Kalathil and Boas 2003, p. 80).

E-government but Not Necessarily E-governance

But successful e-government transactions do not necessarily entail more transparency, accountability, and public participation in government. These three concepts are important goals that need to be specifically promoted within any e-government program in order to achieve a broader goal of better governance. Without a specific focus on these issues, e-government can easily become simply a process through which bad government is mechanized. Indeed, funding for e-government projects may sometimes fall prey to the notion that simply computerizing any kind of process may be sufficient to bring about positive results. In fact, technology should be seen as merely a tool through which government can be transformed to be more citizen-centered (Pacific Council on International Policy 2002).

Governance scholars in advanced industrialized democracies often focus on the ways in which transparency is promoted through regulatory policy. In the United States, for example, public disclosure of information on topics such as food labeling and toxic-pollution reporting represent formal measures of transparency that have undergone several layers of bureaucratic wangling before being formally instituted as law (Graham 2002). In some authoritarian and new democracies in Asia, the rule of law may not be enshrined sufficiently to yield pro-transparency regulations or to ensure their enforcement. E-government, if implemented properly, has the capacity to achieve a similar effect to specific pro-transparency regulation, while also boosting public participation and increasing government accountability. As might be expected, these potential benefits of e-government tend to be most valued in democracies such as the Philippines, India, and South Korea. Authoritarian countries such as China or Vietnam, although embarking on ambitious e-government programs, tend to deemphasize the pursuit of these goals.

In Asian democracies, the drive toward e-government dovetails with government-led and grassroots movements that seek to stamp out corruption. In South Korea, for example, the government took the initiative to streamline regulatory rules that provided middle-level government managers with plenty of opportunities for graft. As part of the revamping, the government also created an online monitoring system to track the progress of government applications, called the Online Procedures Enhancement for Civil Applications, or OPEN. Citizens who use OPEN now can easily determine the status of their applications online, without having to pay bribes to government officials (infoDev 2002).

India has also implemented several e-government programs specifically designed to increase transparency and promote government accountability. The state of Andhra Pradesh, often an innovator in this area, has devised a program through which citizens can quickly and efficiently complete land registration processes. Previously a breeding ground for unscrupulous middlemen who exploited the inefficiencies of the system to extort money from citizens, the land registration process now provides a direct computer interface between citizens and government, eliminating the incentive for graft (Bhatnagar and Schware 2000, p. 48).

In authoritarian countries, however, the mere idea of sharing information between bureaucracies may be unpopular. Indeed, in an authoritarian political environment, many bureaucracies typically seek to hoard, rather than share, information. Many government officials find external transparency, or public oversight of government, a still more threatening concept. Especially in more heavily authoritarian countries such as Vietnam, North Korea, or Burma, senior officials, on their own, will be unlikely to promote e-government specifically to foster greater government transparency or accountability. Instead, e-government is officially lauded as a method of cutting government costs and strengthening state capacity.

The tendency to hoard information and control information flow is prevalent not only in the most severe authoritarian countries in Asia, such as North Korea and Burma, but also in modernized, corruption-free semi-authoritarian countries like Singapore. In Singapore, although the government has implemented an extensive e-government scheme, there is some resistance to the idea of transparency. The government has staunchly resisted calls for a Freedom of Information Act, designed to open government records to the public. Singapore's e-government program may indicate the direction in which other Asian e-government efforts could develop: streamlined, highly efficient government that is essentially opaque for the purposes of stakeholder oversight.

At the same time, although transparency and accountability are rarely stated as explicit goals of an authoritarian country, there are ways to ensure that these goals are built into the design for e-government programs in authoritarian Asian countries. China, for instance, is interested in using the Internet to target corruption, and it has proved to be somewhat receptive to e-government programs devised to promote transparency. Once the move to make more government information available to the public online, it may be difficult for China and other countries to return to a culture of bureaucratic secrecy and unaccountability.

Ideally, as the Internet spreads throughout Asia, better governance through use of ICT will infuse the overall structure of governments. E-government programs are helping to emphasize the potential benefits of decentralized, participatory decision-making within the policy apparatus. Departments that have historically relied on a vertical command structure can now encourage horizontal communication through use of the Internet, thus dispersing power. Bureaucrats are slowly being encouraged to innovate and to work in teams toward an end goal of providing better services to citizens. Yet these changes will not take place overnight, nor will they take place of their own accord. Governments must be prepared to expend political will in order to combat longstanding cultures of bureaucratic secrecy, engrained government practices, and resistance to change.

Next Steps: Crafting Better Policy

E-government has the capacity to cause significant changes in the way that governments all over the world interact with and respond to their citizens. Particularly in Asia, where the Internet and other ICTs are generally being enthusiastically embraced, e-government has the potential to improve governance, foster more public participation in government, and give civil society the information and tools it needs to ensure that government functions efficiently and honestly.

But scholars and policymakers have been slow to recognize and analyze the significance of such developments. For their part, scholars have eschewed extensive analysis of the political ramifications of e-government. Although organizations such as the United Nations, the World Bank, and others are increasingly devoting resources to studying the political impact of e-government, they are doing so with an eye toward practical realities, seeking to isolate best practices and impart those practices to countries in need. Scholarly examination of the political trends at work—whether from an international relations standpoint, a comparative politics standpoint, or even a communications standpoint—is still sparse. There is clearly room for informed analysis in this area, and funding institutions might consider how best to encourage the development of further scholarship as well as specific e-government practices.

The lack of directed study on the subject means that policymakers are heavily influenced by anecdotes generated by the popular press, which tends to emphasize the role of civil society in pushing for governmental transparency and accountability. Although civil society does of course play a vital role in the process, policymakers looking to encourage better governance throughout Asia should remember that progress need not spring solely from the grassroots level. E-government programs in many Asian countries have the potential to create a quiet revolution from *within* the state. While the bulk of overseas attention focuses on civil society campaigners, the work of backroom bureaucrats striving for transparency may also have a significant effect, if multiplied throughout the government structure.

Aid organizations should remember, though, that applying technology to government will not by itself lead to transparency, accountability, and better governance. Specific, local-level e-government programs should be identified and targeted for support within Asian countries. Outside assistance should emphasize those initiatives that not only promote bureaucratic efficiency but also augment oversight by, and input from, the public. In industrial democracies, civil society plays a key role not only in pushing for government transparency but also in interpreting government information for the general public. In more-authoritarian Asian countries such as China, Vietnam, or Singapore, few interest groups are likely to pressure the government for increased transparency on the behalf of citizen stakeholders. Overseas support that specifically seeks to embed transparency within e-government programs may help fill the role that civil society plays elsewhere.

Ultimately, improving governance through use of ICTs in Asia will depend largely on the political will and, in some cases, the political character of the government in question. Internet use by civil society organizations also plays a vital role in reforming governance. Spurring political change through e-government in Asia will prove a complex task, and one that will require more than simply installing user-friendly technology. Yet, with the right mix of scholarship, policies, and development assistance, ICTs certainly can improve the prospects for more transparent, accountable governments throughout Asia.

REFERENCES

Bhatnagar, Subhash, and Robert Schware, eds. 2000. "Information and Communication Technology in Rural Development: Case Studies from India." Washington, D.C.: International Bank for Reconstruction and Development.

Graham, Mary. 2002. *Democracy by Disclosure.* Washington, D.C.: Brookings Institution.

Huntington, Samuel P. 1991. *The Third Wave: Democratization in the Late Twentieth Century.* Norman: University of Oklahoma Press.

infoDev, and the Center for Democracy and Technology. 2002. "The E-Government Handbook for Developing Countries: A Project of infoDev and the Center for Democracy and Technology." Washington, D.C.: World Bank.

Kalathil, Shanthi, and Taylor C. Boas. 2003. *Open Networks, Closed Regimes: The Impact of the Internet on Authoritarian Rule.* Washington, D.C.: Carnegie Endowment for International Peace.

Lee, Chin-Chuan, ed. 1990. *Voices of China: The Interplay of Politics and Journalism.* New York: Guilford.

Linz, Juan J., and Alfred Stepan. 1996. *Problems of Democratic Transition and Consolidation: Southern Europe, South America, and Post-Communist Europe.* Baltimore, Md.: Johns Hopkins University Press.

Pacific Council on International Policy. 2002. "Roadmap for E-government in the Developing World: 10 Questions E-Government Leaders Should Ask Themselves." Los Angeles: Pacific Council on International Policy.

United Nations, Division for Public Economics and Public Administration, and the American Society for Public Administration. 2002. "Benchmarking E-government: A Global Perspective." New York: United Nations Division for Public Economics and Public Administration.

Yang, Dali L. 2003. "State Capacity on the Rebound." *Journal of Democracy* 14, no. 1 (January): 43–50.

Zhao, Yuezhi. 1998. *Media, Market and Democracy in China: Between the Party Line and the Bottom Line.* Urbana: University of Illinois Press.

Chapter 24

Dot-Coms and Cyberculture Studies
Amazon.com as a Case Study

Adrienne Massanari

A Prologue: Jeff Bezos, Amazon.com CEO and
Time *Magazine's Person of the Year (1999)*

In 1999, a remarkable image graced the cover of *Time* magazine. The picture shows an open shipping box. Inside the box is a man's head surrounded by multicolored Styrofoam packing peanuts, a computer mouse, and two leather-bound books. The man is smiling subtly, and his face is lit from the front by a harsh light that creates dramatic shadows inside the box. The interplay of light and shadow is reminiscent of those cast by fluorescent lights, giving the impression that this box has just been opened in an office somewhere. The image's caption reads, "Amazon.com's Jeff Bezos: E-commerce is Changing the Way the World Shops" (December 27, 1999).

The head indeed belongs to Jeff Bezos, CEO of Amazon.com, a large online retailer that had seen staggering sales growth in the years since its founding in 1995. On first glance, the picture seems merely amusing; here is this "zany" CEO who has posed for a photo with his head in a box—certainly an unusual pose for the cover of *Time,* but not really enough to give a reader of the magazine much pause. However, closer examination reveals that the cardboard box looks suspiciously like one used by Amazon.com. Bezos, in effect, has become a product—his image has become a commodity sold by his own company. Just as there are books in this "order" from Amazon.com, there too is Jeff Bezos, smiling leader of this e-commerce company. Interesting, also, is the choice of books that accompany Bezos. They are not the mass-market paperbacks or technical manuals that many Amazon.com customers purchase. Instead, they are leather-bound tomes; they look weighty and as if they belong in a wood-paneled library with leather chairs, floor-to-ceiling bookshelves, and tall ladders for access to the upper shelves. The books suggest that despite his goofy appearance, Bezos has credibility with the cognac-sipping Wall Street brokers who may be receiving this package. The picture both humanizes and distances Bezos from the readers of *Time*. He becomes a perfect embodiment of the late 1990s notion of the dot-com entrepreneur: young, marketable, technically savvy, irreverent, and yet, amazingly, still a member of the "Old Economy" business establishment.

Stepping Back: What Are Dot-Coms, and Why Are They Important to Cyberculture Studies?

The subject of journalists and the popular press for some time, dot-coms and the culture they create(d) have been relatively ignored by many academic researchers. In the years since Netscape went public in 1996, the story of the birth and demise of Internet companies (dot-coms) has dominated media coverage and created its own cultural memes that have rippled out into the collective consciousness (e.g., the Pets.com sock puppet). Although covered in the popular press for some time, dot-coms as unique organizational types are only now being considered by academics. Scholars in organizational behavior (Delbecq and Weiss 2000; Perlow 1998; Schellenberg and Miller 1998), economics (Neff and Stark 2003), anthropology (English-Lueck 2000), and cultural studies (Ross 1998) have examined the characteristics that make dot-coms different from traditional businesses, as well as the culture they engender and encourage. These include an emphasis on innovation, flexible organizational structures, and informal attitudes toward hierarchy. However, few new media scholars are discussing how dot-coms came into being, how they changed our attitudes toward work, money, and business in the 1990s, and the larger social impact they have had on our culture.

While many dot-coms have closed since the collapse of the technology market in 2000, several online companies have successfully remained open, despite waning investor interest and a reduction in consumer spending. One of these, Amazon.com, is considered by many to be the "online poster child for e-commerce" (NetLingo 2002), dominating the online world both in terms of market share and brand recognition. Although it began as "Earth's Biggest Bookstore," Amazon.com quickly diversified its inventory to include, among other things, music, movies, electronics, toys, and housewares. As the company expanded and its stock price soared, the company was mentioned frequently in the press, and Jeff Bezos, the company's founder and CEO, became a dominant personality in both the financial/high-tech community and the culture at large.

One of the more interesting aspects of Amazon.com is the company's unofficial "motto" that Bezos has mentioned in articles written about the company: "Work hard. Have fun. Make history." As I mentioned earlier, dot-coms create a culture where it is the norm to be bright, inexperienced, and young; to work long hours; and to believe that your job is actually an "adventure."[1] Amazon.com's motto succinctly captures these values. What is notably missing from the company's motto is "Make money." Dot-coms provided (possibly) unparalleled opportunities for financial gain through stock option grants to their employees. I believe that "Make money" is explicitly absent from Amazon.com's motto for a number of reasons, but I believe it was indirectly present in much of the company's rhetoric and in the documents it presented to the media (and public). Therefore, the analysis I present in this chapter considers this additional phrase as an integral part of the value system that both Bezos and the company perceive as important.

Methods

As I suggested earlier, academic researchers have spent little time exploring the culture of dot-coms. While there are several possible explanations for this, including the fact that the dot-com era is still a fairly recent memory and only now being investigated by the academy, a significant barrier to research around/in dot-coms is the difficult nature of acquiring information about these companies. How does one gain access to people, documents, and so forth in an environment where the NDA[2] is king? What methods can researchers use to understand a corporate culture that prides itself on protecting its technological innovations—when a small information leak could have vast consequences on a company's ability to dominate the technology market? One option is to explore the discourse that these companies produce for public consumption. For example, one might examine advertisements that were broadcast on U.S. television during the height of the dot-com era or those published in popular magazines at the time. Alternatively, a researcher might study the press releases that a company has produced over time.

For my study, I analyzed letters that Jeff Bezos wrote to Amazon.com shareholders in 1997 and 2001. These letters were included in the annual reports[3] sent to all shareholders and were made publicly available on the company's Web site. As texts, shareholder letters are fascinating artifacts that represent a multiplicity of voices, events, audiences, and themes. They are like a good story in the broadest sense, one that the company's CEO narrates, where certain cultural and social values and events are reified and others are marginalized. I analyzed these documents in light of the company's motto, "Work hard. Have fun. Make history. [Make money.]," because I believe that using this statement as a guiding principle helps tease apart the cultural values that Amazon.com was promoting with its letters. I examined two aspects of the 1997 and 2001 letters: themes present in the letters and the narrator's (in this case Bezos's) use of multiple voices to speak to his audience. The results of my analysis are described briefly in the next section.

Themes Present in Amazon.com's Shareholder Letters

Themes in narratives often implicitly and sometimes explicitly make reference to cultural or social myths coconstructed by both the author and his or her audience. Themes help bridge the gap between the narrator and his or her audience, calling upon and creating a shared reality between the two parties. At the same time, however, this "shared reality" can be used to obfuscate the implicit and unstated purposes of a narrative. As one researcher noted in her myth analysis of annual reports, "the producers of reports obscure the differences between reporting the company's yearly progress and promoting business values that leaders find important" (David 2001, p. 196). Similarly, the themes reflected in Amazon.com's shareholder letters echo the company's own motto, "Work hard. Have fun. Make history." Significantly, "Make money" is missing from this vision, though I propose that this theme is clearly (albeit implicitly) present in these letters—after all, annual reports are specifically written to report on a company's financial well-being (or lack thereof). Amazon.com's shareholder letters express these themes in numerous ways, both implicitly and explicitly.

Work Hard

Bezos encouraged his employees to "work hard" and created a company in which this value was rhetorically expressed in everyday activities. The shareholder letters illustrate this theme in a number of different ways, through the numerous references to how Amazon.com's business practices serve its customers. An overriding theme of both letters is the importance the company places on its customer service. As Bezos writes in the 1997 letter, "We will continue to focus relentlessly on our customers" (Amazon.com 1997, p. 1).

Bezos suggests that successfully "working hard" for Amazon.com's customers requires motivated and committed employees who are willing to make significant sacrifices to ensure the success of the company (Amazon.com 1997). He also conflates "working hard" with "making history"; in his view, the second value is impossible to pursue without the first. In fact, Bezos suggests that the intense and difficult nature of Amazon.com's working environment is viewed as a source of pride for the company (and its employees), noting, "It's not easy to work here (when I interview people I tell them, 'You can work long, hard, or smart, but at Amazon.com you can't choose two out of three')" (Amazon.com 1997, p. 3). By emphasizing the difficulties of working for the company, Bezos taps into the larger cultural myth of the dot-commer who works ridiculous hours in the hope that his or her efforts will be rewarded with valuable stock options. Not surprisingly, in his 1997 letter, Bezos mentions the necessity of each employee "thinking like" an owner; by providing them all stock options, he suggests that he will be able to accomplish this goal and that they will work harder to ensure the company's success (Amazon.com 1997).

In both letters, Bezos speaks directly to and on behalf of his employees. For example, in the closing line of his 1997 letter he writes, "We at Amazon.com are grateful . . . to each other for our hard work." (Amazon.com 1997, p. 3). With this statement, he not only collectively praises his staff for its hard work; he also suggests that his employees are grateful to their colleagues for their efforts. His statements also imply that the company's employees are part of the Amazon.com "family" and as such are expected to make the sacrifices and reap the potential benefits of the company's success. In his 2001 letter, Bezos again speaks on behalf of his employees, noting, "they are, and should be, proud of the accomplishment [pro forma profitability]" (Amazon.com 2001, p. 1). These statements suggest that

Bezos is responsive to his employees' thoughts and feelings regarding their work on behalf of the company. Of course, his broad generalizations suggest only one side of the story, that Amazon.com employees are enthused and energized by the company's progress and their own hard work—perhaps not a completely accurate assessment of their true feelings. Significantly, he makes no mention of the frustrations that some of his employees were likely experiencing because of the company's layoffs in early 2001. However, this is not unusual given the purpose of the letter and its audience.

Have Fun

Perhaps not surprisingly, the "Have Fun" theme is rarely highlighted in the letters. This may have much to do with the genre conventions of the annual report. These documents are rarely light-hearted in tone, and the reports' audience is unlikely to be interested in the numerous broomball games that occurred in Amazon.com's halls. However, Bezos does demonstrate his enthusiasm for the direction that the company is heading, in both the 1997 and 2001 letters. For example, in the closing of his 1997 letter Bezos writes, "We feel good about what we've done, and even more excited about what we want to do" (Amazon.com 1997, p. 3). His use of "we" here is important; Bezos is speaking for the entire company—in effect, impressing upon the letter's audience that all the company's employees are excited and upbeat about their work at Amazon.com. He does acknowledge that much of the company's success has come at a cost—the "sacrifices and passion" of his employees (Amazon.com 1997, p. 3).

Sections of the 2001 letter also emphasize the notion that Bezos is the company's mouthpiece—and that he is somehow speaking for all its employees (more on this can be found in the "Narrator" section below). However, the closing lines of his 2001 letter subtly shift the focus from the entire company's supposed enthusiasm about the business to his own, personal excitement. He writes, "I am happy to report that I am as enthusiastic as ever about this business" (Amazon.com 2001, p. 3). This statement is important for two reasons. First, it reconfirms Jeff Bezos's own personal commitment to the company's success, thereby restating and emphasizing his commitment to the company's investors. Since there was speculation as late as mid-2001 that Amazon.com would be bought out or somehow otherwise not survive the dot-com crash, Bezos's own personal affirmation of his excitement about where the business was heading might have allayed some investors' fears that he would fiscally mismanage or leave the company. Second, it indirectly suggests that Bezos may have not felt comfortable suggesting that all his employees were "having fun," hence his choice to speak only for himself and his own enthusiastic attitude toward the company. In light of the unionization efforts and subsequent layoffs of 2001, it probably would have been presumptuous for Bezos to suggest to his audience (which included both external and internal shareholders) that all Amazon.com's employees were excited about the direction in which the company was moving.

Make History

Perhaps more than any other aspect of Amazon.com's motto, "make history" is emphasized within the company's 1997 and 2001 shareholder letters. This is somewhat surprising given the annual report document's supposed focus on financial data, which suggests that the letters would be more likely to highlight the unstated "make money" aspect of Amazon.com's motto. However, Bezos successfully conflates "making history" with "making money," a point I address later.

Especially in the 1997 letter, Bezos differentiates Amazon.com as a market leader, suggesting that its financial strategies are fundamentally different from other companies' approaches. He comments that this may not be the only approach a company could take, noting, "We aren't so bold as to claim that the above is the 'right' investment philosophy" (Amazon.com 1997, p. 2). Bezos further implies (but does not explicitly state) that only "Old Economy" companies would sacrifice the potential to "build something important" for something as prosaic and commonplace as profits (Amazon.com 1997, p. 3). While he does not minimize the potential for competitors to challenge the company—referring to the necessity of a "crisp execution against established franchised leaders," as if there is some sort of territorial battle being waged—he also reaffirms Amazon.com's potential to dominate the retailing industry while suggesting that it is a large enough market for a number of companies to succeed (Amazon.com 1997, p. 3).

As I mentioned in the "Have Fun" section, Bezos creates a communal and familial atmosphere in his letters. Nowhere is this more clearly stated than in a phrase from his 1997 letter, in which he notes that Amazon.com is creating "something that we can all tell our grandchildren about" (Amazon.com 1997, p. 3). Here is an overt a reference to the "Internet pioneer" myth.[4] He suggests that the company's actions will be so significant and will so completely revolutionize the world that generations of Amazonian grandchildren will hear the tale of the company's successful conquering not just of the online retail market but of the world. Again, Bezos uses the word "we" to suggest that each member of the company is a part of his larger vision for the future.

Bezos places far less emphasis on Amazon.com's potential to "make history" in his 2001 letter. This may have much to do with the simple fact that he believed the company had already made history by surviving the dot-com crash and attaining profitability. However, he makes specific references to the past, implying awareness of the company's place in history. For example, he opens the 2001 letter by noting how the company's goals have changed since its founding. He writes, "After four years of single-minded focus on growth, and then just under two years spent almost exclusively on lowering costs, we reached a point where we could afford to balance growth and cost improvement" (Amazon.com 2001, p. 1). He suggests that the company's vision has progressed to keep pace with external events. The company has now moved past the heady dot-com days of "getting big fast" to confront the more serious issues of the present and future: cost reduction and profitability. Bezos also refers to the company's history-making score on the American Customer Service Index, noting, "we are told that this [Amazon.com's score of 84] is the highest score ever recorded—not just for any retailer, but for any service company" (Amazon.com 2001, p. 1). This achievement signifies that the external business community recognizes Amazon.com's unique role in history, as a "customer company," rather than as simply a mammoth online retailer—a point that would likely make Bezos proud, as he often emphasized this notion in his interactions with the media. To remind investors that Amazon.com remained committed to its mission and its place in history, Bezos even went so far as to include a copy of his 1997 letter in the 2001 annual report. In 2001's closing paragraph, Bezos reifies the future over the present, writing, "There is more innovation ahead of us than behind us" (Amazon.com 2001, p. 3). He goes on to thank investors "for joining us on this adventure," again suggesting the myth of the Internet pioneer.

Make Money/Lose Money

Despite the typical annual report's focus on the presentation and interpretation of corporate financial data, Amazon.com's shareholder letters tend to emphasize the company's commitment to dominate the e-retail market in the long term, which Bezos maintains requires sacrificing short-term profits. This emphasis results in the letters' suggesting that the company is, in fact, "losing money"—the negative counterpart to the "make money" aspect of the company's motto. Certainly, much of Bezos's emphasis on the company's continual loss of revenue is a required part of full disclosure and is legally dictated by the U.S. Securities and Exchange Commission (SEC). However, Bezos suggests that the company's losses are actually part of a larger investment strategy, implying that short-term losses are necessary for long-term growth.

By emphasizing this need to grow and dominate the market, Bezos successfully argues for a new approach to investing, one that emphasizes growth over profits. This strategy is not new; it calls upon (and shapes) the myth of the "New Economy." Especially in his 1997 letter, Bezos distorts "Old Economy" ideas regarding profit and stock valuations (where stock values would directly reflect the company's profits), suggesting that Amazon.com is somehow worth more than its current sales figures reflect. He suggests that investors should consider the long-term potential of Amazon.com (and its vision for e-commerce), rather than focus on the company's short-term losses.

In both the 1997 and 2001 letters, Bezos capably argues that losing money *will actually help the company "make history."* He notes in the 1997 document, "We believe that a fundamental measure of our success will be the shareholder value we create over the long term. This value will be a direct result of our ability to extend and solidify our current market leadership position" (Amazon.com 1997, p. 1). In 2001, he suggests that customer satisfaction is tightly linked to the company's financial success:

> We are firm believers that the long-term interests of shareholders are tightly linked to the interests of our customers: if we do our jobs right, today's customers will buy more tomorrow, we'll add more customers in the process, and it will all add up to more cash flow and more long-term value for our shareholders. (Amazon.com 2001, p. 3)

Though the idea that serving customers well will lead to profits is not particularly revolutionary, Bezos notes that the company's most important asset is what he calls its "consumer franchise." Bezos suggests that Amazon.com's monetary value should be evaluated as much on its ability to attract and serve its customers as on its ability to actually create a profitable business model. In addition, in using the phrase "consumer franchise," Bezos opens up the possibility that the company's customers (or rather, their purchasing habits, Web site click-streams, and other data) are commodities that could be sold at any time—providing yet another source of potential income for the company.

Bezos as a Narrator: A Multiplicity of Voices

There are numerous instances when Bezos (as the narrator) speaks in a number of different "voices"—perhaps in an effort to appeal to the texts' audiences.[5] In this section, I will briefly examine two different voices that Bezos uses in the 1997 and 2001 shareholder letters: Bezos as a financial "visionary" and Bezos as a customer advocate.

Bezos as an Internet and Financial Visionary

One voice that Bezos uses often is that of an Internet and financial visionary. Bezos often speaks using financial terms, citing figures and statistics about the company's growth. More important, he presents himself as an e-commerce visionary. In so doing, he suggests that Amazon.com's financial losses are a necessary first step in its attempt to dominate the retailing industry. In the 1997 letter, he presents his "vision" for the future of the Internet:

> Today, online commerce saves customers money and precious time. Tomorrow, through personalization, online commerce will accelerate the very process of discovery. Amazon.com uses the Internet to create real value for its customers and, by doing so, hopes to create an enduring franchise, even in established and large markets. (Amazon.com 1997, p. 1)

The phrase "accelerate the very process of discovery" is particularly important, as it suggests that Amazon.com is somehow more than simply an online store; instead, the company—as guided by Bezos's wisdom and ambition—will change the lives of its customers. In Bezos's vision, the power of the Internet is in its ability to transcend the virtual—he sees that his online bookstore can (and will) become an integral part of his customers' offline/"real" lives by providing "real value." There is something earnest and idealistic about Bezos's words here. He manages to conflate the acquisition of material goods (books) with personal exploration and discovery, as if Amazon.com provides the (only) key for individuals to explore/exploit the Internet's potential as an information gathering and retrieval system. This approach would certainly resonate with the investment community and press, especially in 1997–1998, since it reflected the oft-repeated belief in the Internet's potential to revolutionize and improve our lives. It also taps into the "exploration" and "navigation" metaphors commonly used to describe the Web-browsing experience, metaphors that were also attached to popular software of that time (Internet Explorer and Netscape Navigator).

In his 2001 letter, Bezos embodies the persona of a financial visionary. He refers to his 1997 letter, devoting several paragraphs to a discussion of the way Amazon.com has approached its financials. Not only does Bezos assume that this lengthy discussion of different accounting techniques is audience-appropriate; he frames the discussion as a minilesson in investing. He writes,

> If you could know for certain just two things—a company's future cash flows and its future number of shares outstanding—you would have an excellent idea of the fair value of a share of that company's stock today. (You'd also need to know appropriate discount rates, but if you knew the future cash flows for certain, it would also be reasonably easy to know which discount rates to use.) (Amazon.com 2001, p. 2)

In this section, he speaks directly to the letter's audience, as evidenced by his extensive use of the word "you." He also demonstrates his financial prowess (perhaps suggesting his past experience on Wall Street?) with his mention of how easy it would be for someone to find out what discount rates apply to a company's stock. In speaking frankly and in the audience's own language, Bezos aligns himself with members of this group, presenting himself as just another investor who is interested in evaluating Amazon.com as a potential investment. He moves from accounting/investment generalizations (as seen in the quotation above) to more specific characterizations of Amazon.com's own potential as investment: "We believe Amazon.com is poised over the coming years to generate meaningful, sustained, free cash flow" (Amazon.com 2001, p. 2). Unlike the previous quotation, in which Bezos appears to speak for himself only, here he invites others to join him in his narration, as demonstrated by his use of the word "we."

Bezos as a Customer Advocate

Bezos also speaks directly to Amazon.com's customers throughout his letters, often through parenthetical remarks addressed to customers or potential customers. This is especially noticeable in his 2001 letter, in which he often refers to site features and enhancements that he believes will entice and retain customers. For example, he emphasizes the company's vast selection of products and compares it to offline retailers: "we now have more than 45,000 items in our electronics store (about seven times the selection you're likely to find in a big-box electronics store), we've tripled our kitchen selection (you'll find all the best brands)" (Amazon.com 2001, p. 1). The parenthetical remarks are directed specifically to the company's customers. Unlike other portions of this letter, where he speaks of the Amazon.com's effort to serve its customers—positioning them as somehow separate and apart from the report's audience—this section draws in the customers, informing them of the company's offerings. Bezos manages to sound earnest in his desire to both inform and market to the letter's audience.

In later sections of the 2001 letter, Bezos incorporates his customer-oriented remarks directly into the text, rather than setting them off parenthetically. For example, in one sentence he describes how customers can access and modify orders they have placed with the company and proceeds to detail how one would go about doing this. He writes, "To find an order, just make sure you are signed in and recognized by the site, and do a regular search on any product in your order. When you get to that product's detail page, a link to your order will be at the top of the page" (Amazon.com 2001, p. 2). It is interesting to note how different Bezos sounds here (and the assumptions he makes about the audience's expertise) as compared to the tone he adopts when writing about high-level financial data and strategic decisions that Amazon.com is making. In addition, the lack of statements he directly addresses to the company's customers in his earlier letter suggests that the audience to which he speaks has changed over time. In 1997, he describes site features very generally, and only as a larger illustration of Amazon.com's commitment to its customers. In 2001, however, Bezos offers a detailed tutorial, as if his readers might sit down at their computer after reading the letter, log on to Amazon.com, and follow his directions step by step.

In speaking as a "customer advocate" in his letters, Bezos accomplishes a number of things. First, the guided tutorial he offers to customers in his

2001 letter suggests that the company is highly invested in its customers' experience—so much so, in fact, that Bezos sees fit to spend a significant amount of time in this important shareholder document acting as a customer-service representative. Second, it suggests that Bezos is not above answering the most insignificant question potentially posed (but in this case not actually asked) by Amazon.com's customers, which can be read as his attempt to set an example for his employees. Third, he implies that despite his billionaire status, he remains a humble and down-to-earth entrepreneur who is still in touch with his customers. Bezos's "hints" manage to sound helpful without making him (or Amazon.com) sound desperate for sales—no mean feat in a letter that suggests that the company is still hemorrhaging money.

Conclusion

Analyzing Amazon.com's shareholder letters suggests important implications for cyberculture studies. First, I believe that these letters suggest a wealth of information about the cultural values that the company considers important. On a larger scale, examining stories as told through these types of primary texts and then contextualizing these texts inside a larger discursive environment can provide researchers with new insights into the business culture of dot-coms. Second, my application of Amazon.com's motto as a lens through which we can understand the company's external communication helps illuminate the complex relationships that corporate discourse comprises. By using Amazon.com's/Bezos's own words to provide the context for my research, I have been able to examine the discourse surrounding the company in a unique way, one that attempts to understand the company's actions and rhetoric through its own professed value system. In so doing, I have illuminated events and stories that may have been marginalized because they did not necessarily "fit" with the company's own vision of itself.

There are much larger reasons for the continued exploration of companies like Amazon.com in the field of cyberculture studies. First, the conflation of home and work that the dot-coms encouraged has had a significant impact on our collective notion of what it means to be "at work" and "at home." As we continue to blur the lines between work and play, there are significant implications for the well-being of ourselves, our families, and our communities. Second, dot-coms have changed our collective relationship to Wall Street, creating an environment where more individuals are intimately familiar with the inner workings of the investment world. Additionally, the collapse of many dot-coms has inspired a general feeling of distrust toward corporations. Third, the dot-coms represented the first wave of online commercialization, and their influence on how we think about and use the technology that undergirds the Internet cannot be overestimated. As the Internet continues to become a common part of everyday life for an increasing number of the world's population, it is imperative that we consider the cultural context in which this technology was created.

NOTES

1. In *The Nudist on the Late Shift*, a book that documents the culture of Silicon Valley dot-coms, Po Bronson writes,

> If I could say just one thing about Silicon Valley, this is it: every generation that came before us had to make a choice in life between pursuing a steady career and pursuing wild adventures. In Silicon Valley, that trade-off has been recircuited. By injecting mind-boggling amounts of risk into the once stodgy domain of gray-suited business, young people *no longer have to choose.* It's a two-for-one deal: the career path has become an adventure into the unknown. (Bronson 1999, p. xxvii)

2. Non-Disclosure Agreement. NDAs prevent employees from taking intellectual property/technology of one company and disclosing it to another.

3. The U.S. Securities and Exchange Commission (SEC) requires all publicly traded companies to file an annual report about the company's financial health.

4. The "Internet Pioneer" myth suggests that the Web was comparable to the American West frontier—a place to be colonized and exploited by pioneers and rugged individualists. As Richard Slotkin (1998) notes, this "Myth of the Frontier" has historically been used not only to explain the expansion of the American colonies westward but also to justify the exploitation of indigenous peoples who inhabited the "wilderness." He writes,

> the Myth [of the Frontier] was called on to account for our rapid economic growth, our emergence as a powerful nation-state, and our distinctively American approach to the socially and culturally disruptive process of modernization. . . . In America, all the political, social, and economic transformations on modernization began with outward movement, physical separation from the originating "metropolis." The achievement of "progress" was therefore inevitably associated with territorial expansion and colored by experience, the politics, and the peculiar psychology of emigration. (pp. 10–11)

In the mid- and late 1990s, the Web became the newest frontier to be "conquered" by (primarily) American "colonists." More specifically, the dot-coms used this appropriation of the Frontier Myth to justify their mass insurgence into and imposition of values onto a new technological realm.

5. This section is influenced by Bakhtin's (1981) work on heteroglossia.

REFERENCES

Amazon.com. 1997. *Annual Report: 1997.*

Amazon.com. 2001. *Annual Report: 2001.*

Bakhtin, Mikhail. 1981. *The dialogic imagination,* ed. Michael Holquist. Austin: University of Texas Press.

Borsook, Paulina. 2000. *Cyberselfish: A critical romp through the terribly libertarian culture of high tech.* New York: Public Affairs.

Bronson, Po. 1999. *The nudist on the late shift.* New York: Random House.

Coupland, Douglas. 1995. *Microserfs.* New York: Regan.

David, Carol. 2001. Mythmaking in annual reports. *Journal of Business and Technical Communication* 15: 195–222.

Delbecq, Andre L., and Joseph Weiss. 2000. The business culture of Silicon Valley: A turn-of-the-century reflection. *Journal of Management Inquiry* 9: 37–44.

English-Lueck, J. A. 2000. Silicon Valley reinvents the company town. *Futures* 32: 759–766.

Lessard, Bill, and Steve Baldwin. 2000. *NetSlaves: True tales of working the Web.* New York: McGraw-Hill.

Neff, Gina, and David Stark. 2003. Permanently beta: Responsive organization in the Internet era. In *Society online: The Internet in context,* ed. Phil Howard and Steve Jones, 173–188. Thousand Oaks, CA: Sage.

NetLingo. 2002. Amazon.com. Available at http://www.netlingo.com/lookup.cfm?term=Amazon.com (accessed 10 November 2002).

Perlow, Leslie A. 1998. Boundary control: The social ordering of work and family time in a high-tech corporation. *Administrative Science Quarterly* 43: 328–357.

Ross, Andrew. 1998. *Real love: In pursuit of cultural justice.* New York: New York University Press.

Schellenberg, Kathryn, and George A. Miller. 1998. Turbulence and bureaucracy. *Journal of Applied Behavioral Science* 34: 202–221.

Slotkin, Robert. 1998. *Gunfighter nation: The myth of the frontier in twentieth-century America.* Norman: University of Oklahoma Press.

Chapter 25

Associating Independents

Business Relationships and the Culture of Independence in the Dot-Com Era

Gina Neff

One version of the history of cyberculture, albeit a simple and condensed version, tells the story of an independent media space for free cultural experimentation that was co-opted by people looking for quick and easy profits during the dot-com boom. Individual innovation and creative drive clearly shaped cyberculture and the World Wide Web since the earliest hacks and first personal homepages. The commercialization of cyberspace, however, involved a shift in cultural values, not just the increasing corporate control of the production of Internet content. The artistic, creative, and culturally rebellious pioneers of Silicon Alley considered the financial investments and their concomitant corporate values "the end of the Web as we know it."[1] How then did they accept the shift toward corporate-owned Internet content?

This case study describes how a shift in the social ties among people who produced Internet content preceded the shift in ownership control. These changing social relationships reflect a shift in values away from independent, artistic production toward a commercialized Internet. The case of New York's Internet industry, or "Silicon Alley," as it was commonly called, charts the shifts in the cultural terrain that preceded the widespread corporate ownership of Internet content production. Before independently owned Internet content companies were "bought out" or "sold out" to corporate financial interests, people in Silicon Alley changed how and with whom they associated at business networking events. I argue that the acceptance and incorporation of corporate financial values into the way Silicon Alley worked depended upon this changing pattern of business associations.

The business history of Silicon Alley has been relatively overlooked in examinations of cyberculture and the dot-com era, even though New York's importance in Internet publishing and online advertising makes this history critical for understanding the evolution of online content. Many of New York's content-oriented Internet companies were founded with an explicit mission to create new forms of culture, forms that opposed those of corporate media or challenged corporate workplace cultures and hierarchical organizational principles (Christopherson 2002; Girard and Stark 2002; Neff 2004; Ross 2003). My research elsewhere addresses how people straddled multiple "orders of worth"—or culturally framed calculations of value, such as financial worth and creative worth—in Silicon Alley and how these different valuations were utilized within the industry as a mechanism for dealing with economic uncertainty (Neff 2004). Did financial worth simply trump creative worth? Did these independent cultural rebels merely sell out for the inescapable allure of potential financial success, exchanging "bootstrapped" or self-financed business models for an association with the burgeoning dot-com financial phenomenon?

In this chapter I argue that the co-optation of these values of independence began well before the first stock offerings on Silicon Alley and well before the frenzy of the stock market bubble. When pressures emerged from investors for culture's profitability and for the rapid growth in the rate of those profits, creative risk-taking was no longer a sufficient mechanism of valuation for any small firm in Silicon Alley, regardless of its level or type of funding. Financial accountability was exacted upon content creators, even those not receiving venture capital or corporate funding. The shifting orders of worth in Silicon Alley, I argue, were the result of cultural changes that occurred within the field.

The Creation of Silicon Alley

The creation of Silicon Alley as both a term and a district was accompanied by contention over the boundaries of the industry—that is, which firms, business models, and technologies would constitute Silicon Alley. Early Silicon Alley was filled with artistic, creative entrepreneurs who attempted to develop interesting, novel uses for a new medium. In 1998, as the first initial pubic offerings (IPOs) were occurring in Silicon Alley, content-oriented firms were being closed. Five of New York's oldest and most visible content sites—Word, ada'web, Charged, Urban Desires, and Total NY—all closed or suspended publication by the time the Silicon Alley online advertising agency DoubleClick held its successful IPO in March 1998.[2] These closures sounded the "death knell for New York's first generation of Web publishers, the generation of people who built Silicon Alley's reputation but ultimately, not its fortune," according to an editor of one of the trade publications covering Silicon Alley (Watson 1998). Arts-oriented Web sites like ada'web, The Blue Dot, and Rhizome pushed the limits of digital art production. Critics likened "webzines" such as Word.com and Urban Desires to high culture exemplars such as the *New Yorker* and *Harper's*. And yet, when Silicon Alley began to experience financial success it coincided with the destruction of this diversity of company types in the industry, as culturally oriented sites were scuttled and digital advertising firms, e-commerce firms, design firms, and consulting firms began to gain recognition in financial realms.

The history of Silicon Alley depicts how many diverse business activities—from business consulting to graphic design to retail sales—became associated under the conceptual umbrella of "Internet industry." The tension between the valuations of art and commerce in Silicon Alley was not unlike that in other cultural fields (Becker 1982; Bourdieu 1984, 1993). In the industry's early years, however, there was a delicate détente between the successful Silicon Alley businesses who sought to popularize the medium and the bohemian artists and writers in New York who sought recognition among the avant-garde for advancing it. This contention not only reveals the symbolic labor involved in building Silicon Alley; it also illustrates how multiple actors with different mechanisms of evaluating worth negotiated (successfully or not) the coalescing of business activities, ideologies, and technological trajectories into a coherent new industrial identity.

Ultimately, financial valuations trumped creative ones, as self-published magazines and self-curated art projects succumbed to pressures to show profitability.[3] By taking the struggle over the definition of the industry as a point of examination, this chapter diverges from other scholars' accounts of the new economy that saw Silicon Alley as yet another form of the "in-dustrialization of bohemia" (Ross 2003, p. 10) or that saw the cooptation of independent, alternative culture as inevitable given the overriding forces of capitalism (the seeming lack of agency on the part of people working within these structures). Instead, the analytic question here is *what* cultural shift occurred within the field that justified—even made acceptable—the loss of independent online publishing in Silicon Alley, especially to people working there.

Social Networking in Silicon Alley

One way to map this shift uses the social networks of Silicon Alley. Social network analysis has long been used to depict elite power structures by analyzing the patterns of relationships among people within a particular field. In cultural industries, this methodology has been used to examine the connections among actors in Hollywood movies (Zukerman et al. 2003), university researchers (Owen-Smith et al. 2002), the American "intellectual elite" (Kadushin 1974), and rap musicians (Lena 2003), among many examples. Social network analysis allows for the examination of *structural* forces of social phenomena, as it allows for examination of the patterns of affiliation among people. The present research on the dissolution of independence of online media and the commodification of content online is no different.

One such structural force is Silicon Alley's deeply embedded ties to corporate America. Some scholars have written extensively about the use of countercultural images and discourse within the new economy more generally (Frank 2000; Henwood 2003; Thrift 2001), but few have examined the history of independently controlled Internet-content companies for insight into the shift from independent to corporate Web publishing. (One notable exception is Indergaard 2004). This shift can be seen as an outcome of the networks of affiliations that embedded Silicon Alley independence within a larger corporate ecology, but examination of ownership and consolidation of Silicon Alley companies would only begin to explain the extraordinarily rapid decline of independent Web publishing. Client-provider relationships, strategic partnerships, investments, and advertising relationships closely tied smaller, unknown companies to larger, well-known corporations from Silicon Alley's earliest years and provided mechanisms for the integration of mainstream corporate values into online publishing.

For small Silicon Alley firms, status could be communicated through relationships with particularly visible or successful corporate clients, advertisers, or partners or through levels and quality of funding, such as funding from a well-known "angel funder" or venture-capital firm. These relationships were announced in press releases, through the trade press, in job advertisements, on company homepages, and within informal networks (such as attendance at particular Silicon Alley events). For example, IBM, a paragon of the hierarchical corporation with traditional, "old-economy" organizational boundaries, was involved heavily in early Silicon Alley, as a client, advertiser, and sponsor for a range of company types including online publishing. The firm's reach was broad: until October 1998, IBM spread its interactive advertising across more than sixty different agencies, including many of the major online advertisers in New York. Different business models—from Web publishing to advertising to e-commerce firms—became associated through such networks of relationships.

Silicon Alley's social relationships were particularly important for gaining information about trends and jobs, for employability, and for developing client contacts. Within Silicon Alley, being good at "networking" was recognized as being important to success within the industry. In its first ranking of the Silicon Alley's top one hundred movers and shakers in Silicon Alley, *Silicon Alley Reporter* ranked entrepreneurs and others in the industry by their vision and execution, fundraising, and a metric called simply "network": "Our final rating, network, is perhaps the most important. The most successful companies in Silicon Alley, and on the Internet as a whole, are those that are able to partner and collaborate (that whole rising tide raises all ships thing)" (Calcanis 1997, p. 5). Networking helped build companies, reputations, and resources.

Events

The structure of New York's Internet industry can be seen as emerging out of a pattern of associations at Silicon Alley events. Such events as parties helped to make work in Silicon Alley and other such centers of cyber production seem like "hot jobs in cool places" (Pratt 2002). The reports of such events were a contemporaneous "who's who" of Silicon Alley, in which new businesses were introduced, personalities created, and associations between business models made. These events and the subsequent reporting of them circumscribed Silicon Alley for the participants in the field. Even in a field that was highly mediated through e-mail lists (such as Silicon Alley's World Wide Web Artists Consortium, or WWWAC, e-mail list), face-to-face business meetings remained important to Silicon Alley.

The earliest trade publications of New York's Internet industry included gossip columns to cover the myriad networking events in Silicon Alley. One column was so successful and visible that it was spun off into a business specializing in Silicon Alley networking. E-mail lists emerged with the sole function of telling people about the Silicon Alley events of the week. These events were so frequent that even after the dot-com crash e-mail services dedicated solely to announcing Silicon Alley events still survived.

Thus, social events helped to circumscribe which businesses and people were legitimate in Silicon Alley. And the reporting of who was at these events helped to circumscribe what companies considered themselves a part of the "community," even for people not in attendance. The reporting on Silicon Alley events form an important historical record of the industry and a rich source of data that is, to date, unmined.

Data and Methods

For this chapter, I use three sources of data: four years of reporting on social events in an online industry newsletter, field notes from research at Silicon Alley events from 1997 to 2001, and archival data on firms, employment, and networking practices within Silicon Alley.

A database of attendance at Silicon Alley events was constructed from all "Cyberscene" social columns from September 1996 to June 1999. These columns were written by Courtney Pulitzer and published, first bimonthly then weekly, in one of the online trade publications for Silicon Alley, *AtNewYork*.[4] These events columns were far from a complete listing of all events in Silicon Alley,[5] but their coverage did extend to the most important industry gatherings, such as meetings of the New York New Media Association and the World Wide Web Artists Consortium. Panels featuring industry leaders were frequently covered, as were networking breakfast meetings; parties celebrating new offices, companies, or products; annual awards ceremonies; and the like. For example, the first column covered the launch party for Total NY, a site jointly owned by America Online and the Tribune Company; less than a year and a half later, the site's "closing" party was also featured. Private events hosted by people working in Silicon Alley, such as birthday parties, anniversary parties, and going away parties, were included in the early years of coverage.

The database created from these columns includes information on 365 social events in Silicon Alley with the names of 2,767 participants (1,799 unique people), for an average of 7.6 people named per event. Of these people, 98 percent were able to be identified by company.

Companies were then coded into industry sectors. For the Internet industry, two subcategories were constructed on the basis of the primary business of the firm. The "content companies" category consists of companies that produce Web sites that were based on a model of magazine publishing or of music or arts distribution. Seventy-one Silicon Alley content companies are included in this data. The "Internet startup" category consists of companies that are engaged in e-commerce, consulting, advertising, business-to-business, or other Internet-related business. The people who were reported to be at a particular Silicon Alley event were coded as having been there together. The resulting social network matrices were then analyzed using Ucinet and depicted using Netdraw.

Industry Association

These data allow for analysis of the relationship between Silicon Alley firms to other industries. The number of times that people from particular types of companies—be it advertising, finance, or the arts—were mentioned as being at Silicon Alley events is summarized in figure 25.1. The number of people from the arts field who were reported to have attended Silicon Alley events declined over time. There were sharp increases in the number of people from public relations and advertising firms attending Silicon Alley parties beginning in the 1996–1998 period; later, in 1998–1999, there was a sharp increase in the number of people from business services attending Silicon Alley events.

In the network pictures in figures 25.2–25.5, the relative strength of the association of people from different industries and subsectors at the same events can be analyzed. In these figures, the strength of the lines between industry "nodes" represents the relative number of times that representatives of those industries attended the same events.[6]

In 1996, the strongest relationships—defined here as the highest incidence of attending the same parties—were between Internet-content firms and other Internet companies, along with arts, print media, and technology companies. Notice that in figure 25.2, finance is an isolated node: no representatives of financial firms were mentioned as having attended Silicon Alley events in 1996.

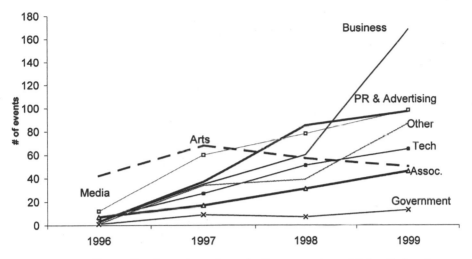

Figure 25.1. Silicon Alley Event Attendance by Representatives of Other Industries

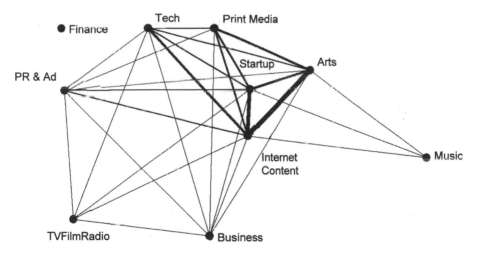

Figure 25.2. 1996 Industry Affiliations of Attendees at Silicon Alley Events

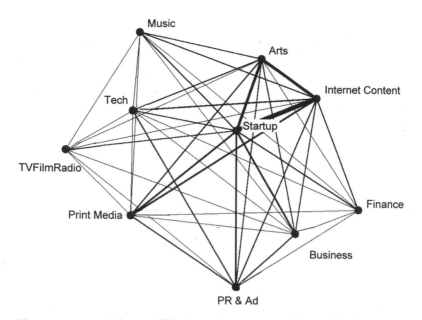

Figure 25.3. 1997 Industry Affiliations of Attendees at Silicon Alley Events

By 1997, the ties among Internet-content companies, other Internet-startup companies, and the arts formed the strongest set of relationships in Silicon Alley, as evidenced by the bold triangle between the three industries in figure 25.3. In that year, finance entered the Silicon Alley scene. Although seventeen employees of financial firms attended events that year, other industries were significantly more important to the Silicon Alley social scene. Representatives from public relations and advertising, print media, and technology all attended Silicon Alley events more often than people from the business and finance sectors.

By 1998 (figure 25.4), the relationship between Internet-content and Internet-startup firms remained strong, but these subsectors began to show a split in the strength of their affiliation with other industries. People from startup companies were more likely to be at events with representatives from technology, business, and finance companies than were people from content companies. While public relations and adverting firms remained important to both subsectors, the relative importance of the arts declined.

By 1999 (figure 25.5), representatives from many industries attended parties with startup companies. All industries had weaker ties to content firms than to startups. Arts, by this point, has gone from being one of the

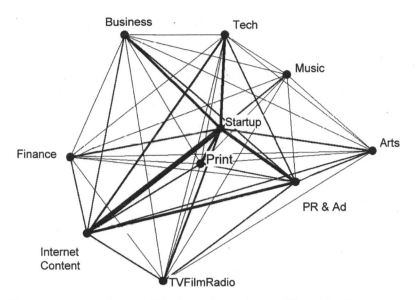

Figure 25.4. 1998 Industry Affiliations of Attendees at Silicon Alley Events

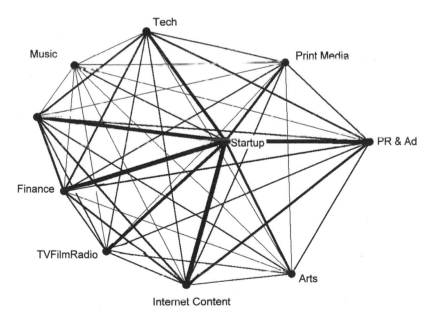

Figure 25.5. 1999 Industry Affiliations of Attendees at Silicon Alley Events

most important industries associated with Silicon Alley to one of the least important.

In the earliest years of Silicon Alley, arts and media were circumscribed as being important within the social events of the industry. Representatives of print media, arts organizations, and public relations and advertising firms were a part of the Silicon Alley social scene by 1997. People from finance- and business-related companies did not become strongly circumscribed as part of the Silicon Alley scene until 1998.

These events represent samples, of a sort, of the most visible members of Silicon Alley who attended the most newsworthy events. Clearly, marginal players within the industry or from other industries would have been underreported in the "Cyberscene" column, if reported at all. What is clear from this data is that certain individuals and company types emerged as central in the reporting of Silicon Alley social events. At a party in November 1997 someone turned to Pulitzer and said, "This is a good party; everybody's here."[7] That comment can be evaluated structurally: Who is "everybody" within an emerging field? And, more important for this research, how does that recognition of who is "everybody" get created?

One limitation to these data is that they do not necessarily show other types of power wielded within Silicon Alley. Just as the more marginal players may have been underreported, the most powerful may have been more likely to be covered when they did venture out. People from outside Silicon Alley may not have been as important to the social scene and, thus, to its reporting. Certainly, Microsoft chairman Bill Gates would be recognized as a technology leader, but he is only listed in this database once and at an event for which no other attendees were reported in the column. Thus, these data reflect the resources and prestige garnered through "networking" at social events in Silicon Alley, not necessarily power and other resources in Silicon Alley.

Overall, these figures show the consolidation and the beginning of the dissolution of Silicon Alley through its social events. What is powerful about these figures is that they graphically depict the consolidation of industry types at a series of events. Given that the social columns did not report all attendees of the events, nor did it cover all events in Silicon Alley, the consolidation among Internet-startup firms shown in figures 25.4 and 25.5 most likely reflects an even tighter linking within the industry that occurred during this time.

Conclusion

People working in cultural industries struggle to balance the tension between commercial and artistic values. This is not to argue that the dot-com boom and bust could have been prevented by a focus on artist output in Silicon Alley. Early pioneers mixed work for sale with work for art. Enterprises focused on cultural production came to be associated with corporate media and technology companies under the conceptual umbrella of "dot-com." Many individuals working in both kinds of firms—independent and corporate—were part of the same social circle of production within Silicon Alley from the industry's earliest days.

However, the tension among the heterogeneous interests of Silicon Alley begins to emerge in the pattern of associating at Silicon Alley events. This is not to argue that the dot-com downfall could have been prevented with a continued heterogeneity of evaluative principles as embodied by the dichotomy of creative and financial values. Rather, creative values were used in Silicon Alley to prepare the ground for profit-making. In examining how content companies and other kinds of Internet businesses affiliated with sectors outside Silicon Alley, this chapter shows that before the financial success of Silicon Alley companies, a cultural shift occurred that enabled the co-optation of independence.

Independence is often deeply embedded in a corporate ecology, as it was within Silicon Alley. These networks of relationships are a more powerful tool for examining the history of independent cultural producers, as networks exert a strong influence on how value is calculated and how business models are associated and compared. Models of media analysis that focus solely on the structures of ownership and the ties among corporate entities will fail to capture how social association creates the cultural precedent for economic transitions. In this sense, this examination of the business relationships within Silicon Alley has implications for understanding corporate control of media more generally, as well as for understanding who draws the boundaries of authenticity and innovation within cultural fields.

NOTES

1. Nicholas Butterworth, cited in Grigoriadis 2000.
2. In fact, content and design became seen as untenable business models for

the Internet in light of the rise of e-commerce, and companies scrambled to define their work in other terms. In March 1998, one of the editors of *AtNewYork* called "web shop" the "two dirtiest words in Silicon Alley" (Chervokas 1998).

3. For an excellent first-person discussion of this push for online profitability, see the interview with Word.com editor Marisa Bowe in Kait and Weiss 2001.

4. The publication of these columns in *AtNewYork* continued until 1999, when they began to be published independently by Pulitzer on her own Web site.

5. "Bernardo's list," Bernardo Joselevich's weekly e-mail containing "internet-industry events & parties," featured over fifty events in New York City per week in March 2001, a full year after the beginning of the dot-com crash. In contrast, *AtNewYork* covered two to three events per issue in 1999, the last year that it reported events in its e-mail version.

6. For simplicity's sake, industries with very few ties to Silicon Alley, such as government and education, are excluded from these representations.

7. Mark Tribe, of Rhizome, to Courtney Pulitzer at the Feed Magazine Party in November 1997. Fittingly, Pulitzer "turned around and spied Nick Butterworth," the founder of Sonic Net (Pulitzer 1997).

REFERENCES

Becker, Howard S. 1982. *Art Worlds.* Berkeley: University of California Press.

Bourdieu, Pierre. 1993. *The Field of Cultural Production.* New York: Columbia University Press.

Bourdieu, Pierre. 1984. *Distinction: A Social Critique of the Judgement of Taste.* Cambridge, MA: Harvard University Press.

Calcanis, Jason. 1997. "1997's Silicon Alley Reporter 100." *Silicon Alley Reporter* 1:10 (October).

Chervokas, Jason. 1998. "In the Evolving Internet Industry, Web Designers Need Not Apply." *AtNewYork* 3.30 (March 27).

Christopherson, Susan. 2002. "Project Work in Context: Regulatory Change and the New Geography of Media." *Environment and Planning A* 34(11): 2003–2015.

Frank, Thomas. 2000. *One Market under God.* New York: Doubleday.

Girard, Monique, and David Stark. 2002. "Distributing Intelligence and Organizing Diversity in New Media Projects." *Environment and Planning A* 34(11): 1927–1949.

Grigoriadis, Vanessa. 2000. "Silicon Alley 10003." *New York* 33(9): 28.

Henwood, Doug. 2003. *After the New Economy.* New York: New Press.

Indergaard, Michael. 2004. *Silicon Alley: The Rise and Fall of a New Media District.* New York: Routledge.

Kadushin, Charles. 1974. *The American Intellectual Elite.* Boston: Little, Brown.

Kait, Casey, and Stephen Weiss. 2001. *Digital Hustlers.* New York: HarperCollins.

Lena, Jennifer C. 2003. "Meaning and Membership: Samples in Rap Music, 1979–1995." Unpublished manuscript, Vanderbilt University.

Neff, Gina. 2004. "Organizing Uncertainty in Silicon Alley, 1995–2001." Ph.D. dissertation, Columbia University.

Owen-Smith, Jason, Massimo Riccaboni, Fabio Pammolli, and Walter W. Powell. 2002. "A Comparison of U.S. and European University-Industry Relations in the Life Sciences." *Management Science* 48(1): 24–43.

Pratt, Andy C. 2002. "Hot Jobs in Cool Places: The Material Culture of New Media Product Spaces; the Case of the South of the Market, San Francisco." *Information on Communication and Society* 5(1): 27–50.

Pulitzer, Courtney. 1997. "@ the Scene: Why Silicon Alley Is a Real Community." *AtNewYork* 3.7 (October 17).

Ross, Andrew. 2003. *No Collar: The Human Workplace and Its Hidden Costs.* New York: Basic.

Thrift, Nigel. 2001. "'It's the Romance Not the Finance That Makes the Business Worth Pursuing': Disclosing a New Market Culture." *Economy & Society* 30(4): 412–432.

Watson Tom. 1998. "Where Content Is King: Portrait of a Figurehead." *AtNewYork* 3.27 (March 13).

Zukerman, Ezra W., Tai-Young Kim, Kalinda Ukanwa, and James von Rittmann. 2003. "Robust Identities or Nonentities? Typecasting in the Feature-Film Labor Market." *American Journal of Sociology* 108: 1018–1074.

About the Contributors

Espen Aarseth is Principal Researcher at the Center for Computer Games Research at the IT University of Copenhagen and Adjunct Professor in Media and Communication at the University of Oslo. He is also editor in chief of *Game Studies* (gamestudies.org), and he initiated the Digital Arts and Culture series of conferences.

Nancy K. Baym is Associate Professor of Communication Studies at the University of Kansas. She is the author of *Tune In, Log On: Soaps, Fandom and Online Community.* She is a cofounder of the Association of Internet Researchers, which she served as Vice President from 1999 to 2003 and President from 2003 to 2005.

Greg Elmer is Bell Globemedia Research Chair, School of Radio TV Arts, Ryerson University, Toronto. He is the author of *Profiling Machines: Mapping the Personal Information Economy,* editor of *Critical Perspectives on the Internet,* and coeditor (with Mike Gasher) of *Contracting Out Hollywood: Runaway Productions and Foreign Location Shooting.*

Kirsten Foot is Assistant Professor in Communication at the University of Washington. She coedits the "Acting with Technology" series at MIT Press, and as codirector of WebArchivist.org, she is developing new methods and tools for studying social and political action on the Web.

Anthony Fung is Associate Professor in the School of Journalism and Communication at the Chinese University of Hong Kong. He received his Ph.D. from the School of Journalism and Mass Communication at the University of Minnesota. His research interests include cyberculture, political economy of communication, popular culture, gender, youth, and cultural identities.

Blanca Gordo is a Ph.D. candidate in the Department of City and Regional Planning at UC Berkeley, where she studies the relationship between technology and development at the community level in urban pockets of poverty within growing regions. Her dissertation examines new forms of social and technical inequalities introduced by technology, social processes, and community governance structures with potential for positive change.

Stine Gotved is a cultural sociologist who obtained her Ph.D. with a dissertation on cybersociology. Currently, she is affiliated with the University of Copenhagen, Denmark. Her fields of interest include online communities, mediated sociality, time and space relations, mediated interaction, and urban sociology.

Emily Noelle Ignacio is Assistant Professor of Sociology at the University of Washington at Tacoma and the author of *Building Diaspora* (Rutgers University Press). Currently, she is researching the impacts of transnational migration and new technologies—such as satellite television and phone texting—on non-Tagalog Filipino communities in Chicago, in the hope of adding to discussions about assimilation, multiculturalism, transnationalism, and race/ethnicity.

Steve Jones is Professor of Communication, Research Associate in the Electronic Visualization Laboratory and Adjunct Professor of Electronic Media in the School of Art and Design at the University of Illinois–Chicago and Adjunct Research Professor in the Institute of Communications Research at the University of Illinois at Urbana-Champaign.

Shanthi Kalathil contributed her essay while based at the Carnegie Endowment for International Peace. She is the coauthor of *Open Networks, Closed Regimes: The Impact of the Internet on Authoritarian Rule.* Kalathil is currently a Democracy Fellow at USAID's Office of Democracy and Governance under World Learning's Democracy Fellows Program.

Beth E. Kolko is Associate Professor of Technical Communication at the University of Washington, where she is Director of the Ph.D. program. Her research focuses on technology, culture, and design, with a basis in rhetorical theory. She is the editor of *Virtual Publics* (Columbia University Press, 2003), a coeditor of *Race in Cyberspace* (Routledge, 2000), and the author of numerous articles and book chapters. She currently leads a National Science Foundation grant that measures the effect of ICT on society in Central Asia.

Madhavi Mallapragada is Assistant Professor in the Department of Communication and Culture at Indiana University, Bloomington. Her research interests include cybercultures, satellite television, and postcolonial and diaspora studies. She is currently working on a book that deals with the constructions of Indian American identities on the Web.

Alice Marwick is a Ph.D. student in the Department of Culture and Communication at New York University, where she studies social technology and emerging media. Alice divides her time between Brooklyn and Seattle and writes a blog about feminism and technology.

Adrienne Massanari, a doctoral student in the Department of Communication at the University of Washington, has worked as a usability specialist and information architect for several dot-coms and for an educational technology initiative. She is interested in the unique ways groups use emerging technologies and how these uses change communicative practices.

Bharat Mehra is Assistant Professor in the School of Information Sciences at the University of Tennessee. Mehra's work addresses community informatics issues surrounding the needs of minority and underserved populations, social justice and social equity, service learning and action research, empowerment and the digital divide, situated studies of technology use, cross-cultural learning, and international perspectives in U.S. education.

Lisa Nakamura is Assistant Professor of Communication Arts and Visual Culture at the University of Wisconsin, Madison. She is the author of *Cybertypes: Race, Ethnicity, and Identity on the Internet* and is working on a new book, *Visual Cultures of the Internet,* forthcoming from University of Minnesota Press.

Gina Neff is Assistant Professor of Communication at the University of Washington in Seattle, where she teaches classes on the relationship between technology and organizations. Currently, she is completing a book entitled *Venture Labor: Work and the Burden of Risk in Innovative Industries,* which addresses the experience of uncertainty within jobs in the new economy. She is also a coeditor of the collection *Surviving the New Economy,* which is forthcoming from Paradigm Publishers.

Kate O'Riordan has published research on gender, sexuality, and digital media, and her research interests include the material/theoretical dynamics of bodies and technologies. She is currently working on a research project at the Centre for Social and Economic Aspects of Genomics, Lancaster University, while on secondment from the University of Sussex.

David J. Phillips is Assistant Professor of Radio-Television-Film at the University of Texas–Austin. He studies technologies of privacy, identification, and surveillance. His publications include "Texas 9-1-1: Emergency Telecommunications and the Genesis of Surveillance Infrastructure" (forthcoming in *Telecommunication Policy*) and numerous papers exploring the relations among policy, economics, ideology, culture, identity, and technology.

Wendy Robinson teaches multicultural and mobile communication in the Department of Communication Studies at the University of Michigan in Ann Arbor. She writes on cyberculture and electronic mobility and has chapters forthcoming in books published by Routledge and Peter Lang. During the dot-com period, she worked in corporate communications.

Christian Sandvig is Assistant Professor of Speech Communication at the University of Illinois at Urbana-Champaign. He received a Ph.D. in Communication from Stanford University. In 2002 he was named a "next-generation leader in science and technology policy" in a competition of the American Association for the Advancement of Science.

Heidi J. Figueroa Sarriera is a psychology professor at the University of Puerto Rico, Río Piedras. She was assistant coeditor of *The Cyborg Handbook* (1995), edited by Chris H. Gray, and has published articles and book chapters on cyberpsychology, technoculture, and gender construction. She is the editor of the online journal *TeknoKultura* (http://teknokultura.rrp.upr.edu).

Frank Schaap is a Ph.D. student at the Amsterdam School of Communications Research at the University of Amsterdam. His research focuses on the process of construction and the implications of gendered identity in various online environments.

David Silver teaches in the Department of Media Studies at the University of San Francisco. He is the founder and director of the Resource Center for Cyberculture Studies and the codirector, with Sarah Washburn, of the September Project, an effort to foster distributed acts of civic participation that take place annually on September 11.

Jonathan Sterne teaches in the Department of Art History and Communication Studies at McGill University. He is the author of *The Audible Past* (Duke University Press, 2003) and numerous articles on media, technologies, and the politics of culture. His next book is on the mp3 as cultural form. He is also an editor of *Bad Subjects: Political Education for Everyday Life,* one of the oldest publications on the Internet.

Fred Turner is Assistant Professor of Communication at Stanford University. He is the author of *Echoes of Combat: The Vietnam War in American Memory* (2nd ed., University of Minnesota Press, 2001) and *Counterculture into Cyberculture: How Stewart Brand and the Whole Earth Network Transformed the Politics of Information* (forthcoming, University of Chicago Press).

McKenzie Wark teaches media and cultural studies at Eugene Lang College and the New School for Social Research. He is the author of, among other works, *A Hacker Manifesto* (Harvard University Press, 2004).

Index